M000031286

HAPPY, JOYOUS, AND FREE

ONE MAN'S JOURNEY AND GUIDE TO ULTIMATE SPIRITUAL HEALTH

Juris S.

ISBN 978-1-63630-864-7 (Paperback)
ISBN 978-1-63630-865-4 (Hardcover)
ISBN 978-1-63630-866-1 (Digital)

Copyright © 2021 Juris S.
All rights reserved
First Edition

The excerpts from *Alcoholics Anonymous*, the Big Book are reprinted with permission of A.A. World Services, Inc. ("A.A.W.S."). Permission to reprint these excerpts does not mean that A.A.W.S. has reviewed or approved the contents of this publication, or that A.A.W.S. necessarily agrees with the views expressed herein. A.A. is a program of recovery from alcoholism only—use of these excerpts in connection with programs and activities which are patterned after A.A., but which address other problems, or in any other non A.A. context, does not imply otherwise.

All rights reserved. No part of this publication may be reproduced, distributed, or transmitted in any form or by any means, including photocopying, recording, or other electronic or mechanical methods without the prior written permission of the publisher. For permission requests, solicit the publisher via the address below.

Covenant Books, Inc.
11661 Hwy 707
Murrells Inlet, SC 29576
www.covenantbooks.com

This book is dedicated to the following:
God. Without His love, power, grace, and mercy,
none of this would be possible. May God be
revealed and glorified in these pages.
My magnificent, amazing wife, Kim, who demonstrates the
no-matter-what-ness of God's love to me. May we continue
to seek God's will for us and the power to carry that out,
continuing to live this dream life that God has designed for us.
My spiritual fathers, Gary B. and Brady Cooper. Thank you
for investing in me to earnestly seek and come to understand
the one true God. May the wisdom that you have transmitted
to me be clearly conveyed to others in this book.
The courageous, kind, wise, and loving men and women
of Alcoholics Anonymous. Your welcoming embrace has
saved my life and taught me how to find heaven on earth.
May we continue to carry the message, help save lives, and
share our discovery of this beautiful thing we call life.

Be happy for this moment.
This moment is your life.

—Omar Khayyam

This is the day that the LORD has made;
let us rejoice and be glad in it.

—Psalm 118:24 (ESV)

CONTENTS

FOREWORD

The United States is facing an addiction epidemic for the last thirty years. Addiction, including alcoholism and tobacco use, is leading cause of death and disability in our country—more so than cancer and heart disease combined. Over these past thirty years, there have been few advances in the treatment of addiction as compared to other major diseases. As people, we want a quick fix—a pill, a scan, radiation, an ablation, or other high-tech treatment modality to treat what ails us. We certainly do not want a spiritual remedy for a lethal disease. And yet, as we read in *Happy, Joyous, and Free* by Juris S. that is exactly what works best. This spiritual program known as the twelve-step program of Alcoholics Anonymous has helped millions of people recover from every type of substance and process addiction. Juris S. presents a strong argument backed by studies that illustrates how he recovered from alcoholism and addiction by working the original twelve-step program, and as a result, developing spirituality.

My relationship with Juris has taken many forms as it has evolved, mirroring his recovery journey. Today, I am happy to call him a friend. We first met when I was in the role of his treating physician as he was being admitted for alcoholism. My initial impression of Juris as he entered treatment, which he accurately describes in "90 Days at the Ranch" was something like "he's not going to get recovery." It is a good thing that first impressions are often wrong. The term "recovery" in this sense means the basics of surrender and spirituality. Physicians, as a rule, are difficult to treat. They do not easily submit to the patient role. Their inherent feelings of inflated self-importance and white coat get in the way. Juris was no different. In fact, he exemplified the reasons that physicians are difficult to treat. Initially, he did not want to give up his doctor identity, which is

9

sometimes referred to in the treatment field as MD—Medical Deity. He had too much to lose. At least, that is what he thought. In reality, and as he so eloquently describes in this book, he had much to gain.

On first appearance, Juris is a formidable human specimen with many apparent and noticeable attributes. He is relatively tall. He is a bodybuilder, a former male model, and an orthopedic spine surgeon with a successful practice. He has a loud voice and distinctive laugh. But his values, like his muscles, were superficial. On the surface, he had the American dream. It looked like he had everything anyone would ever want. But just below the surface, he was broken. His world was fractured. That fracture compounded to the surface while on a Florida family vacation. Prior to admission for treatment for the disease of alcoholism, he had just returned from this vacation, with his life and family in utter chaos. Alcohol caused events to occur in Florida that precipitated his crash, a rock bottom, and the end of his life as he knew it. That crash was also the catalyst for his recovery. His world, along with his family's, was about to be turned upside down for the better.

Happy, Joyous, and Free is his amazing story of transformation. A change in values from superficial to meaningful. From slowly succumbing to the lethal disease of alcoholism to grabbing recovery with every ounce of strength. From his isolation, incorporated by atheism, to a powerful Christian walk with his God.

Among many elements, this book illustrates how the author learned, grasped, and internalized spirituality from and through the twelve-step program process. Like many in recovery, the twelve-step process introduced him to a Higher Power, who he calls God. He discusses all sides of spirituality and even equates spiritual fitness to physical fitness.

I have witnessed amazing changes in Juris while our paths have crisscrossed from when he was admitted for treatment to the present. I was his physician during his treatment. More recently, I am the medical director of the physician health program that has monitored, supported, and advocated for him in the five years subsequent to treatment. Suffice it to say that I have a firsthand knowledge of his story and his journey of recovery.

Fear always exists when one of our monitored physicians goes public with their story as in writing a book because it can reflect poorly on the person and our program if their recovery is interrupted by a public relapse. In a similar notion, that is one reason that Alcoholics Anonymous is an anonymous program. Therefore, when Juris approached me with his book, I should not have been enthusiastic about him publishing it and agreeing to write this foreword. However, I was enthusiastic and excited because the public needs education about Alcoholics Anonymous and twelve-step recovery, and his journey is a powerful testimony of its effectiveness. It is a given that no person can guarantee that they will not relapse. Spirituality and surrender are the bedrock principles of a good recovery program. These components of Juris's recovery program are solid, and I have confidence in his continued recovery—one day at a time.

Happy, Joyous, and Free is a passionate recovery story based on spirituality and the twelve steps of Alcoholics Anonymous. He travels from a spiritual death to a full and happy spiritual life on the wings of a twelve-step program that revealed to him his Higher Power. His recovery and spiritual journey have changed his, his family's, and his patients' lives—all for the better. It has been a privilege and honor to have been a part of and a witness to Juris's recovery journey.

Enjoy the story of spirituality and recovery from the lethal disease of alcoholism in the pages of this book, *Happy, Joyous, and Free*, by Juris S.

—Michael Baron, MD, MPH
Medical Director, Tennessee Medical
Foundation Physician Health Program

1

ABUNDANT LIFE

When I was five years old, my mother always told me that
happiness was the key to life. When I went to school, they
asked me what I wanted to be when I grew up. I wrote down
"happy." They told me I didn't understand the assignment,
and I told them that they didn't understand life.
—John Lennon

Happy. Joyous. Free.

All my life I wanted to be happy. When I was younger, I did
not really think about being joyous and free; but as I stand today, I
know that all three of these things are dependent on one another. I
do not remember ever having a conversation with anyone specifically
about how to be happy, joyous, and free as a child and young adult.
I merely knew that deep down inside, all I really wanted out of life
was to be happy.

Growing up, I looked around at the people in my life and
tried to figure out how to accomplish this. The message I received
from my parents and others, TV and movies, was that in order to be
happy, one had to be "successful." "Success" became defined for me
in my childhood as having a prestigious occupation that earns a lot
of money and a nice house in the suburbs with a wife and kids. Most
of my adult life has been spent in the delusion that achieving those
things would finally grant me happiness. Simply put, a delusion is a
false belief. This false belief drove my actions and behaviors for many
years.

I chased happiness in all the things that the world promised would bring me to it. I sought fulfillment and satisfaction from life in my image, career, fame and notoriety, sex, drugs, alcohol, and relationships. I had the "American dream"—beautiful wife, kids, nice house, fancy cars, respected status in my career, and money. And yet somehow, some way, I was not satisfied. I had momentary feelings of happiness, but I did not have continual abundant joy and inner peace. To the world, it appeared as though I "had it all," and yet I was disenchanted with life. I wondered why I felt there had to be more when I had attained everything I thought I ever wanted.

No matter what I obtained, it was never enough, even when I met or exceeded the goals that I set for myself. There was always something greater that I wanted, and all my "successes" ended up falling flat. It was never enough.

I grew up atheist. My parents never talked about God. We never went to church. My life was mostly centered around academics, which is probably my strongest gift. However, being intelligent is also my worst enemy.

Because I excelled in school, I felt superior to the people around me. I was particularly adept at math and science. This drove my belief that science could explain everything in the universe. If it had not been explained through science yet, I believed that it was certain that it would be. I came to believe that it is not scientifically plausible that there could be an ethereal being called God. It was not logical, so therefore, He must not exist. I was not quiet about my atheistic beliefs and often used my intellect to belittle and berate those who would present me with the concept of God. The truth is that I never investigated God. I just dismissed Him because I was my own god and was "succeeding" in most everything I set my mind to.

Why did I rail against God for most of my life? The answer is simple.

If there is a God, then I would not be in control.

Through my journey, I have come to discover that not only is there a God, He is fiercely interested in me and my life and has plans for me that are beyond what my limited human mind even had for myself. The issue of whether or not God exists is not an evidence problem. For me to come to believe in an almighty God, I made a thorough investigation into the life, death, and resurrection of Jesus. What I found turned my life upside down, and for the better. Not just better, but the BEST life I could possibly have. The evidence surrounding these events is irrefutable. I realized that faith and science are not opposites; they are inextricably linked with truth. If the man of Jesus could be brought back to life, that proved to me that God must exist. Once I had that spiritual awakening, my entire life and everything I believed was set on a new trajectory.

The paradox that I have discovered is that by relenting control of my will and my life over the care of God, my life is more than I could have expected or achieved on my own. Surrendering control allows me to let God direct my life, and I can enjoy every step of the journey. I am finally happy, joyous, and free as a direct result of me NOT managing my own life.

Through my long, circuitous journey, I have discovered that true happiness, joy, satisfaction, freedom, and fulfillment in life can only come from living in the truth. Truth applies to all people, at all times, and in all circumstances. Truth never changes, never evolves, never falters. Although it would seem intuitive to me that I would know the truth being educated as a physician, it took me many years to find it.

The purpose of this book is to share my experience, strength, and hope, through my journey to help others be happy, joyous, and free, and find an abundant, extravagant life. Heaven is not a destination. I have found much of heaven and live a life now that I could not have even imagined. Heaven is not just somewhere we go when we die. Someday is too far away for me. Thinking about where I will go when I die does not have any immediacy to me. I am there today.

If you have one foot in yesterday and one foot in tomorrow, you are pissing on today.

In His unrelenting pursuit of an intimate relationship with me, God gifted me with the disease of alcoholism for which the solution is not medical, but spiritual. Alcoholism is a medical disease, classified in the Diagnostic and Statistical Manual of Mental Disorders (DSM-5) produced by the American Psychiatric Association. It is the standard classification of mental disorders used by mental health professionals in the United States. Because it is a medical disease, it is something that my medical mind can assess and process. I can study and analyze it in medical terms, and it makes intuitive sense to me.

However, the solution for this medical disease is not medical at all. It is spiritual. There is no procedure or medication that can effectively treat this disease. The most effective treatment for alcoholism is the original twelve-step program described in the book *Alcoholics Anonymous.* I have read that the reported success rate is 10 percent. Based on my experience and observation as well as recent published Cochrane review, this is not true. The reported success rate is 10 percent because the compliance to treatment is 10 percent. From a medical perspective, the success rate for any disease in which only 10 percent of the patients are taking the medication is going to be 10 percent or less. It is not a fault of the treatment (Alcoholics Anonymous or AA); it is the willingness of the individual to comply with treatment.

God used this specific disease to bring me to Him. Although I had accepted Jesus as my savior in 2010, my surrender to God did not occur until I went to rehab in 2015. In this book, I delineate how the program of AA accelerated my journey toward God through Jesus Christ. What I hope to achieve in this book is to reveal to others how the program of AA can be applied to the Christian life no matter what the individual struggles with. AA gave me the clear, direct blueprint to follow Jesus effectively, which finally brought me to the abundant, extravagant life that I have today. I want this for everyone.

Because of my experiences and background, I incorporate recovery, spirituality, psychology, and medical science. I draw from everything that I have seen and heard throughout my life to practically demonstrate how I obtained the ultimate contentment of life, fullness of joy, feeling of complete security and safety, and freedom from judgment or condemnation in all situations and circumstances. It is the best feeling I have ever had, and it is my prayer that others can find the same by learning from my journey. I share much of what I wish someone would have taught me at an early age.

There are many spiritual and practical truths that have helped me along the way. In this book, whenever I present one of these, I put it in bold so that it can be easily seen and remembered. I consider these spiritual and practical truths to be modern-day proverbs. These are pronouncements that have had a profound impact on me spiritually, mentally, and emotionally. These truths will impact a person in different ways depending on the condition of their heart in the moment and circumstances in life. However, the one thing that never changes is the fact that these statements are immutably true.

Truth is the only thing that will lead a person to the best life possible—the life that God has ordained for you. You can fulfill your ultimate destiny that has been predetermined by the creator of the universe, and not of yourself. The results will blow you away. You will achieve and gain more than you ever dreamed you could. You will look at your life over time and realize that you had never seen, heard, or imagined anything so beautiful as the way your life unfolds over time.

I had no idea how magnificent, enjoyable, and satisfying my life could be.

2

TRUTH

2+2=4

Two plus two equals four. It has always been four. It is four today. It will be four tomorrow. It will always be four. It never changes. It does not care about how you feel. It does not care where you are from. It does not care who your parents are. It does not care what language you speak or what color your skin is. It does not evolve or change with the times. It is the truth. It applies to all people, in all situations, at all times.

If a person lives his life in the delusion that two plus two equals five, it is not going to end well. He will never make it in school. He will never be able to hold down a job. He will never be able to keep money in a checking account. He will have difficulty going anywhere or doing anything wherever he goes.

He will believe the world is against him. "They are wrong!" he will say. He is unwavering in his belief that two plus two equals five. It is likely that his parents encouraged him to believe this. They told him, "Yes, son. You are right. You can believe two plus two equals five. If it feels right to you, it is YOUR truth and that makes it okay." He will likely be angry at God and at the world. "Everyone is against me!" Maybe he will even cry out to God, "Why, God, why? Why does two plus two equal four! I don't understand!"

This analogy may seem silly, but it is the way many people lives their lives. I lived my life in this manner, ignoring and suppressing the truth for most of my life. The truth has been presented to the world in the Bible, but many people reject it, or even if they accept and learn the truth, they do not apply it to their lives. If the truth of two plus two is known, but not applied, the result is the same.

The Bible contains the truth. It applies to all people, in all situations, at all times. If applied, it leads a person to eternal life. And that abundant, extravagant, joyful, happy, heavenly life begins here and now on earth, when these truths are known and lived by. Eternal life is not a destination. It does not start when your body is dead. It begins today. Merely knowing the truth of the Bible and not applying it is as useless as not knowing it.

Truth may not be able to be understood sometimes, but that does not make it any less true. Truth may not feel like the right thing to a person, but that does not make it any less true. Truth may even seem completely contradictory to a person's logic, but that does not make it any less true.

Going against truth will never satisfy a person's spirit, even if in the moment, it seems like it will. Going against truth will never lead to joy, even if a person believes that it will and even if the world is condoning and encouraging it.

This has been my experience as well as my observation and many, many other people's experiences. I was on a happiness quest. I was looking for whatever would make me happy in that moment. "Do whatever makes you happy." "If it makes you happy and you are not hurting anyone else, then it's okay." That way of living only ends in destruction from my observation and personal experience.

If you want to be truly happy, if you truly want to have joy, if you truly want freedom, you need to be on a truth quest, not a happiness quest. Not only finding the truth but applying it and living it out daily. It will never let you down. Truth never changes.

It really is that black and white. You can argue with it. You can fight it. You can ignore it. You can learn it and not use it. No matter what you do with the truth, what is will always be what is. Either it is or it isn't. It does not need to be understood. It needs to be accepted and used appropriately. That's it.

It's simple, but it is not easy. Truth sometimes does not make sense to the human mind and emotions. In fact, a lot of truth is counterintuitive. It is illogical based on our patterns of thinking. It is in direct opposition to much of what the world would teach and have you believe.

It is my prayer that I can help others find the truth. My story is the most emphatic demonstration of God's power in my life. I lived in a delusion for most of my life, and the results were disastrous. I pray that in reading my story, your journey to the truth is accelerated and you can experience the fullness, peace, and joy of life that I have found.

Let me present you with this hypothetical scenario. The ten most influential, brightest, progressive orthopedic spine surgeons in the world collaborated and wrote a book about spine surgery. These are surgeons who have had extensive training over an extended period of years. They also have many years of practice in the diagnosis and treatment of patients with spinal conditions requiring surgery. Throughout the world, they are considered the absolute authorities regarding spine surgery because of their intimate knowledge of the subject and firsthand experience.

I obtain a copy of the book. Although I am a good, talented spine surgeon, I would not be considered internationally known. I am very progressive in my surgical techniques, but most would not consider me to be on the investigative forefront of spine surgery. I start to read this book, and I come to a few places where things do not make sense to me. I cannot understand the point they are trying to convey, or it does not fit with the way I currently practice. Because of this, I decide that the whole book is worthless, and there is absolutely no reason that I should learn or follow the instructions set forth in this book. After all, it does not make sense to me, and it is not in accordance with what I am currently doing. I am intelligent and have had many years of education and experience; therefore, I know what I am doing, and since I do not like or agree with what is written, I disregard it.

What would you think of my thought process? Does it sound rational? Since I am highly qualified, does that give me the right to disregard the information contained in this book written by people who have much greater knowledge in experience in the same field?

I believe that you, as well as most people, would state that I am an idiot with this line of thinking. I would agree with that conclusion. However, isn't this what most people do with the Bible?

We human beings think that because we have a pulse, have been taught by our parents, teachers, coaches, and other people of limited intelligence (compared to God), we somehow have the capacity to make good decisions about our lives and how we need to live them. None of my academic qualifications, however, prepare me to make proper decisions about how to live the best possible life. Most people would agree that because of my education and training, I should be fully equipped to make those decisions, but what I have found is that I am totally incapable of making the best decisions regarding life without proper direction and training. Life decisions. Relationships. Marriage. Parenting. Sex.

This is the reason many very intelligent, successful people have a difficult time surrendering to God. In fact, the more educated or worldly successful a person is, the harder that person will fight against the gospel because it does not make logical sense. We feel that because we have achieved high levels of success, accolades, wealth, or power, we obviously can make good decisions about basic life choices regarding relationships, marriage, parenting, or sex. What we fail to realize is just because we have attained a high level of worldly success in whatever endeavor does not qualify us to make good decisions about life. This is humbling to admit because it would stand to reason that living a good, satisfying, enjoyable life would be something basic. However, achieving the best quality life for ourselves is not intuitive, and the majority of the world does not receive any kind of basic instruction for these elementary life skills. As a matter of fact, we learn mostly from those around us who have failed at most of these things. In order to learn how to live the best life possible, it is necessary to go to the experts, just as we would in any field of study. Even better, to go to the being that created that life and has the plans for each and every one of us already laid out, plans to prosper and not to harm. That being is God.

The Bible is God's Word. It is a book about God by God. God is the one who created everything. He created my life. Your life. Everyone's life. It stands to reason that the best entity to consult regarding how to best live and order one's life would be from the being who created it. It makes perfect sense when stated that way. Anyone can understand that logic.

Unfortunately, many, many people disregard the Bible because they do not understand one thing or another. Let's say I took a person off the street and gave them the spine surgery textbook that I described earlier and had them read it. They come across something they do not understand. Because of this, they decide that the book must not be true. Does that make any sense at all? The book was written by the ten experts in spine surgery in the world. Obviously, there are going to be things in the book that the average person does not understand. But that does not mean the book is not true.

This is the situation many encounter with the Bible. The words of that book are from the creator of the universe, God. The one who has knowledge of ALL things. It was written by people who spoke to God. People who heard from God. The New Testament is written by people who knew Jesus, God's begotten son, who was God in the flesh. It was written by people who saw firsthand what Jesus (God) did. It was written by people who did extensive research and investigation into Jesus's life if they were not present firsthand during His life. Therefore, in the same manner that the spine textbook was written by people who have the highest education and experience about spine surgery, the Bible was written by people who have firsthand communication with, observation, and experience or who did thorough research about God and Jesus. Who are we to say that we can define and know God in comparison to the experts who wrote the Bible?

A God we human beings can understand is a God we can control. After all, if I understood everything about God, what He does and why He does it, why do I need a God at all? A God that can be completely understood is a God that we can control, which is the natural desire of a human being. We all want to be our own God. Accepting a God that we do not completely understand is an acknowledgment that we are not in control.

Early in recovery, a friend of mine suggested that I stop asking why. Why is not a good question for me when it comes to life. By asking the question why, there is an unconscious undertone of nonacceptance. Rather than taking energy to determine the cause of whatever life situation is going on, it is far more beneficial for me to accept that situation and seek God's wisdom to navigate it. God can do whatever He wants whenever He wants, and for me to ask why to the creator of the universe is an exercise in futility. My life operates far better when I seek to understand His nature and characteristics and look to Him to navigate life.

Although far less expansive and impactful, the analogy of people's view on spine surgery is similar. The vast majority of people do not understand spine surgery, nor do they have any need to, until something happens to them where it may benefit them. Many people do not believe in spine surgery because of something they have heard or seen from another person, who is usually not a spine surgeon. However, when a person NEEDS spine surgery, all of a sudden, a person becomes willing to seek it out, surrender to it, and have it done because the pain is so great that they cannot bear it anymore. They do not even care that they do not understand it completely because they are so eager to be rid of the pain. Spine surgery existed prior to this time and will exist after this time. The principles of spine surgery have been true and will continue to be true.

And so it is with God. He has always existed and will continue to exist, irrespective of a person's belief or understanding of Him. He will be available to help when one becomes willing to seek Him and surrender to Him because the pain of life is too great to endure by one's self. The reward that God will effect in that person's life will be directly proportional to how surrendered that person is to God's will for him/her, just as much as a person's recovery from spine surgery is contingent on how compliant one is with the surgeon's instructions. The pragmatic analogy of spine surgery is a limited but illustrative corollary to the presence of God in a person's life.

I have extensive knowledge in one specific subspecialty of a subspecialty of medicine, and that qualifies me in the world to be labeled as intelligent. But I have very limited knowledge of cardiology, pulmonology, hematology, radiology, general surgery, etc. And that is just medicine. I have extremely limited knowledge of physics, chemistry, marine biology, etc. And that is just science. I have almost no knowledge of musical composition, art, social sciences, political science, etc. Therefore, what do I really know?

Not much.

I accept that there are going to be certain things in the Bible that I will never understand on this earth. Just because I do not understand these things does not mean that they are not true. The qualifications of God are far superior to mine that there is no possible way I could understand everything that happens and why.

The primary struggle I have each and every day is this: **remembering and realizing that there is a God and that I am not Him.**

Humility. I know my place in the universe today. I surrender to God. He is the author of my life. The author of your life. Of every single human being's life that has ever existed. He knows the story from beginning to end of each and every one of us. Would it not stand to reason that if I want to live the best possible life, get the most enjoyment, and have the most peace, I need to know and talk to the being who created my story and wrote it? The one who has ultimate authority over my life?

This is the paradoxical truth about life: **"Maximum freedom in life comes from submission to authority"** (Brady Cooper).

This is seen physically in the case of the judicial system. If I do not submit to the laws of this country, and I am caught and convicted, I will be placed in prison. My freedom will be limited. This is obvious. Any person can understand this.

In the spiritual realm, the same holds true. God's credentials are these: creator of the universe and all things, sovereign ruler, absolute final judge. This is an authority I do not have issue surrendering to today. If I do not submit to the laws of God, my spiritual freedom, my lasting sense of peace and serenity, will be limited. No matter how I justify and rationalize my behavior, since I am (and we are all) created in the image of God, there will be a spiritual discontent that I will feel internally when disobeying God's laws, whether I recognize it or not. Sin in our lives does not make us bad people. Sin in our lives makes us human.

This is how my alcoholism progressed. I would suppress or ignore the fact that I was not doing the right thing, whatever it was in that moment, and that spiritual death slowly crept over me. Not wanting to feel the guilt and shame associated with that, my drinking increased to the point where I could never drink enough to eradicate that feeling deep within me. God knew what was best for me, and what I needed so the circumstances and events that finally sent me to rehab were exactly what I needed to be rescued from spiritual death to eternal life.

Ravi Zacharias has said, "Sin will take you further than you want to go, keep you longer than you want to stay, and cost you more than you want to pay." That is exactly where my alcoholism took me. But I also realize that it was exactly what I needed to be broken in my journey to become fully dependent on God for EVERYTHING in my life.

Knowing God and having deep effective spiritual experiences with Him is the only way that I have any chance of following the instructions set forth in the Bible. Many of them do not make sense to my human mind. They do not feel good to me in the moment. Being a human of limited intellect, my only experience is the moment. I cannot see the rest of the story. I cannot comprehend the wound to my spirit and soul when I operate outside the instructions in the Bible. They are commandments because they come from the ultimate authority of life itself, God.

This is how alcoholism is overcome. How any sin is overcome. Deep and effective spiritual experiences.

> We have found much of heaven and we have been rocketed into a fourth dimension of existence of which we had not even dreamed.
>
> The great fact is just this, and nothing less: That we have had deep and effective spiritual experiences which have revolutionized our whole attitude toward life, toward our fellows

and toward God's universe. The central fact of our lives today is the absolute certainty that our Creator has entered into our hearts and lives in a way which is indeed miraculous. He has commenced to accomplish those things for us which we could never do by ourselves. (*Alcoholics Anonymous* [a.k.a. the Big Book], 4th ed., 25)

How to achieve these spiritual experiences is what Alcoholics Anonymous has taught me. It gave me a clear and direct pathway to surrender and follow Jesus maximally. My walk with Jesus has deepened my spirituality beyond sobriety to abundant life. This process can be utilized by any person (substance abuse disorder or not) to achieve eternal, abundant life.

It is my prayer that anyone who reads this book will find the same peace, joy, serenity, happiness, and freedom that I have found. I did not find this path on my own or with my decision-making. God has directed my steps all along the way, whether I believed in Him or not. Without hesitation, I can attest to the fact that I live in heaven today. Not someday. TODAY.

I pray that you will find much of heaven and be rocketed into a fourth dimension of existence of which you have not even dreamed as I have. You have no idea how great your life can be, and it is my hope that you will find and fulfill your God-given destiny and experience how grand life really is.

Heavenly Father, I pray that through my story, others will seek and find You. I pray that truth is revealed. I pray that the delusion of the promises of this world is stripped away and found empty. I pray that my reader's journey will be accelerated toward You, and they too will find heaven in the here and now. I pray all these things in the mighty and powerful name of Jesus. Amen.

3

EVERY SINNER HAS
A FUTURE, EVERY
SAINT HAS A PAST

I was born in Chicago on August 11, 1975. My mother is from Latvia, which is a country on the east side of the Baltic Sea. Most people have heard of Lithuania and/or Estonia, but the response I typically get when I tell people this is "Where in the heck is that?" My dad is from Japan, and of course, everyone knows where that is. Both my parents are proficient in math and science. My parents are physically small because they grew up after World War II in countries that had few resources, but all my cousins on both sides are very tall, most over six feet. I have been very fortunate and blessed to have great genetics for math and science, and large physical stature. The combination works rather well for me, and I appreciate my heritage.

My mother was born in Riga, the capital of Latvia. She only lived in Latvia for a short period, however. When Russia occupied Latvia after World War II, she and her family fled Latvia and lived in refugee camps in England and Germany. Eventually, they came to the United States to Chicago, where she went to college. They all stayed in the Chicagoland area, as there is a large Latvian population there. She had one sister, my aunt Irene, who was part of my life growing up.

My father was born in Sapporo, which is in Hokkaido, the northernmost island of Japan. He thinks our ancestors are the Ainu, which were Eskimos who emigrated to Japan. He thinks this because we have an unusual amount of body hair for Japanese people. This may or may not be true, but I find it interesting. He had two brothers and two sisters and grew up in post-World War II Japan. I do not know a lot of the details, but I do not think they had much growing up. I know very little about his father, my grandfather. My dad did not have kind things to say about him, and it seems he may have been an alcoholic based on what little I know. My dad attended Waseda University in Tokyo, which is the Japanese equivalent of Harvard. He studied architecture because he loved art and design but thought that he needed to do something practical to make a living using those skills.

He originally came to the United States for an internship in Chicago. His thought was that Japan, having very little available land, does not have many opportunities for design and construction of new buildings, but America does. He planned to come to the United States for a year to explore architecture and then return to Japan.

My parents met through a mutual friend in Chicago. My mom likes to help people explore new things and introduce new experiences to them. So naturally, my mom was interested in taking my dad around Chicago and showing him everything. They started playing tennis together and eventually married and had me. My dad did not end up going back to Japan, and our family began its life in the city of Chicago.

My mom had a degree in chemistry and worked as a chemist at Baxter labs when I was very little. I do not know exactly when, but she became a teacher and taught science most of my life that I can remember. She is always teaching, even to this day. I remember her showing me the periodic table when I was in elementary school and having me memorize the elements.

My dad did architecture his whole life. He had many jobs with many different firms throughout the years, which he blamed on the economy. He told me to never be an architect because one's job goes up and down with the economy. If times are good, people are building, and an architect will have work. If there is a recession or depression, no one is building, and an architect will have no work. He did

28

not have very good communication skills, some of it being language, but a lot of it being that he was not able to read or process emotion from people. Since he is not sensitive to what he is saying to a person, he can easily offend someone, and not even realize he did so. That also played a part in why he changed jobs often.

He told me to be a doctor because it does not matter what the economy is doing; a doctor will always be "successful." In fact, if there is a recession, more people get sick! That made good sense to me as a child, but I really cannot say that it was my heart's desire to be a doctor until I was in college.

Japanese people in general are very driven to succeed in education and career. My dad wanted to succeed and did what he could to help me succeed in life, in his worldview. I remember him teaching me algebra, specifically the communicative and distributive properties with variables, when I was five or six years old. I remember crying about this and my mom pleading with him to stop because I was too young to learn that material. But he persisted. I don't know if I ever got it or not at that age, but when I was being taken to the local junior college in seventh and eighth grade for algebra, I do remember feeling as though I had seen it before. I understood it very easily at that age, and probably because of the fact that I was exposed to it at a young age.

My dad was very practical. I was very good at baseball at age eight, and I told him I wanted to be a professional baseball player. He told me directly, "You will never be a professional athlete. There will always be someone stronger, faster, and better than you in athletics; so you can get rid of that dream right now. You can play sports and have fun, but you will never be a professional. You need to spend your time studying and learning in order to be successful in life." Remember, I was eight when I was told this. Yes, it is a very practical advice. Only 0.0296 percent of children will become professional athletes, but I think there may have been a kinder, gentler way of communicating this to my eight-year-old self.

I realize now that was God guiding me toward my destiny. Neither my mother nor my father was a superb athlete, so I did not have the genetics to be a transcendent athlete. It is a realistic expectation that I would not be a professional. Even though I resented him at the time for that comment, I can look back and see the powerful hand of God directing my steps. In reality, it would have been more appropriate for my dad to tell me that I would never be an orthopedic spine surgeon. There are only just over one hundred spine fellowship spots each year in the United States. The odds of being a professional athlete are higher than that of being an orthopedic spine surgeon based on numbers. But he just knew to push me into academics, and whatever path I took, would be successful in his eyes in that endeavor.

I succeeded in the academic arena very well. God has created me to be book smart. That is not an arrogant statement. It is just true. Michael Jordan does not apologize for being good at basketball, and I am not apologizing for being book smart. I say this now, because you will find out later why this is not necessarily a positive attribute in all aspects of life.

I always finished my homework as quickly as possible. I remember my second-grade teacher actually chastised me for doing this one time. "You think you're so smart! You think you can do your work so fast." Actually, I didn't think that. I did do that.

At some point in the middle of second grade, I was promoted to third grade. This is not something I see happening very often today. I don't know any people who also did this except me at that time. That is how I draw the conclusion that God made me very, very smart, because I continued to excel and be at the top of the class, even though I was about one and a half years younger than my classmates.

Thinking about this as an adult now, socially, it must have been very difficult for me to assimilate to a whole new class, with all new older peers. They all knew that I was the "smart" kid who just got put in third grade. I do not remember the social transition being difficult, but it must have been. I may have forgotten much of what I do not want to remember, or maybe it just was not that hard. Either way, I was the "smart Asian kid" in an almost all-white suburban school of Chicago.

The thing is, I did not have to work very hard to assimilate information. I just got it. I became upset at a friend of mine when we were about college age when he told me that he and his friend used to make fun of me when they passed my house, saying that I was studying spelling books. That was just it. I did not have to study hardly at all. I just absorbed information the first time around. I cannot say that I had an exceptional work ethic at that age, or even throughout my schooling. I was just blessed to be able to learn and memorize information easily.

I played many sports growing up (tennis, hockey, baseball), swam on the swim team, and went snow skiing throughout my childhood. I rode my bike and rode skateboards frequently. I built ramps with my neighbor, and we rode and jumped for hours at a time. We also bowled a lot. We would get a pass for unlimited bowling over the summer at the bowling alley across the street from our neighborhood. In all these sports, I was always very good, but not top tier in anything. My relationship with sports was appropriate, in my opinion. No sport dominated my life, and I was never pushed into a higher level for a "scholarship." I formed bonds, made friends, and was active with sports; and they were a part of my life but were not the focus or goal of my life.

From an external view, and from all accounts, I felt that I had a great childhood. Every need was met. I participated in many different activities and did not have many restrictions. I never felt like our family needed anything, and I was happy most of the time from what I can remember. My parents were not overtly affectionate in front of me (I do not think they were when not in front of me either). They were stable. My mom taught and cooked; my dad worked and came home and went to the study to do more work. There was never any alcohol or drama in my house. I was an only child, so I played with my neighbor, who was two years younger than me.

We never talked about God. There was a Catholic school called Holy Ghost that my neighbor went to that was behind our neighborhood. I thought that was strange. They had to wear uniforms, and there was this churchy building in the front. I never talked to anyone about it and was not really interested in it at all, except I knew Joe went there, and he had to wear a uniform.

I was the only Asian in a pretty much all-Caucasian suburb. From at least second grade onward, I was the subject of a lot of Asian jokes. A lot of eye pulling from the sides to make slanty eyes and taunting. I would tell my parents about it. My mom is very passive, and she just told me to not take any notice. My dad would say the same thing. Basically, I just stuffed those feelings of being different away and tried not to feel them.

I was a very responsible child, and since I always made straight As, my parents trusted me. I never got in trouble at school or at home. I just had the inherent sense to do the right thing (at that point in my life) so that I could succeed, whatever that meant to me at that age. Because of this, I think I was about eleven years old when I would ride my bike to and from school and come home to an empty house. I was a latchkey kid. Both of my parents worked until about five, so I would come home and do basically whatever I wanted. Most of the time, that consisted of me riding my bike or skateboard around outside.

A couple of memories stand out to me in the sixth grade. I do not have many conscious memories of things in my childhood, so the fact that I can remember the details of these events demonstrate to me that they were significant and affected my thinking about life and the world. These events shaped my worldview and fueled my actions and behaviors well into my adult life.

One of these times that I remember is the time I had my first beer. My parents rarely drank, so it wasn't like I was exposed to alcohol, or my dad gave me my first drink. I remember going to my friend's house. His parents also were not home after school. He didn't live far from the school, and we rode our bikes to his house. It was there that I had my first beer (Old Style) and smoked my first cigarette. This experience was not particularly transformative, as I've heard other alcoholics describe. I don't remember loving it or it even changing the way I felt. Old Style is low-quality beer, and I was not particularly fond of it. Cigarettes also did not have any particular effect on me at that time either. We drank a couple of beers, smoked some cigarettes, and shot BB guns at things that afternoon. It was fun, but I had no specific desire to do it again. We were boys being boys and doing things that we were not supposed to be doing. I could take or leave a drink at that point, so I would call myself a "normal" drinker, as normal as a drinker could be at age eleven. When my parents came home later, they did not know about any of this. I wasn't drunk, and I didn't smell like cigarettes, so life went on as usual. The next time I drank wasn't until I was fifteen.

I always made the honor roll. I made straight As all my life. It was something that just came naturally to me. I did not have to study long hours; I was just able to do it. This, I know today, is a massive gift from God.

Probably the most traumatic experience of my childhood happened that year also. There was another kid at school, who, for reasons unbeknownst to me, wanted to fight me. I was bigger than he was, and it seemed like a fun thing to do, so I agreed. One afternoon, after school, we went to a park in town. I had not told anyone about the fight, but there were about five other seventh graders there who had heard about it somehow and came to see the tussle. One of them lived in my neighborhood. We were not particularly good friends, but we did know each other and sometimes rode bikes and jumped ramps together.

The fight started. We wrestled to the ground, and I hit him in the head and face a couple of times. I am not a violent person and had never hit anyone before, so it was not like I made him a bloody mess or did any real damage. The seventh graders were cheering and shouting. I do not have any recollection of what they said. I finally let my opponent up, and he ran to a house across the street. "Come over here," he said. "This is my house."

I said, "I'm not coming over there. Why would I come over to your front yard? What if your parents are home?" I left, and so did the seventh graders. We did not leave together. We all went on home and went about our day. Again, my parents did not know anything about what happened. They didn't ask; I didn't tell them.

The next day at school, I was feeling good about myself. Not excessively prideful about the fight, but I knew I stood my ground, and at the very least, I wouldn't get picked on as much as I had proven myself physically the day before. Before school started at Wood Dale

Junior High School, all the kids wait in the parking lot outside before they open the doors to the gym. I was standing outside when all of a sudden, another sixth grader put me in a headlock and wrestled me to the ground. He was in the "cool kid" group and was somehow friends with the boy I fought the day before.

"Why did you tell your friends to come to the fight?" he said.

"WHAT? I didn't tell anyone to come!" I shrieked back.

"You told your seventh-grade friends to come to the fight so if you started losing, they would come in and rescue you!" he said.

"I didn't do that! I just showed up, and they were there! I swear I didn't tell anyone to come!" I shouted, head still in a headlock in front of the whole school.

"Whatever! You told them to come because you were scared! You shouldn't have done that!" he shouted.

I do not recall what else was said or how long it lasted, but it seemed like I was in that headlock in front of the whole school forever. It was probably a good five minutes. Finally, he let me loose. I wasn't hurt physically, but I was completely dejected. I felt like everyone was looking at me and laughing. It was the most humiliating thing that had ever happened to me in my childhood.

It was at that moment I thought to myself, *I'll show them.* I was determined to succeed at every level and make sure everyone would know about it. I wanted to make sure I succeeded well beyond what all of them could ever do academically. I also had dreams of being bigger and stronger than everyone else so no one could ever make me feel that way again. I was incensed, and I was going to do everything in my power to make sure they would feel as bad about themselves as I did that day. My life from that day forward was all about performance, appearance, and control.

Shortly after that, I remember another incident that shows the desperation of this awkward, intelligent kid, trying to fit in and be accepted. I had always got straight As. God had gifted me to do well in school, and I never struggled in this area. Because of this, my name was always on the high honor roll. In junior high school, they would put the names and certificates of the people who made the high honor roll in a glass case in the front of the school as one walked in through the front doors. I was continually being made fun of for getting good grades (children will do anything to bring someone down), and it was something that I did not like. I decided to purposefully get Bs during that semester. So I did. Since I always knew the right answers, it was easy for me to provide the wrong answers and control what my score would be.

When my report card came out, my parents asked me a few questions but just told me to do better. There was not much of a discussion about it. The principal of my school called me into the office the next day.

"What are you doing?" he asked.

"What are you talking about?" I said, as if I had no idea what was going on.

"You always get straight As. Is there something going on that I need to know about? I don't understand how you could have gotten Bs last semester," he said.

I proceeded to tell him how I did not want my name up in the front of the school on the high honor roll because I didn't want the other kids making fun of me. He told me to NOT purposefully get lower grades and that if I made the high honor roll, they simply wouldn't put my name up there. As obvious and ridiculous as this all sounds, that had never occurred to me before. It is foolish to try to not do well when I was fully capable, and there was an easy solution to this problem. But I didn't have anyone to talk to about how I felt, about how things ever affected me. My parents did a great job of raising me, but the area in which they lacked was emotional support and spiritual direction. This caused me to bury any emotion that was negative and figure out a solution myself to rectify the situation.

I did not know it at the time, but that was the genesis of many pathologic but very successful coping mechanisms that would serve me into my adult life. I had this vision of myself that was bigger than life, and all the people who hurt me would covet what I had and envy me. They would know that I was not to be messed with. They would wish they would be as successful as I would be. I was in charge of my image, reputation, and success; and I would do whatever it took to achieve this grand vision, and eventual delusion.

A lot of alcoholics and addicts have similar stories. The problem with this is that no matter how much is achieved, no matter how big and strong a person becomes, no matter how much money a person makes, no matter what accomplishments and accolades are garnered, it is NEVER enough. It is a constant quest to prove to someone else, anyone else, that I had value.

Never having been taught anything about God, or what the Bible says about me, I had no idea that I had value just because God created me. I did not know that I was wonderfully and beautifully made. I did not know that the creator of the universe knew the number of hairs on my head and had planned my entire life before I was even born. It was up to me, all me and only me, to prove that to the world. That is a daunting, impossible task for anyone to undertake.

Taking the playbook from my parents, success meant having a good job. Success meant being able to live in a nice house and material things for myself and my family. Success meant having enough money to go on nice vacations. Success meant having a family and appearing to the world that I had my life in order. Success meant portraying myself in such a way that everyone liked me and wanted to be around me.

I went on this quest to show everyone how great I am and how incredible I could be. I excelled academically and went to a boarding school called the Illinois Mathematics and Science Academy (IMSA). It is a public school that attracts the top students from the entire state of Illinois. It was founded in 1985 and takes students from sophomore through senior year. When my family learned of this school, there was no question that my dad wanted me to go there. My mom was not quite as excited about me living away from home at age fourteen, but she did value academics as well and agreed. I did my freshman year at the local public school and applied to IMSA. I got in, and off I went at age fourteen to boarding school about an hour from our home.

IMSA is an incredible educational institution. They treated us as if we were in college. Attendance was not taken, and there were no bells to alert us to go to the next class. Of course, we were all the top students throughout Illinois, so the majority of us went to class and did what we were supposed to do to be academically successful. I took classes such as organic chemistry, advanced chemistry and physics, and calculus and systems theory, classes that are normally offered at college. By the time I got to Northwestern, the classes were pretty much redundant, which made it easy for me to excel there.

While I am forever grateful for my experience and relationships that I developed at IMSA, there was one huge void in my life by going to school there. While we had residential assistants who were grown men to supervise us in our dorms, I lacked a solid male mentor to guide me in life. My dad did not provide much in the way of life or spiritual guidance, so I can't say that I would have been any better off at home for those years. Even though I was intellectually capable of taking care of myself and excelling in school, I needed a male mentor to teach me how to live life appropriately. I believe that every teenage male needs a strong male mentor, preferably his father, but if not him, then at least another adult male who lives life well to guide and lead him.

An education of the mind without an education of the heart is no education at all. (Aristotle)

That is what I was getting at IMSA. A premier education of the mind, but zero education of my heart. This is not a fault of the institution. I never sought spiritual or emotional assistance because it was never prioritized to me as a child.

My concept of being a successful male adult was taught to me by whatever I saw in movies and TV. I believed that in order to be a success, I needed to have a reputable occupation that garnered me a tremendous amount of money, have a beautiful wife and family, be physically strong and dominating, and enjoy the fruits of my labor with lavish parties and vacations. Since I did not have athletic prowess but was academically gifted, I thought the best way for me to accomplish this was to be a doctor. Even back then, I did have a heart to help people, so being a doctor seemed like the obvious career choice for me.

My real drinking career began when I was in high school. My friends and I were all on the swim team throughout our childhood, so we all became lifeguards at the neighborhood pool. I never drank at IMSA. Alcohol wasn't easily available, and the stakes were higher there. I definitely did not want to get kicked out of that school. My drinking in high school was over the summer and on weekends when I came home.

The first time I got really drunk I was fifteen. One of the older lifeguards had a party at his house. I rode my bike there because I rode my bike everywhere. I remember drinking Dr. Peppers. A Dr. Pepper is when you drop an amaretto shot into a glass of beer and drink it as fast as you can. It tastes exactly like Dr. Pepper. I do remember liking that, and I also did like the feeling of getting drunk at this point. I could say what I wanted to say to girls or anyone, and I truly didn't care about what anyone thought of me. It removed the fear of what other people thought of me. It took away the inhibitions, and I could say whatever I wanted. I definitely remember liking the way it made me feel.

Having no tolerance, and naïve to the effects of alcohol, I got ridiculously drunk. I don't remember much of what happened at that party. I was told later that I was passed out on the couch, and they gave me bowl to throw up in. They told me it was my "million-dollar bowl," so I wouldn't let go of it to ensure that I would have it when I vomited. When I finally came to, it was two in the morning. This was in the era before cell phones, so my parents had no idea where I was or what happened. I rode my bike home in a daze at two in the morning. My parents asked me what was wrong, and I just told them I was tired. The absurd lies we tell to try to get ourselves off the hook. Like they had no idea I was still drunk.

But since I always did well in school, and because I was mostly responsible, the only punishment I received after that was I now had a curfew at midnight. Since my parents did not grow up in the United States, I am fairly certain they did not understand the gravity of this situation. They probably had no idea that high school kids go to parties regularly where alcohol is served, and many appalling things happen. Because my performance was so good in school, they were willing to look the other way if I was not getting in trouble with the school or the police. That is the lesson I learned from this. If I perform well in what society expects me to do, and protect that, then it does not matter what I do on my free time, as long as I did not get in trouble.

I drank regularly over the summers and on weekends. I always made sure to make it home before midnight to keep my parents off my back. My drinking habits were definitely different than most of my friends. Drinking alcohol was not about enjoying it. I drank to obtain the feeling that I desired from alcohol. I was drinking to be the better version of myself I always wanted to be. Bold. Courageous. Able to say or do what I was thinking without holding back. The problem was that when I was drunk, I was NOT a better version of myself. I was just able to express myself without having the fear of what other people thought of me.

4

COLLEGE AND MEDICAL
EDUCATION

I applied to several prestigious universities and decided to go to Northwestern University near Chicago. Even though I was only forty-five minutes from home, I rarely went home to see my parents during college. I majored in biomedical engineering because I did not want to be a biology teacher if I did not gain entrance into medical school. I thought that if I at least get a degree in engineering, I could still have a successful career doing that instead. Fortunately, being a biomedical engineering major parlayed well into my future career in being an orthopedic spine surgeon.

I drank a lot in college. When I say a lot, I mean A LOT. There are many nicknames I have accrued over the years, but one I was bestowed in college was Juris "No Moderation". "No Moderation" did not just apply to my drinking. It applied to everything I did in life. Whatever it was, be it working out, academics, or drinking, I would either not do something or do it all the way. This pattern of thinking in extremes like this is typical for most alcoholics. Since we have fear of failure or fear of what other people will say, we will avoid doing certain things we think we may fail at. But at the other end of the spectrum, if we commit to something, we will throw everything we have into it to do it as perfectly as we can because we are looking for the praise from other people in order to feel good about ourselves. When we do not achieve the standards that we have created in our own minds, and others critique our performance, that will often lead an alcoholic to drink to drown out that negative feeling.

Before classes start at Northwestern, the freshmen arrive for what is called New Students' Week. It is a week of orientations, getting to know the professors and campus, and settling in to college life. What it really is, however, is a massive week of partying with kids who just left home for the first time and are out on their own. The fraternities threw huge parties to try to allure new freshmen to join them, and alcohol was abundantly available.

I knew the exact moment when I knew that I was going to be an Alpha Tau Omega (ATO). My friends from the dorm and I went to the parties they were having around campus, so we went to a lot of different fraternities. I remember walking by the chapter room at ATO that week. I saw at least fifty kegs stacked up in rows along the wall, and I was thinking to myself, *This is the place I need to be.* I knew that ATO was a party fraternity, and that was what I was all about. However, we were not really much of a party fraternity in the sense that we would throw big parties, and lots of girls would come over, and everyone would have a really wonderful time. We were more of an Animal House-type fraternity where we would throw parties, and not very many girls would come, because we were always too drunk or too high to be appealing to anyone with any sensibility.

I drank at least three days a week, but I always took care of my grades. Notice I did not say I took care of going to class. Sometimes I would go, and sometimes I would not, but because of the excellent preparation I got at IMSA and my academic abilities, I was always able to obtain the high grades necessary for me to get into medical school. My friends and I road-tripped to Mardi Gras in New Orleans my sophomore, junior, and senior year. My sophomore year, we left that Wednesday to go down, and I brought my organic chemistry books in the car to study for the test I had that Monday when we returned. A real genius idea, I thought. However, there was an ice storm in southern Illinois, and we were in two cars. We got separated, and I ended up in the car that did not have my books in it. Needless to say, I did not study at all. After three days of hard partying and little sleeping, we returned that Sunday night where I promptly went to bed. I completely aced that test. I have just been fortunate that God has blessed me with the ability to do well in school, and that is how I got away with my drinking for so long. The downside of this ability is that I was able to avoid the harsh consequences of my drinking because I was able to make up for it in other areas. Areas that the world would label me a "success."

I met my first wife when I was in college. She was in this advanced science program that a friend of mine from IMSA was in. We met the first week of college but did not start dating until late freshman year. We dated on and off during college but ended up getting back together again the semester before graduation. The cook of my fraternity was this great guy named JT. He was an older African American man, and he was hilarious. He told me at that time that I probably was not going to find a better woman than her. We were both going to medical school and be doctors. She was attractive and had a great personality, and we got along very well. In my mind, where performance, appearance, and control were the primary drivers, I decided that he was right. We would be two successful doctors married to each other. We would have our standard 2.2 average American children and live a wonderful life in a huge house in the suburbs. Everything I had in mind to be the success I had envisioned myself to be.

I went off to University of Illinois College of Medicine, and she went to a different medical school because she lived in a different state. We got married during medical school, which facilitated her transfer to University of Illinois, and we could be together. Looking back now, I can see the manipulation of the whole situation by me. I was definitely not ready to get married and really had no idea what a good marriage entailed. But I wanted to continue down this path of the vision of a successful life I had built up in my mind. To have the life that everyone else would envy. I would "show them."

I did not drink much in medical school. My wife and I studied, did our rotations, and generally had a good time and life together. I was happy throughout that whole experience. We matched at University of Miami for residency together in the couples match. She became a pediatric resident, and I was an orthopedic resident.

The orthopedic residency program at that time fit my personality very well. The vast majority of the residents were guys who worked hard, were athletic, and worked out. One of the first-year rotations was spent in the orthopedic emergency room, which we called the Pit. A third-year resident rotated with us, and the shift was from 7:00 AM until 6:00 PM. During that rotation, we took all the consults from the emergency room and trauma, and that is where we learned to stabilize fractures and put casts and splints on—basic orthopedic stuff. There was a weight room in the medical school building across from the hospital. When the ER and trauma consults were slow in the late morning, a required part of that rotation was for the pit boss (third-year resident) and pit boy (first-year resident) to go work out. Being the workout fiend that I was, this fit in perfectly with my personality and lifestyle.

I went out and partied some when I was a first-year resident. We went to some clubs, and I drank, but it was not a lot that year. There were a couple other older residents who were known for going out and partying a lot, through the night, into the next morning. I could not understand how they did that.

I found out. I met some of them late in my first year and started to party with them. That was when I was introduced to cocaine and ecstasy. I will never forget the first time I tried ecstasy. We were out around eight in the morning on a Sunday at a club with an outdoor terrace where the parties would routinely go into Sunday afternoon. A friend of mine gave me some. I felt AMAZING. I danced on the speaker with my shirt off, smiling like crazy. One girl that we hung out with pointed at me and said, "You are so happy!" And I was. It was the best feeling I had ever had up until that point. I chased that high for years afterward with all kinds of combinations of drugs and never recaptured that feeling again from drugs.

The dirty little secret about ecstasy is that although you reach an intense high and feel very happy because of the dopamine release, two days later, your body is depleted of dopamine; and I found myself crying in the shower for no good reason. I accepted this as part of it. It was worth that to experience the high and happiness that I felt from it for several hours.

From that point forward, I partied a lot. My attitude was that if I was going to be on call and work all night sometimes, I would party hard and stay up all night other times. My wife was a pediatrics resident and then worked in the pediatric emergency room, so I would mostly go out on the nights that she was on call or have a night shift. Sometimes I would go out when she was home and be out all night and into the next day. She never gave me a hard time or questioned me. I was faithful in my marriage during that whole time in Miami, despite being at clubs with all kinds of models and scantily clad women. I just wanted the attention. I did not have to have sex with a woman, as long as I could sense that she wanted me. I was very proud to be married and be faithful, and I bragged on my wife for "letting" me do what I wanted. On the nights I spent home with my wife, we had good times together.

When I entered treatment in 2015, I was evaluated for everything including sex addiction. Although I didn't qualify as a sex addict, they told me that I had the potential to become one. One quality of a sex addict is that desire to be lusted after. I definitely had that. I know that I have the potential to become addicted to any substance or behavior.

In 2006, we went to Chicago where I did my spine fellowship at Rush University Medical Center. My wife worked at the children's hospital doing emergency room work. That year, I did not drink or party much. The only times I would go party would be when I would go out of town and meet my Miami friends in Miami or Vegas. The first part of my fellowship year was difficult for me. Spine surgery is so much different than any other orthopedic surgery. When I finished my residency in Miami, I felt that I was a very skilled surgeon. During my first six months at Rush, I felt like I had lost the ability to operate. I had difficulty learning the anatomy and techniques, and it was frustrating. This likely had an impact on my drinking/drugging. I had to achieve the next level, so I did not want anything to interfere with the advancement of my performance. Performance, appearance, and control were my life; so at that time, I still had the ability to limit my drinking.

Our marriage was good, and my wife got pregnant that year. Everything was going according to my grand plan of life. I graduated my fellowship, and we moved to Murfreesboro, Tennessee, to begin our careers and this wonderful life I had envisioned.

I had made it. I was finally "showing them." I became extremely busy very quickly. Money was rolling in, and we had a beautiful house in an up-and-coming neighborhood. Life would now be perfect, and we would ride off in the sunset together, happily ever after.

5

WORK: MY FIRST ADDICTION

Something changed. I was still very selfish, and I wanted what I wanted right when I wanted it. My wife started to expect me home more often. She was not as allowing when I wanted to go to Vegas or Miami to party with my friends. I did not drink at all in Murfreesboro at that time and did not seek out any drugs. I saved that for the times when I went out of town. I had a reputation to protect. I was Dr. S, successful spine surgeon, and I could not let anything tarnish that veneer. My wife did not like that I was working so much. However, as I saw it at the time, I needed to work very hard to provide all the things that I wanted for our lifestyle. I had this beautiful daughter at home, but instead of feeling the need to spend time with her, I felt that I had to make more money to give her a wonderful life. I worked many hours and became very "successful." I provided above and beyond what anyone would ever need monetarily. But I neglected my wife and daughter during that time. I felt like I needed to get out of town every couple months or so to really let loose.

My wife and I started drifting apart. I took any negative comments from her as personal attacks. Looking back, they were not attacks. I did not learn this until much later in recovery, but when my wife is complaining to me, she is actually telling me what she needs from me. Now I am much more spiritually aware, and I can more often discern my wife's needs from her complaining. But having no relationship with God at that stage in my life, all I heard was complaining, mostly about and directed at me. I was so wrapped up in myself that I could not understand why she was complaining so much.

Living in that darkness, separated from God, and believing the lies the world will tell you, I convinced myself that I was obviously married to the wrong person. She and I were too different, and I did not want to live my life unhappy being married to her. I would complain about my marriage to anyone who would listen and heard what I wanted to hear. *You deserve to be happy.* You do not deserve that kind of treatment. Anyone who is married to you should be telling you how great you are all the time. I was hearing how great I was from everyone else, and I did not feel that I was hearing that from my wife. I convinced myself that our daughter would be totally fine. It was better for her to grow up with us divorced, rather than in a marriage where we were not happy and did not love each other anymore. I envisioned her having this great life with her mom during her parenting times, and the times she would have with me would be far better if I did not have to deal with her mother. Today, I can tell you those are all lies that the enemy tells us to encourage our disobedience toward God.

My divorce is my personal contribution to an imperfect world and to the suffering of many people. God did not cause this suffering. I did. My selfish, evil heart. Although I do not regret my divorce because it is part of the story that has led me to eternal life with Jesus, I can see how selfish divorce is and how there is ALWAYS pain associated with it. My ex-wife and I have just about the best arrangement and relationship I think divorced parents can have, but there is still a hurt for her and for my daughter and for me. There are times I cannot take our daughter on vacation with the rest of my family due to the parenting plan. There are things she misses out on with me and her siblings. She is remarkably well adjusted, but I know there is a certain level of pain associated with this that I have caused.

God does redeem all things. My daughter does know and has stated that without the divorce, I would not be the father I am today in Christ. Everything that has happened on my journey has led me to Jesus, and I know beyond a shadow of a doubt that nothing was in vain. However, being human, I do feel guilt at times about the actions of my past.

6

FAME: MY NEXT ADDICTION

God has given me an unusual ability to eat large quantities of food at a very fast rate. In 2008, I was ranked among the top 10 competitive eaters in the world. It was not the path to fame that I would have chosen, but nonetheless, it had its benefits and got me on ESPN. My competitive eating career fueled my craving for attention and fit perfectly with my drive for performance, appearance, and control.

I always knew I could eat a lot. It amuses me when I tell people about this, and then they proceed to tell me how much they can eat. The most I have ever eaten in one sitting was at Thanksgiving in 2007 or 2008. I weighed myself before and after the meal. In one hour, I consumed seventeen pounds of food and liquid. To me, that qualifies as "a lot."

In Miami, every year one of the orthopedic hardware companies would take the graduating residents out to dinner at Don Shula's steak house for a celebration. It is a rite of passage of manliness that each orthopedic resident would order and consume a forty-eight-ounce porterhouse steak.

That night, for dinner, I had the usual appetizers and bread, drank about eight beers, ate TWO forty-eight-ounce porterhouse steaks (yes, ninety-six ounces), standard side dishes, chocolate cake, and apple cobbler. "No Moderation" was in full display. The staff there was stupefied and said they had never seen that before. They have plaques up on the wall for everyone who finishes the forty-eight-ounce porterhouse. I asked where the plaque was for ninety-six ounces of porterhouse. They replied that they didn't have one. I told them they better get one!

My entry to competitive eating began in 2006. My wife and I had moved to Murfreesboro, and I saw that they were having a Krystal hamburger eating contest at the Tennessee State Fair. Krystal hamburgers are small sliders, similar to White Castles in the North (although Krystals are FAR better, even when eating vast quantities of them quickly). I went to the fairgrounds, and in order to qualify for the qualifier, there was a two-minute contest, and the top finishers of that would be allowed to compete in the eight-minute qualifier for the Krystal finals, which are held in the birthplace of Krystal—Chattanooga, Tennessee.

I had seen competitive eating on TV, so I knew that I had to break the burger in half and dunk it in some kind of liquid to make it easier to swallow. God has gifted me with the ability to eat or drink things without having to taste them. Back in my bodybuilding days, I would drink tuna shakes that consisted of two cans of tuna blended in lemonade Crystal Light. Blend till frothy, then chug. So as disgusting as it sounds to the average person to dunk a Krystal burger in water or drink, then slam it down, it really did not bother me at all to do that.

I had never practiced this before. I was just there to see what I could do. In the two-minute qualifier, I ate fourteen Krystals in two minutes, and the winner ate seventeen in two minutes. My total was good enough to qualify me for the contest.

I remember the guy next to me in the eight-minute contest was the same one who beat me in the two-minute qualifier. I kept glancing over at him because I figured he would beat me since he did the day before. Around the four-minute mark, I saw him basically stop. I kept going. My friends in the crowd said he just could not go anymore, and he was staring at me in awe for the last four minutes. I ended up getting second with thirty-three Krystals in eight minutes. The guy who beat me was "Humble" Bob Shoudt, a veteran on the circuit who later became one of my good friends in competitive eating.

After the contest, the people who ran the contest (International Federation of Competitive Eating [IFOCE] at the time) ran over to me and said, "No one just shows up and just does that!" They could not believe it. In 2006, that was about the sixteenth best total ever recorded in competitive eating for Krystals. I had not practiced one time. In actuality, the first Krystal I ever had was at the contest the day before. They took a picture of me and put it online talking about the great "newcomer" to competitive eating, and what a great future I had in it. There were comments on competitive eating websites about me.

My ego just swelled. *Wow*, I thought. If I could do this well without ever even practicing or knowing anything about this sport (and it is a sport, not a lifestyle), how much higher could I go? Performance. Appearance. Control. Perfect. At my orthopedic group's annual retreat, they put my picture from that contest up on the big screen for everyone to see. The president of the group at the time announced my accomplishment, for anyone who did not hear about what their new partner had done. Some of my partners found this interesting and fun. Most of them did not, but I did not care. What I did on my free time had no bearing on what kind of physician I was, and we had some arguments about it, but I pressed on. I needed to achieve whatever kind of fame and attention I was going to get for this.

The Fourth of July Nathan's Hot Dog Eating Contest was televised every year on ESPN, so in my constant quest for the next thing to achieve, I set my sights on that.

Training for competitive eating is not dissimilar from training for a bodybuilding show. There is water training where one drinks a gallon of water as quickly as possible. Do NOT TRY THIS AT HOME. My body could tolerate a gallon of water without getting water intoxication, but I am telling the reader, DO NOT DO THIS. A gallon of water is seven pounds. Eventually, I was able to do this in thirty-five seconds.

The other aspect of training is actual food training to teach the esophagus to swallow large pieces without gagging. It also expands the stomach. This really is not much different from weight training. When you lift weights, you stress and damage the muscle. Then between workouts, the body repairs that damage, and the muscle grows. For whatever food I was training for, I would replicate the contest to work on speed. Then I would continue to eat for an hour afterward to work on stomach capacity. I would do this on every third day leading up to a contest. On the days I did not do this, I would just drink protein drinks, less than one thousand calories per day. That way, I could still stay lean, because of course, if I didn't look good doing this as well as placing high, what was the point? I did extra cardio and my usual weight training. On the day of the Nathan's contest in 2008, I was probably in some of the best shape I had ever been in up to that point.

I had moved my way up in the ranks where they invited me to Las Vegas, all expenses paid, to do a three-contest series that was going to be televised on Spike TV. The plan was really coming together. During the second Spike TV event, I placed the best I had ever done, and the irony of this story is hilarious. Every year, for Thanksgiving, my mom would make this cranberry Jell-O to go with the turkey. Every year, she would tell me I needed to eat some because it was so delicious, and I would love it. And every year, I would tell her no, I don't like cranberry. Well, guess what? This contest was going to be televised on Thanksgiving when it finally aired. My group of eaters was going to eat…cranberry sauce! I almost fell on the floor laughing when they told us. But like I said before, I can eat whatever without really tasting it, and I had to excel, so it was on.

I finished second in that contest, eating 11.11 lbs. of cranberry sauce in eight minutes. I was elated. This meant that for the third contest, which would air during halftime of the Super Bowl, I would be in the group with the top 8 eaters in the world. The attention I would get from this would continue to grow and fed my desire to continue to rise. The attention I was getting was filling that God-sized hole in my heart and made me feel good, at least for a while.

Competitive eating is part sport and part professional wrestling. The top competitors take the major contests very seriously and are trying to win. With my side job as an orthopedic spine surgeon, I knew I could not devote the kind of time it would take to get me to the top. Therefore, I took every opportunity I could to be outlandish and attention seeking. I cut my sleeves off my shirts for every contest. I needed to be lusted after. I needed to be known as the competitive eater who had a model physique. I adopted the nickname Dr. Bigtime (Bigtime was one of the nicknames I had in residency). I had a hat made with Dr. Bigtime on it in Asian lettering, and MLE (Major League Eating) on the back, so it would show when I turned the cap backward during the contests. I was very much in control of my image. I wanted to show everyone the version of myself that I thought would be most impressive. It did not matter to me that the sport was competitive eating. The fact that I was a doctor and fit, and this was ridiculously ironic, was amusing and enjoyable to me.

For the last Spike contest, where I had to eat ham with the top eaters, I knew I would not place top 5. It was a large ham on the bone and very difficult to eat quickly anyways. When the camera came to me during the contest, I grabbed that ham and started going crazy. I was spinning it around, gnawing at it like a wild boar, ham flying everywhere. The announcer said, "Look at Dr. Bigtime, going crazy with that ham! He's really getting into it! Man, that's wild!" I finished last in that contest, but that did not matter to me. I put on a great show and portrayed this wild, crazy, manly, buff doctor to the world; and I just knew that people would love it. And they did. And it fed my ego more and more and more and more. God-sized hole being filled with attention and accolades from people.

I flew a lot of places to do eating contests. I would take Friday off if I needed to because most of the contests were on Saturdays. My wife at the time really did not give me too much of a hard time about it. Maybe she just had given up, or maybe I just blocked her complaining from my mind. I was focused on work and competitive eating at this point. I had my beautiful one-year-old daughter at home, and I was flying all over the country chasing this thing. I was completely consumed with myself, my image, and garnering as much fame as I could.

I qualified for the 2008 Nathan's Hot Dog Eating Contest by winning a qualifier event in New Orleans. The IFOCE pays for the airfare and hotel to New York City for all the contestants who are in the finals held at the original Nathan's in Coney Island. I really felt important and satisfied now.

Since I knew I was going to be on ESPN, I had my entrance planned out. This was about the image I wanted to project to the world. I had brass knuckle rings custom made that had BIG on my right hand and TIME on my left hand that I would be able to put up to the camera when it would come to me. I would make my entrance with my shirt off to display my physique. My shirt would go back on for the contest, but I had the sleeves cut off just right. I had Yves Saint Laurent sunglasses that would give me a Terminator kind of look. An eight-by-ten picture of my daughter was pinned to my shorts because I wanted her to get on camera as well. In my delusional mind, I wanted her to potentially get some of the attention I was getting, and that somehow would make up for me being an absent father.

I ended up finishing ninth with a total of twenty-nine hot dogs and buns in ten minutes. I was happy with this total, but more importantly, I was pleased with my presentation of my image during the entrance and contest. I could not wait to see the contest on TV to see how it all turned out.

During one part of the contest, the camera panned to me, and the announcer said, "Look at S over there. Thirty-two-year-old spine surgeon, lives in rural Tennessee. He has an affinity for the expensive things in life, Ritz-Carltons, bottle service at the table. They don't have that at the Applebee's in Murfreesboro, so if he can win or place today, he'll be out on the circuit full-time. Expense accounts, lots of pretty girls, and fancy hotel rooms." The camera was on me in full glory. The caption read, "Juris S., Orthopedic Spine Surgeon and *Men's Health* Model." I thought that was hilarious, and just what I was seeking. The image I wanted to project. I just knew that this would be the start of something big.

I flew home the next day, just waiting for the calls to come in requesting interviews, fitness magazine features, or television appearances. I had done some modeling while in Miami and was in several fitness magazines and catalogs. I was certain that the media would be clamoring to talk to this orthopedic spine surgeon, fitness model, and professional competitive eater.

Of course, none of that happened. Most of my friends had seen the contest, but I did not get the kind of attention that I was expecting. I felt like no one really cared about this. The truth is, no one really did. All that work and effort I put in for people to look at me, and it was basically all for naught. I was not going to become famous. The fame I was seeking was not to the level that I wanted. Yes, I did get some comments here and there; and even to this day, some people will mention my competitive eating career. But chasing this fame left me empty. Unsatisfied. It did not fill that God-sized hole in my heart. I felt happy for a while, but in the end, that feeling was fleeting and empty. I had controlled my performance and appearance just the way I wanted, but it did not produce the results I was looking for—the attention and compliments of people.

My competitive eating career was great, and I am very thankful for it and the lessons it has taught me. I had wonderful times going to the contests and making friends with the other eaters. I did enjoy the journey along the way, but it was never about the journey for me at that time. I wanted to get in the Nathan's finals and get on ESPN, then everything would be grand. It was all about the destination. Once I got there, I never found the satisfaction in life that I was looking for in it. Looking back now, I can see how insane it was for me to think that way.

7

MY ANGEL

I will never forget the first time I laid eyes on my beautiful wife. My senior partner in Nashville would come down to my office to do a clinic one day a week. She worked for him as his physician assistant. I went up to the office to talk to him one day, and that's when I saw her. I had NEVER seen someone as beautiful as she is. Remember, I used to live and party on South Beach where there are models around every corner, and she was more stunning than them all. I was absolutely blown away. She was the one in the hospital that every male doctor wanted to be with. Truthfully, I do not even know how I was able to talk to her. The circulating nurse in my operating room formerly worked at the hospital where she worked at. I came back to the OR after meeting her, and I said, "You never told me she looked like that!"

I was absolutely in lust.

Every Wednesday, I made sure I would come up to the office and talk to her. I think because I was a surgeon, and she was a PA for our group, she would talk to me. We found out that we both liked to go to Vegas and had a lot in common. She was and is drop-dead gorgeous. We would talk and laugh, and our personalities meshed. I thought to myself, *If I could get a girl like this to marry me, then I have truly arrived.*

One day, I got enough courage to ask her out. Much to my surprise, she said yes. I couldn't believe it. I was over the moon. You mean you actually want to go out with me? Even though I was a successful spine surgeon and former model, I did not have any confidence in myself. I was still this scrawny kid that got picked on who never got the girl.

We started dating, and it was pure fire. We had the best times together, and our relationship grew. We traveled to different cities to see concerts, went on extravagant vacations, and spent just about every day together. In the *Meaning of Marriage* by Tim Keller, he suggests that the best way to find a suitable marriage partner is to find someone that when you see what God is doing in their life, it excites you. Although I did not believe in God, I believe that my future wife could sense something inside my heart that was genuine. She could tell that deep inside all those layers of bravado and machismo, I have a servant's heart. It was just that my actions and beliefs were misdirected.

Our lust grew into love, some of it genuine, unconditional, agape love, and probably more of it the transactional affection that our culture is so accustomed to. The transactional affection of which I speak is that type of "love" where a person believes he/she is doing something to serve and love the other person, but the underlying motive is a ploy to eventually get what that person wants from his/her partner. She also came from a background where performance was praised, and appearance and control were the primary drivers for behavior. Transactional affection will never lead to a fulfilling marriage, but unfortunately, it is what that majority of marriages today are based on. This is why the divorce rate is 50 percent. Although this transactional affection will work for a period, eventually the other person will fail you, and you will stop getting what you expect from the actions you think you are doing out of love (service without expecting anything in return) but actually doing to get what you want (transactional and manipulative).

We got married on October 23, 2009. It was a beautiful beach wedding under a canopy in Lido Beach, Florida. My wife loves that area of Florida, and that is where we spent many rendezvouses when we were dating. The only people in attendance were my mom and dad and her mom.

Finally, I had everything I had ever wanted. I had a supermodel, loving, kind wife; a thriving spine practice; a beautiful daughter from my first marriage; a fully customized BMW 550i; and a beautiful house in the suburbs. Now I could really be happy. What I did not understand at that time was all of that without God, and a relationship with Jesus, means that I had absolutely nothing. My life was still about performance, appearance, and control, which meant that there was still something to achieve to prove something to somebody.

My favorite character in the Bible (other than Jesus) is Solomon. This is because my life and journey parallel his. I denied myself no pleasure but still felt empty. I did not have peace, serenity, and the pure joy that I have in my life today, although in my delusional mind, I was convinced that I did.

> And whatever my eyes desired I did not keep from them. I kept my heart from no pleasure, for my heart found pleasure in all my toil, and this was my reward for all my toil. Then I considered all that my hands had done and the toil I had expended in doing it, and behold, all was vanity and a striving after wind, and there was nothing to be gained under the sun. (Ecclesiastes 2:10–11 ESV)

8

COMING TO BELIEVE, BUT NOT FOLLOW

$\mathbf{M}$y wife moved to Murfreesboro with me. I continued to thrive and grow in my spine practice, and she kept her job as a physician assistant for my partner. She had been saved as a teenager and wanted to find a church in Murfreesboro. She would go to church when we were dating, and I never went with her. It was something she did, and I wanted no part of it at the time. She lived this verse:

> Likewise, wives, be subject to your own hus-
> bands, so that even if some do not obey the word,
> they may be won without a word by the conduct
> of their wives when they see your respectful and
> pure conduct. (1 Peter 3:1–2)

She never pushed me to go to church or talked about Jesus with me. We actually had this conversation.

"You know I don't go to church," I said emphatically.

"Well, you know that I do," she replied.

"Well, that's fine as long as you know I don't," I retorted smugly.

"Well, that's fine as long as you know I do," she responded.

That was it. We had an understanding. She looked online at the churches in Murfreesboro and found New Vision Baptist Church. She asked me to look at the website, so I did. She stated that was the church she was going to go to.

COMING TO BELIEVE, BUT NOT FOLLOW

After she had gone several times, one Sunday morning, I told her that I would go with her. I had absolutely no interest or belief in God at this point. I just wanted to spend more time with her. I was impressed with the building and the professionalism of the service. I liked all kinds of music, and the music they played I thought was actually pretty good.

The head pastor, Brady Cooper, gave the message that day. I cannot remember any specifics of the Scripture or what the message was about, but the one thing I do remember is that this was the first time I had been to church where there was actual teaching. Growing up in Chicago, I had gone to church a handful of times with some of my friends. The services were very confusing to me. There was a lot of chanting, standing up, sitting down, Scripture reading, no explaining; and I really had no idea what they were talking about. I heard Jesus's name mentioned, but there was no teaching or explanation of who He was or why He came to earth.

This was the first time I ever remember someone telling me that Jesus was an actual PERSON who walked on the earth. This was news to me. I had always thought that Jesus was a mythological figure much like Zeus that was created by people to tell stories or whatever to brainwash people. For the first time in my life, I had "ears to hear." This is how I know beyond a shadow of a doubt that God must reveal Himself to a person. Until he/she has "ears to hear," no amount of evangelizing, begging, pleading, explaining, shaming, or berating someone with God or Jesus will have any effect. In fact, it may drive a person further from God, if the truth is not shared in love. Forcing Jesus on people creates atheists. I know this because that is what happened with me.

We Christians are very good at sharing truth, but truth without kindness is abuse, not love. "You are going to hell if you don't accept Jesus" is NOT a good opening line to share Christ, in my opinion. We must first share love, as my wife did, before we can share truth or the subject's heart will not have been opened by God to receive it.

Truth without love is brutality, and love without truth is hypocrisy. (Warren Wiersbe)

Brady had a great way of explaining and teaching that resonated with me. This started me to really contemplate the truth of whether or not Jesus really was a person. I thought about the huge statue of Jesus outside of Rio. I knew that there were more followers of Jesus than any other religion, which made me think that maybe, just maybe, there was some truth to this story. Either Christianity is the biggest hoax in the world, or it is the absolute truth. I started asking questions to my wife. Being humble, and knowing her limitations, she would tell me if she did not know something and told me to make an appointment with a pastor if I genuinely wanted to know the answer.

New Vision is a massive church. It has over six thousand members and dozens of pastors on staff. Right in line with my massive ego and pride, I decided I needed to make an appointment with Brady, the head pastor of the entire church. Being as arrogant as I was, anyone in a lower position could not give me the answers that I needed. Also, I had many objections to religion; and being as intelligent as I was, I was certain I could have that meeting and shoot down everything he threw my way. In my defense, however, Brady's teaching resonated with me; so I thought that he would be the best person to talk to.

I made an appointment, and graciously, he agreed to meet with me. My intellectual guns were loaded and ready for battle. I came into his office, sat down, and started to go through every objection I had with organized religion. I talked about all the holy wars that have been fought and all the people who have been killed in the supposed name of God. I talked about Christians who would tell me that I was going to hell because I did not believe in Jesus and the way in which these supposed "good Christians" lived their lives. In the opening of a song on a DC Talk album, the singer states, "The number one cause of atheists in the world are Christians." This had been absolutely true in my life. I believed that I was a "good person." After all, I was a doctor. I helped people. And these Christians would steal, cheat, lie, backstab, and take advantage of others, then claim their supposed "good" status by stating that they were Christian. Unfortunately, many Christians profess the name of Jesus to others but do not follow the golden rule: treat other people the way you want to be treated. They do not love and serve others and use Jesus for their own personal gain, whatever that might be.

Brady explained to me that I could not base Jesus, who He was or how He lived and what He did, on other people. The purpose of Jesus coming to earth was, in fact, because NO PERSON can be perfect; live a sinless, selfless life; and be loving, kind, and gentle at all times. Jesus came to earth as God's perfect son to reconcile broken people (NOTE: THIS MEANS ALL PEOPLE) back to God.

He used this analogy. Suppose I were making an omelet. I put eleven perfectly good eggs and one rotten egg in the bowl. I then mix it around and serve it to you. Would you eat it? I mean, there are eleven perfectly good eggs in it. What is the problem? That represents sin in a person's life. I trusted and judged myself by the 98 percent of the time when I was a "good" person, helping people, being kind. If a perfect holy God did in fact exist, my life would be like that omelet.

This made sense to me. Although I believed myself to be a "good" person overall, I was not perfect. I did not tell the truth all the time. I definitely drank when I went out and partied to get drunk. I was not kind and loving to all people at all times. How would I know if my good deeds outweighed my bad deeds? I had an innate sense of right and wrong, so where did that come from? Therefore, I conceded on this point that I needed to investigate Jesus Himself, rather than base my views of Christianity on other people who claimed to be Christians. Did Jesus really live without one sin? Not one lustful thought? Never once got angry out of selfish intention? Obeyed His parents 100 percent of the time?

I talked about what I believed at the time, to be the absolute strength of science, and its purported ability to explain and manipulate nature and life. I explained my belief in the big bang theory and how science has supposedly figured out the beginning of the universe down to the first fraction of a nanosecond. As to my belief in whether God existed or not, he used this analogy. He said, "I saw you sit down in that chair when you came in. Before you did that, you didn't walk around the chair to check the legs. You didn't shake the legs to make sure it would hold you up. You had faith that the chair would be strong enough to support you. You take things on faith all the time." This was true based on what I just stated about the beginning of the universe. Even if science could explain everything up until the very first fraction of a second, I still had to have faith in science that it would eventually be able to figure that detail out. It was not a certainty and could not be proven as truth, and therefore, I had as much faith in that as other people had in what was written in the Bible. In *The Knowledge of the Holy* by AW Tozer, he states, "Every man lives by faith the nonbeliever as well as the saint; the one by faith in natural laws and the other by faith in God. Every man throughout his entire life constantly accepts without understanding."

Today, I have found science to be a flimsy reed upon which to build one's faith. In medicine, what we believed to be true in the past has not always stood the passage of time. In fact, our theories in medicine, even if based upon sound scientific logic, do not always prove to be true when put into practice. There are a million examples, but I will give you one that has transpired just in my career as a physician. Less than twenty years ago, medical science believed that beta-blockers, a heart drug used to slow heart rate and control blood pressure, should never be used in heart failure. Back then, it was almost considered malpractice if a physician prescribed those drugs in a patient with heart failure. This makes logical sense. If the heart is failing, then slowing the heart rate and bringing blood pressure down would seem to be the last thing you would want to do in a patient whose heart was not pumping blood well. Within the past several years, we have found that beta blockers INCREASE the life span of patients with heart disease and is now considered to be the standard of care. This is the exact opposite of what we believed not even two decades ago. Therefore, my absolute belief in the strength of science and its ability to eventually explain every single thing that happens in life and the world was not a strong argument.

Science changes all the time. Truth does not. Truth applies to all people, at all times, in all situations. The fact that the Bible has not changed in almost two thousand years is strong evidence that it contains the truth. The Dead Sea Scrolls, which were discovered in the 1960s, prove that what is written in the Bible has not changed over that time. It is the most popular book in the world, translated into the most different languages, and read and studied by the most people than any other book in history. Some would argue that Christianity is a Western religion, but only 13 percent of the earth's population is Caucasian. The majority of the world is not Western, nor Caucasian, but the Bible is still the most popular book in the entire world.

Finally, I went into my last point that Christians are against everything that is fun and enjoyable in the world. They are against drinking, cursing, and sex, among other things, I believed at the time. Brady explained that Christians are not against any of those things, per se. Jesus was not against drinking; in fact, He drank wine. The first miracle was Him turning water into wine. Jesus came to cleanse people of their sin, and drinking is not a sin. Drunkenness is a sin. Christians believe that sin leads to spiritual death, separating us from God, and thus prevents a human being from living the best life possible, the one that God intended for that person. He also explained that God is not at all against sex. In fact, God created sex. God wanted me to have as much sex with my wife as possible.

Wait a minute. Now he had my full attention. My mind was blown.

God wants me to have sex?

God created sex for procreation, connection between a husband and a wife, and pleasure. Yes, pleasure. God wanted me to experience that pleasure, but within the confines of marriage, under the parameters that He knew were best for my enjoyment of it. He analogized sex to fire. God also created fire, which has many purposes that are beneficial to the world. However, everyone knows that it is not a good idea to just start fires wherever one pleases. Sex is the same way. Sex is good and wonderful and pleasing, but when sex is not used within the confines of marriage between a husband and a wife, it has damaging consequences to a person, physically, mentally, and, most of all, spiritually.

Brady had piqued my interest in taking this investigation further. He directed me to two books: *The Case for Christ* by Lee Strobel and *Mere Christianity* by C. S. Lewis. Both books were written by former atheists who became Christian. I agreed to read those books because I wanted to see if there was really something to this.

Around this time, at church services, New Vision used to have a choir made up of talented singers from the church. I remember always seeing this elderly lady in the front row. She had been attending New Vision for many years. Whenever she sang, she would always have this look on her face of complete peace and joy, as if she never had a bad day in her life. This intrigued me. I did not know anything else about her other than the fact that she sang in the choir. But whatever she had, there was something inside me that wanted that same feeling of peace and joy. Even though by all accounts I would have stated that I was very happy at the time, there was a longing for something deeper and more meaningful than what I was experiencing.

For me to come to believe in an almighty God and creator of the universe, I had to first research and investigate the events surrounding Jesus's life, death, and resurrection. There are seven billion people on the earth today, which means that there have been hundreds, if not thousands of billions of people, who have ever lived. I could not even tell you who the president was one hundred years ago, much less anything about someone who lived almost two thousand years ago. The fact that many, many people around the world are still talking about this one man meant to me that He had to be different than anyone who had ever lived.

Every Sunday, throughout the world, billions (yes, billions with a *B*) of people all over the world gather to study the book about His life. This one single man. Almost two thousand years later, people still quote His teachings and can call Him by name, Christian and non-Christian. The details of His life are still intricately studied and discussed. There is no other person who ever lived who can claim that kind of notoriety.

Another thing I thought about was Christmas. At least in the United States, the whole world pretty much comes to a complete stop on Christmas Day. It is a very strange thing to see the Walmart parking lot totally empty on Christmas Day. All to celebrate the birth of this single man. For my entire life, I celebrated Christmas with my family yet never put any thought into why this day is so significant.

In thinking about this in the context of Jesus being an actual person who walked the earth, it is amazing to me to think about the fact that people around the world celebrate His birthday without a second thought.

It does not matter what religion, nationality, or spiritual belief that a person has; the whole earth acknowledges the concept of time based on Jesus's birth. Anno Domini (AD) means "in the year of our Lord Jesus Christ." BC means "before Christ." Every time a person writes the date on anything, anywhere in the world, the date is based on the birth of this one man, Jesus. In today's culture, human beings feel as though we have the right to make choices on all kinds of things that simply cannot be changed. I cannot decide, just because I feel like it or because it makes sense to me or even if I can get a group of people to agree with me, that today is August 11, 2000. If I wrote that in a medical chart or on a check, people would think that I was simply insane. Today's date is today's date, and it is a truth that the whole world accepts. Yet there are so many other things that are true that the world rejects and tries to manipulate and change that cause a tremendous amount of chaos in people's lives.

The Case for Christ far more eloquently explains the evidence for Jesus's life, death, and resurrection. Belief in Jesus is not blind faith but based in science AND faith. And the science is strong. There is not anything to dispute that Jesus actually lived and walked on the earth. The miracles are more difficult to explain with evidence, but the fact that there is no historical record refuting that these miracles happened suggests that they actually did happen. Even most famous atheists agree that Jesus "appeared" to at least five hundred people after His death. They argue that all those people had the same delusion at the same time. If this were to be true, that would be a miracle as astounding and equal to the resurrection itself. Therefore, I chose to believe in the scientific evidence that Jesus really did live, He really did die on the cross, and He rose bodily from the dead three days later.

The evidence that Jesus was killed by crucifixion and was bodily resurrected is very strong. There is not one verifiable writing that issues a statement of recant regarding the event of the resurrection.

65

The easiest way to prove something did not happen would be to have it in writing by someone, ANYONE, stating that they were there and it did not happen. That does not exist.

Christianity and the Bible are true because of this historical event. Many people say that it is not possible for a dead human being to be brought back to life. That belief is not enough evidence to disprove the resurrection. Every day in medicine we see things that we think are not possible. People who have cancer that just disappears. People who are told by the "experts" that it is impossible for them to walk again and then are running marathons years later. The fact that a person does not think that this could be possible proves nothing.

Similarly, many people say they do not understand how a person could be physically dead and then be physically brought back to life. There are so many things in life that we do not understand, but that does not mean they are not true. Many people do not understand orthopedic spine surgery, but when they need it, they are more than readily to believe that it is true and that it exists for their good. Many people do not understand quantum mechanics, but that does not mean that it is not true. Many people do not understand how an airplane lifts off and flies through the air, but that does not mean they will not get on an airplane and fly. Therefore, understanding of how a dead body can come to life is not enough evidence to prove the resurrection did not happen.

After having come to believe in the resurrection of Jesus Christ, being Juris "No Moderation," I was all in. Because I believed Jesus was who He said He was, I came to believe in an almighty God and creator of the universe. I conceded that there were things that I would not be able to explain. I accepted Jesus as my savior and Lord on February 14, 2010. It was Valentine's Day. Brady's sermon on the absolute, unconditional love of God moved me, and I prayed to receive Christ that day. I went public with my belief with baptism on March 21, 2010.

Now, follow Jesus. That's all I had to do. The only problem was I had no earthly idea of what that meant or how to do it. My acceptance of Christ was merely the first step of an incredible journey that I am still on today. From this point, my life didn't get easier. IT GOT

HARDER. There is a difference between ignoring the truth and suppressing it. I never acknowledged God and Jesus prior to this point in my life, so it was easy for me to live only for myself and indulge in sin, not realizing the spiritual consequences of it. Now that I knew the truth about God and Jesus, and the fact that I am selfish and self-centered leading me to sin, my heart had to find a way to suppress that truth. The Holy Spirit dwelt inside of me. I felt a spiritual conviction of my sin. I had no idea how to develop a relationship with Jesus to be rid of that. I had no idea where to start. I had come to believe, but I still had yet to receive.

9

HUMAN DOING

My wife was the most stunning, beautiful bride in the universe to me. I remember standing out on the beach (under the canopy) and watching her walk out to me. To this day, I refer to my wife as my "Heavenly Wife" because I had never seen, heard, or imagined any woman to be so beautiful and radiant as my wife was that day, and every day going forward.

We settled into life in Murfreesboro. She continued to work as a physician assistant for a while, and I continued my career as an orthopedic spine surgeon. We went to church every week and started volunteering in the preschool area. We joined a small group that consisted of blended families. We started to DO everything we thought we needed to do to be "good Christians."

I really dislike the term "good Christian." That term implies some type of moral superiority. I prefer the term "strong Christian." The term "good Christian" is an oxymoron. By claiming to be a Christian, I admit that I have a sin nature and, therefore, am incapable of being a "good person" on my own. By being a Christian, I am admitting that I am weak in my flesh and therefore can only perform good works through Christ who is in me. Therefore, by definition, if I claim to be a Christian, I am not a "good Christian." Any "good" that comes from me is not from myself, but rather from the Holy Spirit abiding within me.

I became a "human doing." Now that I believed in Jesus, I did what the people in the church told me to do in order to follow Jesus. However, I did not do EVERYTHING I needed to do in order to follow

Jesus. I did what I wanted to do and still had strong opinions on what was necessary and what was not.

One thing I never did from 2010 when I got saved until 2015, when I entered rehab, was pray. My thought process was that if God knew everything that was going to happen from beginning to end, He knew what I wanted and what I needed and had promised to care for me, why do I need to pray? What was the point of talking to God if He had everything predetermined? The problem with this logic is that since I never talked to God, I never developed a *relationship* with God. I believe that people exist in China, but since I never talk to them, I obviously do not have a relationship with them. Similarly, I believed in God; but since I never talked to Him, I did not have a relationship with Him. I neglected to do the MOST important thing I needed to do that leads to eternal life.

> And this is eternal life, that they know you
> the only true God, and Jesus Christ whom you
> have sent. (John 17:3)

Eternal life is not about catching heaven and missing hell. Eternal life is about KNOWING the only true God through Jesus Christ so that I could live in heaven TODAY.

If you want to know the purpose and meaning of a painting, you must talk with the artist. Similarly, if we want to know what our true purpose is and direction for our lives, we must communicate with the one who created us, God. Using my own will, I continued to try to determine the best path for my life, without consulting my creator. Without praying to God, I could not discover my true purpose and destiny in God's will, which led me to greater levels of frustration as I continually fought to exert my will in what I thought was best.

I would not pray, but I went to church, was in a small group, and served in the preschool ministry, so I felt that I was doing well. I became the accidental pharisee that I had always hated. Since I have been blessed with the ability to memorize things and logically explain my thought processes, most in my small group also thought

I was doing well. I would soak up all the compliments about how I was doing as a husband and as a father and how I was being such a "good Christian."

The one person who knew the truth, and it was driving her crazy, was my wife. I started working long hours again shortly after we got married because I wanted to be "successful" and give my wife and family everything they wanted. We had difficulty getting pregnant, so my wife had to go through four rounds of in vitro fertilization (IVF) to get our three beautiful children. IVF is EXTRAORDINARILY difficult for a woman. Not only is it very physically painful because of many shots and procedures that she had to endure, it is an emotional roller coaster with amazing highs when successful, but mostly terrifying periods of waiting and hoping that everything is going to work out.

Our first round of IVF, she got pregnant but miscarried shortly afterward. I was still a terrible husband and not a godly man, and I did a poor job of supporting her emotionally through this. In my defense, I had not been taught properly how to really love (service without expecting anything in return) another person, nor had I been taught about emotions or how important emotional support is in a marriage.

I handled this problem like I had learned and handled every other relationship problem in my life prior to this: I threw money at it. We hired a couple of nannies so my wife would have the help she needed, I believed. I continued to work long hours, and we tried to go on the same vacations we did when we were dating to Florida and other tropical locations.

None of this was making her happy. She would complain that I was never around and how our marriage was not turning out anything like she had envisioned. She would complain about me going to the gym, and I would fight back by telling her I was not going out and partying with my friends in Miami and Vegas like I used to. She had stopped working because we felt the stress of work contributed to her first miscarriage and our difficulties in getting pregnant. She was giving up so much for us and our family, and I was giving up nothing, even though I felt like I was.

I felt like I was working hard, earning money to provide what she and our family needed. I was paying money for nannies to give her the help that she was asking for. I was not going out of town partying in Vegas and Miami like I used to. I did cut my hours down at work to some degree, and every time I did that, I felt like I was doing "all I could" to help her and our marriage.

What I could not hear and what she was really saying was "I want you to be my husband and be there for me emotionally and support me."

What I heard was "You are not a good husband and father. Everything you do is not enough. You are not making me happy."

This was the same message I felt like I received toward the end of my first marriage. I thought to myself, *How in the world did I end up here again?* I felt inadequate and worried that I might be divorced...again! No matter how much I did, I never felt like I was doing enough, and it was driving me insane.

Feelings are not facts.

The fact was that my wife was still with me, loving me, and telling me what she needed from me. The feeling I had was that she was telling me I was not good enough. Making decisions based on feelings versus facts leads to disaster.

This is when the reason for my drinking changed. When I used to go out and party, I was preparing myself to have a good time; and I thought that by drinking and doing drugs, I would have a better time. Now, when I drank, I was drinking because I needed to feel better. I felt inadequate. I felt unworthy. I felt ungenuine/two-faced. I maintained this image at work to be the perfect surgeon, perfect father, and perfect husband, when in reality, I knew I was falling short in two of those categories.

I became the Christian hypocrite who drove me away from Christianity for so long. I would go around telling people that the most important thing to me was God, then family, and then work. In reality, it was just the opposite. My work was the only thing that I was preserving. I was destroying my wife and children when I would drink excessively at home because I needed to feel better about myself. I would never drink on workdays because being a spine surgeon was my higher power, and I was not at the point in my disease where I was going to put that in jeopardy. For whatever reason, I had enough moral code within me to not put my patients in danger. I am very thankful my disease did not take me that far.

Because I was not going to do anything to damage my career, my drinking was largely limited to weekends and vacations. On Friday afternoons, I would stop at the liquor store and buy a bottle of vodka. It got to the point where I would open that bottle as soon as I got it and start drinking it on the drive home. I was doing my best to hide this excessive drinking from my wife, but she was not fooled. The mental exhaustion of drinking excessively and trying to not drink excessively in front of her was killing my soul. I was drinking to deal with life on life's terms, and toward the end, I could never get drunk enough. The tragic irony of this is that even though I was drinking to deal with life, my excessive drinking was the root and cause of most of the problems in my life!

> So our troubles, we think, are basically of our own making. They arise out of ourselves, and the alcoholic is an extreme example of self-will run riot, though he usually doesn't think so. (*Alcoholics Anonymous*, 4th ed., 62)

That was me. I felt as though I was doing everything for everyone, yet the truth was, the only person I truly cared about was myself. Yes, I was doing a good job taking care of my patients, but that was not out of a sincere and genuine loving heart. Being a doctor was my job. I was good at my job, but that did not mean I cared about anyone else other than myself. I was destroying my wife and children at home, the people in my life who were most dear to me.

I made the realization one day that I was an alcoholic about two years before I went to rehab. My wife was pregnant, so she was not drinking at all. I made the commitment that I was also not going to drink while she was pregnant. I did well on this promise for about seven months. I had to go to a dinner in Nashville for work. It was on a Friday night, so I did not have to work the next day. I thought that I would have two drinks with dinner that evening and come home, and my wife would be none the wiser. We lived about forty-five minutes from Nashville; and on the drive up to the restaurant, I said to myself repeatedly, "I'm going to have two drinks." I must have said this at least a thousand times, trying to prepare my mind. I had demonstrated to myself many times in the past that I had tremendous willpower in other areas, so I thought that by doing this, I could easily limit myself to two drinks that evening.

I arrived at the dinner and started by ordering a cocktail. One cocktail turned into another cocktail, and then another. My willpower had vanished completely. When dinner started, there were bottles of wine on the table; so I of course had wine with my dinner, like everybody else. The only difference between me and everyone else is that I continually kept refilling my glass about every five to ten minutes. By the time I left, I had to have had at least twelve drinks before making the forty-five-minute drive home. I really do not have much recollection of the drive home, only that I had a Tesla at the time, and I am certain I was driving well over 100 mph at times.

I came home and promptly threw up all over the sink in our master bathroom. My wife was asleep and woke up to the ruckus. She asked what was wrong with me, and of course I responded, "Nothing!" I cannot remember most of the details of our exchange, only that she was very angry, and I had no defense to anything she said.

I was completely demoralized. I had willpower to study long hours to get through my medical training. I had the willpower to not eat fattening food pretty much whenever I set my mind to it. And yet with alcohol, I had absolutely no ability to control the amount that I drank. If I never started, I could manage to not drink that day; but if the first drop of alcohol hit my lips, I had lost the ability to control the amount that I would eventually consume. The Big Book says that alcohol is "cunning, baffling, and powerful"; and that was definitely my experience at this point in my life.

Alcoholism/addiction is continued use in the face of adverse consequences.

Since I continued to drink, and the consequences for me with my wife and family were continuing to get worse, I knew beyond a shadow of a doubt that I was an alcoholic. Being a physician, I know from medical school that an alcoholic cannot have even one drink. And yet there were times when my willpower was nonexistent, and I would start drinking, even if there was absolutely no good reason to. On Saturdays, I would remember waking up, promising myself I would not drink that day. And then by as early as midmorning sometimes, I would see a bottle of vodka and think to myself, *I need to have a drink. Just to relax. To have a better time hanging out with my wife and kids this weekend. I deserve it. I've worked hard this week. I can have a couple of drinks. I'm certain this time will be different.* And inevitably, it would end up the same, and I would be drunk in short order.

This is how sad and pathetic I was at this point. Truthfully, at my core, I did not even feel good enough about myself that I was worthy to spend time with my wife and kids. I convinced myself that it really was no different than when I would go out and party with my friends in Miami. My family and I were home over the weekend, and we were just spending time together, so why not drink and have a better time? The only flaw in this thinking is that my wife and kids were NOT my friends in Miami. I was no longer the boy I was then, and I was a man who needed to lead and be present for them. And I was not, and deep in my heart, I knew that. It was killing me, and I did not know how to stop it.

This went on for two years. Horrible weekends at home, totally nightmarish vacations to Florida, sometimes only with my wife, and sometimes with the whole family. I look back on that time, and I am amazed at how God protected me and my family, despite my best efforts to destroy everything.

As bad as weekends were, vacations were a hundred times worse. If I was on vacation, I would really "enjoy" myself and drink with impunity since I did not have to be sober to go to work. This all culminated in the vacation where I hit rock bottom (note, however, that every rock bottom has a trap door). We went to Siesta Key with the whole family, as we had done many times in the past. We also went with a friend of ours from church and her daughter. A couple of days in, they left because they could not take the chaos I was creating. My daughter from my first marriage who was eight at the time came with us as well. She was so scared a couple of days into the vacation that she texted her mother about what was going on. A friend of her mother's came to pick her up. This is one thing that really sticks with me. I had fought so hard in years previous to get more parenting time with her. Yet here I was with the gift of having her on vacation with us, and I had no problem letting her go back to her mom in the middle of the vacation. Somewhere, deep in my heart, even I knew it was not safe; and yet I could not stop drinking.

I do not remember most of that vacation, but of what I do remember, it was a nightmare. My wife and my ex-wife got in touch with a doctor from Murfreesboro who was in recovery and over twenty years sober. He talked to me several times during that vacation, telling me I needed to quit drinking, but his words had no effect. He had planned an intervention for me that Saturday with another man in recovery, as we were supposed to get back Friday.

That intervention never happened. I was in such bad shape that my wife did not think we could make it through the airport and get on a plane. She called my seventy-six-year-old mother. She flew down and then helped us make the eleven-hour drive back to Tennessee in the minivan we rented.

Here I was. A successful orthopedic spine surgeon. Portraying this image of being this great, strong family man. Yet I had to have my seventy-six-year-old mother help me drive my family back from our vacation. This is the epitome of pathetic. Alcohol had brought me down to my knees and was a foe that I could not beat. Drinking was once a source of great temporary happiness and had now become the source of all the pain and destruction in my life.

Every addiction starts with the pursuit of pleasure and ends in the avoidance of pain.

The pain I was feeling, however, was all created in my mind. I always had this feeling that I was not good enough, no matter how much I accumulated or accomplished, and that is what primarily drove me to drink. Living a life of performance, appearance, and control will inevitably lead to devastation of one's life, in some form or fashion.

It's a gift that the intervention never happened. Alcoholics/addicts in full-blown addiction cannot hear rational thought. I would have never agreed to go to treatment if I sat down with them and we talked. I knew I had a problem, but I did not know what the solution was. Furthermore, at that point, I was not willing to do whatever I needed to do to get sober, unless I was forced.

As we were driving the van home that Sunday evening, I knew I would be tired and not in the best shape to operate that Monday morning. I called the hospital and spoke with the nursing supervisor on the way home. I asked her to cancel all my cases on Monday. She informed me that I did not have any cases on the schedule. Incredulous, I asked her to check again because I knew I had a full surgical schedule for at least the next month. She looked and told me that I did not have any cases scheduled for the whole week, but she could not give me an explanation why.

Puzzled, I then called my physician assistant. He told me that my group had been made aware of what was going on in Florida and that I had to talk to the CEO to find out what I needed to do. I called him, and he told me that I needed to do a five-day evaluation at a treatment center before I would be allowed to return to work.

Either you can be humble, or you will be humbled.

I was number one in collections for my entire group. I was at the busiest point in my career. My career was my higher power, and as such, it was the only thing that I was preserving. And now, it was threatened. It could all be taken away from me if I did not comply with my group's request.

> "One definition of bottom is the point when the last thing you lost or the next thing you are about to lose is more important to you than booze. That point is different for everyone, and some of us die before we get there." (*Alcoholics Anonymous*, 4th ed., 425).

God knew what He was doing in my life. Alcohol was the one thing in my thirty-nine years of life that I could not control on my own. To get sober, I needed to surrender to His will and His plan, and not mine. My plan to get sober over the past two years was not working.

I started making phone calls. I found out there were only three treatment centers in the area that had treatment programs approved for physicians to complete to be in compliance with the Tennessee Medical Foundation (TMF), an advocacy group for physicians in recovery. I had heard about the advocacy groups of physician's health programs for alcoholic/addicted physicians. I always thought that those programs were great for those people. Now, I was one of those people who would need them.

10

REHAB (BORN AGAIN)

I found a treatment center on the other side of Nashville called the Ranch that had availability. They did not take admissions on Sunday, so I arranged to come in that Monday morning for my five-day evaluation. That Sunday evening, my mom helped us get the whole family situated at home. That would be the last night I spent at our house for the next ninety days.

Monday morning, I packed my bag with five sets of clothes because I was certain I would be coming home after my five-day evaluation. There was no way I would be able to stay any longer than that, I thought. I had an extremely busy spine practice to return to. Also, I had four children and my wife that I needed to take care of at home. I knew I had a problem with alcoholism, but I surmised they would set me up with some outpatient therapy, maybe some counseling, and I would be on my way.

I drove myself up to the Ranch, about a one-and-a-half-hour drive. I had a lot of different feelings on that trip. I was fearful because I really did not know what to expect, but part of me was also excited that I was actually going to be evaluated for this problem of alcoholism that I knew I had but did not know how to recover from. There was also a sense of relief that now my alcoholism was out in the open, and I would be getting the help I so desperately needed.

On the drive up there, I debated how much of my drug history I would be willing to share with them. It had been many years since I lived in Miami when I had been doing a lot of cocaine and ecstasy. I tried to rationalize to myself that since I had not done those drugs in a long time, and alcohol was really my problem today, there was no point in telling them all the details. I also did not want to divulge that much information because I surely did not want to stay longer than five days.

However, something inside me knew that was not the right thing to do. I was finally going to a treatment center to get help for my alcoholism and addictions, and if I did not tell them the whole story, I would be only hurting myself. After a long debate with myself in my head in the car, I vowed to tell them everything I had ever done in regard to my drug and alcohol history. I did not know it at the time, but this was one of the first spiritual awakenings I had on my journey. The Big Book states that the treatment of alcoholism and addiction "demands rigorous honesty." Although I had never read that before, in my heart I knew that if I was not totally honest, I would not get better.

I arrived at the Ranch, parked my car, and walked into the administration building. That was June 22, 2015. I did take one picture with my phone from my car, which I have to this day. It's called the Ranch because it really is a beautiful ranch, with rolling hills and horses and lush countryside. The people who greeted me were very friendly, and I filled out all my paperwork and checked in. They showed me to my room in the medical detox building. I took my suitcase in there and settled in.

11

THE FIRST FIVE DAYS

The first five days in rehab, I was COMPLETELY cut off from the outside world. I was not allowed to speak to any of my family members at all. They could call and check on me in the medical unit, but they were not allowed to talk to me, and the staff was not allowed to tell me if they even called or not. My head was spinning thinking about my busy practice and what was going to come of that. I wondered how my group was handling my situation and how it would be when I came back and moved all those surgeries around. I also worried about my wife and four children. I needed to be home for them and take care of them.

Looking back, all this thinking was completely irrational and insane. I was doing a terrible job of being a husband and father. I was at work way too much, and when I was home on weekends, I was completely drunk. This inflated sense of self-importance is a delusion that many alcoholics live in. The thinking that I was so important that if I was not there, my family would fall apart. The truth is that me being with my family as an active alcoholic was the primary malady tearing my family apart.

Of all my experiences, nothing forged my faith in God more than those first five days. I was not allowed to talk to anyone on the outside. My mind was spinning trying to figure out how to control anything outside of rehab. For those five days, not only could I not do anything about any of it, I was not even allowed to KNOW anything that was going on outside of rehab. I had a choice: to go insane or truly trust God to take care of what He said He would take care of—everything.

This was the first time in my life where I was aware that I had zero control of my life. Notice I said that I became aware of the fact that I had zero control. The truth for me, and for all of us, is that control of our lives is an illusion. We have the ability to make choices and decisions that affect our lives, but the actual control of our lives is not ours.

To give you a simple example, let's say you have plans for an all-day outdoor excursion one Saturday you have off from work. You plan all the details of your day down to every excruciating last detail. Then Saturday comes, and it is a torrential downpour of rain all day long. All your plans and designs are for naught. Who really is in control?

I knew that I had to do everything the rehab center said for me to return to work. My CEO told me that my group's board was aware of my situation and mandated that I had to do my five-day evaluation before I would be allowed to return to work. At that time in my life, my career was my higher power. That was the only thing I was preserving and protecting. I had no problems being completely intoxicated around my wife and my kids, but I would never be in that state for work or even the night before I had to work.

God has a way of stripping or dangling one higher power in front of us for us to come to the realization that we are completely dependent on Him. I truly believe that all the circumstances that brought me in rehab was God's way of snapping me on the neck and saying, "I want a relationship with you." As I said earlier, I came to the belief in God and Jesus, but I never prayed. If I never prayed or talked to God, even though I believed, there was no relationship there.

I was still running on self-propulsion. I turned some areas of my life over to the care of God, but there were others that I felt as though I needed to keep control of. It gave me a lot of comfort as a spine surgeon to turn my work over to the care of God. I always do my best and performed the surgeries as flawlessly as I could. But medicine is not an exact science, and there were times when the operation would be perfect, but the patient's symptoms did not improve. I spent a lot of hours and sleepless nights going over those surgeries again and again, trying to figure out why the patient did not get better. Everything was perfect, I would think. The screws, the hardware, the decompression, every technical detail of the surgery was perfect. Once I came to the belief in God, I realized that the outcome of the surgery was not up to me. My role was to perform the surgery, to the best of my ability that day, and the rest was up to God. Turning my patients and my practice over to the care of God comforted me knowing that I just had to do my best with God's help, and He would determine the outcome.

Turning the care of my wife and children over to the care of God was something I did not relinquish before I went to rehab. Being an orthopedic spine surgeon can be a very dangerous thing for a person who does not have his ego in check. All day long, patients are coming to me for answers. I prescribe what is medically necessary and recommend surgery when appropriate. Nurses, hospital administrators, and hospital staff almost invariably say yes to whatever command or request a spine surgeon has. All day long at work, people are doing what I tell them to do, when I tell them to do it.

It was NOT that way at home, yet I placed that expectation on my wife and family as well. When my wife was not doing what I thought she should be doing, I had feelings of resentment, and oftentimes, I would let her know. This would lead her to fight back against me, continuing to damage our relationship. I would take her comments personally, which always led me back to my feelings of being inadequate and not worthy. A lot of my drinking was driven by the need to medicate those feelings because I had no mechanisms to cope with them in a healthy manner.

It was at this time I was introduced to the Tennessee Medical Foundation (TMF), an advocacy group for physicians with substance abuse disorders and/or mental health issues. They have a Physician's Health Program (PHP) where we are monitored with random drug tests and are required to go to recovery meetings as well as a specific recovery meeting for health professionals. I remember learning about these groups in medical school. At that time, I thought, *Wow. That sounds like a great program for those people.* Now, I was one of those people, something I never thought would happen to me.

Today, the term "those people" does not exist to me. If I hear those words coming out of my mouth, I pause and check myself for the judgment that lies beneath it. All human beings, everywhere around the world, no matter what their circumstances, situations, choices, or decisions they make, are created in the image of God. I am connected to every living human being on the face of the earth, and therefore, I have learned that there is no such thing as "those people." We are all people, together as one people.

The TMF advocates for alcoholic/addicted physicians in recovery. There are other states where if a physician goes to rehab, his/her license is revoked, and he/she will no longer be able to practice ever again in that state. Once again, God's hedge of protection was all around me because I did practice in a state with such a program. The Tennessee State Board and the TMF recognize that alcoholism/addiction is a disease. As such, if the disease is being treated appropriately, the physician is allowed to continue practicing medicine. It is akin to allowing a diabetic physician to continue working if being treated appropriately.

The risk to the public is obviously much higher with alcoholic/addicted physicians, and that is why organizations like the TMF are so critically important. As long as I could stay in compliance with the TMF, which basically means that I am treating my disease, I knew that I would be able to return to the practice of medicine in Tennessee. The TMF's PHP, I believe, is the paradigm for PHPs and I pray will set the standard for these types of programs throughout the United States to fairly treat alcoholic/addicted physicians.

I spoke with the director of the TMF at the time. He said if I completed treatment satisfactorily and entered into a five-year contract with the TMF, my license and ability to practice medicine would be assured. Even though I never prayed or talked to God at this point, He continued to build my faith in His role as protector and provider in my life.

I also had several conversations with the CEO of my group. They were in a conundrum as well, trying to figure out how to manage and distribute my patients while I was out. He was very encouraging and assured me I would be able to return to the group. In my first week in rehab, he also told me that they had a shareholders' meeting with all the physicians in my group, and he made the announcement that I was in rehab for alcoholism.

Awesome, I thought. Now EVERYBODY in my group knows. What I did not realize at the time was that was a tremendous gift. When I returned, I would not have to figure out who knew and who didn't. I didn't have to watch what I said or try to explain what happened and why I disappeared for ninety days.

My alcoholism was no longer a secret. I did not have to keep hiding it. Although it never affected my work, after I processed it, it was truly a relief to know that my disease was not something I would have to hide or explain. Thankfully, since I was in a group with other physicians, they all realize that alcoholism is a disease, not a grand moral failure or glaring character defect. They all understood that I was sick and was getting the treatment that I needed, and after that treatment, I would return to work in much better shape that I had been in before.

On my third day, I had a four-hour evaluation with a psychologist. Basically, I had to tell him everything that happened within the past couple of years that had led me to this point. I had filled out some paperwork with my drug/alcohol history, so he had that as well. After I had been talking for a while, he stopped me and said, "Juris. How do you know when an alcoholic is lying?" I told him I didn't know. He said, "When his lips are moving," implying that I was not being truthful.

What a jerk! I thought. How he could say I was lying? I was doing everything in my power at that point to tell the whole truth and nothing but the truth. What I did not understand at the time was that as an alcoholic in active addiction, I had been lying to so many people for so long, I was incapable of telling the whole truth. Most importantly, I was lying to myself. I did not have the awareness of myself and my situation to be able to tell him the truth. The fact was, even though I had made a decision that I desperately needed help and that I committed to tell the truth, I was manipulating details of my story or leaving things out with the hope that he would not commit me to treatment longer than five days. I was trying to control my situation and outcome, rather than leaving it up to the will of God.

I did not outwardly express my displeasure at his comment, thankfully, and the interview continued. I did state to him that I did believe, without a shadow of a doubt, that I was an alcoholic. I had enough awareness of my situation to know that was true. But I kept trying to convince him that it was not that bad. I was still a successful surgeon. I was still married and had four beautiful children. I had never been arrested or had a DUI (only by the grace of God). All of that explaining just meant that I was a functional alcoholic. My life was unmanageable, although I was unwilling to admit it at that point, and I was destroying my family while preserving my career.

He told me about Alcoholics Anonymous. He pointed me to the first sentence in the chapter "How It Works" on page 58. It says, "Rarely have we seen a person fail who has thoroughly followed our path." He told me that in all his years as a psychologist, he had NEVER seen a person fail who had thoroughly followed the program of AA. The key word is "thoroughly." Thoroughly means doing everything suggested by the program virtually guarantees that a person will stay sober. Hundreds of millions of people all over the world have proven this to be true, over the past eighty-five years, and the fellowship keeps growing. It is also supported by scientific evidence now by a Cochrane Review that was published in March 2020.

Failure was not an option for me. I had to get sober. I had to get sober to regain my career. I had to get sober to save my marriage and family. Therefore, I bit in to that truth and held on to it with a death grip. This was my first act of faith.

Human nature says I will believe it when I see it. Faith says I will believe it, and then I will see it. (Joel Osteen)

My human nature for my entire life before entering rehab was to rely on the experiences of my past where I had enough willpower to stop myself from doing other things. My willpower to stop drinking alcohol toward that end was nonexistent. That was baffling to me. For a real alcoholic, such as myself, using willpower to try to stop drinking alcohol is akin to using willpower to try to stop diarrhea. It is not possible. I had lost the power of choice in drinking. I had to have faith in something, anything, that would enable me to stop drinking. That power had to come from outside of myself.

From my observation and experience, the observation of many I have come into contact with in the mental health field, and medical studies, AA is the most effective treatment for alcoholism/addiction, if followed THOROUGHLY. For two years, I knew I was an alcoholic. I just did not know what the solution was. I was never taught that in medical school. I see alcoholics and addicts in my practice all the time, and I had never suggested to them to go to AA. Being a physician, I always thought the treatment was medical, with counseling and medications and such. I did not know what rehab entailed. I thought there would be a bunch of counseling and therapy sessions. There is a lot of that in rehab, but the ultimate, long-term solution to alcoholism/addiction is the spiritual program of AA. The treatment is spiritual, not medical. Everything I know today to help other alcoholics/addicts, I was not taught in medical school.

Another thing he told me that resonated with me and sticks with me to this day is that sobriety had to be my number one priority every day. If I did not stay sober, I would lose my career, my family, my possessions, anything that was important to me.

Anything I put in front of my recovery, I will lose.

I could understand this because for two years, getting sober was one of the things on my to-do list, but it was never number one. I had to go to work, take care of the kids, go to the gym, and, oh yeah, get sober. That was not working. I was about to lose everything.

After our discussion, I had to do some psychological tests. I had to do a Rorschach test. This was very amusing to me. A Rorschach test is a projective psychological test that uses a subject's interpretation of ten standard black or colored inkblot designs to assess personality and emotional tendencies. I remember learning about this test, which was developed in 1927, in medical school. At that time, I thought that it was an interesting test for "those people" with mental health disorders. Now I was one of "those people" again.

We concluded my evaluation, and I went back to the Ranch. On my fifth day there, I had a meeting where they were going to tell me their findings and what their treatment plan was for me. After my first few days, it was becoming obvious to me that I was going to get at least thirty days in rehab. I was slowly surrendering to that fact and starting to process it.

The head psychiatrist called me into a room. In that room was the head psychiatrist, the medical doctor at the rehab, the head administrator, the psychologist, and one or two other staff members. The head psychiatrist said to me, "Juris, usually when there are this many people here, it isn't a good sign." *Great*, I thought. I sat down and braced myself, and he said that they were recommending sixty to ninety days of treatment.

WHAT? HOLY CRAP! I couldn't believe it. I was incredulous. I almost passed out and fell out of my chair. However, I didn't get angry. I didn't say anything. I just sat there and listened.

I had never had a work issue, a DUI, or other legal issue, so my thinking was that they would just prescribe some outpatient treatment, and I could get sober and go on with my life. What I did not understand is that physicians get MORE treatment because the public risk is so high. The statistics for success for thirty versus sixty versus ninety days of treatment definitively show that ninety days of treatment carries with it the highest rates of success. Today, I am overwhelmingly grateful for those ninety days at the Ranch. Very few alcoholics/addicts get that kind of opportunity. That ninety days spent away from my family, career, and life were necessary for me to have continued success in sobriety and all aspects of life.

After they finished talking, I told them that was fine and that I needed to go home to pack a suitcase. I had only packed for five days, because in my delusional thinking, I knew that was all I had to do. They asked me not to do that, and I asked why. "Because the majority of people who do that end up dead or in jail." I guess people who do that go out on their last bender, and it usually doesn't end well. The slow process of surrendering my life and my will continued, and

I agreed that I would not go home, and my wife would have to bring my belongings.

After the meeting, we departed, and the medical doctor (who is also in recovery and had been to rehab) pulled me into a room. He said, "You know, Juris, when they say sixty to ninety days, they really mean ninety." *AWESOME*, I thought. More surrender. I started to process the fact that I would be completely removed from everything in my life on the outside for the next eighty-five days (I had five under my belt) and proceeded to accept my circumstances.

He also told me that he had never seen someone accept this kind of recommendation the way that I did. He said he was cussing and yelling and fighting everyone when they told him that. My reaction was a result of one of my pet peeves. As a spine surgeon, I have twenty-six years of educational training in my life. After high school, I had four years of college, four years of medical school, five years of orthopedic residency, and a one-year fellowship dedicated exclusively to the surgical treatment of spine disorders. When I see patients and recommend surgery, I will take the time to show them the imaging and explain what needs to be done and why it needs to be done that way. I will gratefully answer any questions the patient might have regarding the surgery. Then there are times that after I go through all that, the patient will say to me, "Well, I don't think that surgery is a good idea because I read on the internet..."

I was NOT going to be that patient. I had enough awareness to know that I did not know ANYTHING about the treatment of alcoholism/addiction. In that room, I was sitting with many people who have been educated on, learned about, and have had a plethora of experience treating alcoholics/addicts. They were the experts. I was not. Thankfully, I had enough humility at that point to know that I did not know what was best for me, and they did.

I was employing a spiritual principle that I learned about much later in my recovery. Alcoholics have a hard time accepting whatever situation they are in. In recovery, the Big Book states that "acceptance was the answer to all of my problems today." It is from one of the stories in the back of the Big Book by another physician. Going beyond that, I have been taught not only to accept everything, but to embrace it.

Embrace the suck.

The fact that I was going to be separated from my wife and family for ninety days was going to suck. I would not work for ninety days, which in itself sucks, but also that loss of income was going to really suck. A lot of things in life are not pleasant and, in fact, suck. But that is the truth of this thing that we call life. By not just accepting things as they are, and not as I would have them to be, but embracing them is transformational in the mindset of an individual. Finding the joy in any situation, even if it sucks, keeps me in a constant state of peace and understanding, which helps me to minimize or eliminate the unpleasant feelings that arise in me.

I embraced the suck of ninety days of treatment so much that my wife became irritated with me. She found out that I was having such a good time in rehab that she developed a resentment to me because I was not worried about what she had to deal with and what was going on in the outside world. It was not that I did not have concerns about those things. It is the fact that I knew I had absolutely no control over anything happening outside of rehab, so I had to make the conscious choice to trust God that He was taking care of them. And that is exactly what happened.

And so it began. Reflecting on those first five days in rehab, I can see the incremental surrender of my will and my life over to the care of God. How God stripped perceived control of my life from me and set a plan for my life that I had no input on. How God started the journey that would prove to be the best thing that had ever happened to me. What seemed to me to be the worst possible scenario turned out to be the biggest blessing in my life. All of this confirms that, on my own, I do not know what is best for me; but God does. Now that is the TRUTH.

12

SPIRITUALLY DEAD

When I entered rehab, I was very much physically alive. Physically, I was in almost the best shape I had ever been in my life. My workout regimen and diet (other than drinking) were very much controlled so that I could project the image of perfect health to attract the attention and praise of those around me. To some degree, in my mind, I probably thought that I could offset the damaging effects of my drinking with exercise and diet. I was not the type of alcoholic who drank every day because I wanted to protect my career. The detrimental effects of alcohol to my health and image were not as great as they would have been had I drank every day.

At that time, out of over fifty orthopedic surgeons, I was number one in collections. My career and reputation were at an all-time high. This is proof of the fact that work was my higher power, something I put above God. Jesus said, "For where your treasure is, there your heart shall be also" (Matthew 6:21). It also contributed to my delusion that I was in control and that my life was manageable. I had no close friends at that time who would hold me accountable for my actions outside of work. Purposefully on some unconscious level, although not intentionally, I had separated myself from any close relationships with godly men. Therefore, the message I heard was that I was supremely successful and could not possibly have a problem that I could not handle.

However, I had reached my bottom. I was very much spiritually dead. I had no relationship with God. I never prayed. My heart was bankrupt. Although I was very intelligent and could recite the

Scripture easily, none of those words penetrated my heart because of my drunkenness and sin that had separated me from God. I had head knowledge of the Bible, but none of that made the twelve-inch journey deep down into my heart. Reading and memorizing the Bible, although helpful, is distinctly different than studying the Bible, especially with a godly mentor. This was something I had never done, or even considered, and it left me spiritually dead.

In the Bible, the tree of knowledge of good and evil brought forth life from the fruit that it bore. It also brought death to Adam and Even when they ate it upon the suggestion of the serpent. That which brings forth death can also bring forth life. This is the point at which I found myself. I was spiritually dead, but that spiritual death was necessary to bring forth the abundant, extravagant life that I would eventually find as I journeyed along the path that God had set forth for me. The realization of spiritual death, I believe, is necessary for a person to step into and embrace full surrender to God's will. If there is any lurking notion that a person can cling to some semblance of spiritual life on his/her own terms, he/she will be unable to fully surrender everything to God.

God will put a limp in your life to remind you that you are fully dependent on Him

I had been able to control and manipulate so many things in my life to a great degree of success. Drinking alcohol was the one thing in my life that I could not master. There was no amount of willpower, promise, or resolutions to myself that would stop me from drinking. I was completely powerless and knew that I needed help. What I did not realize was that help had been available to me all along. I had never thought that I could have access to the power of almighty God if I just came to Him and surrendered to His will, not mine.

People do not like the word "surrender." When most people think of surrender, they think that they are losing. This thinking is flawed. If a person or entity is at the point where surrender is necessary, that person or entity has already lost.

Surrendering is not losing. Surrendering is joining the winning team.

My way of living was obviously not working. If it had been working, I would not have been asked by my group to have a five-day evaluation for alcoholism and then received ninety days of treatment. **No one comes into rehab on a winning streak.**

I had enough awareness to realize that this was true. The time had come for me to do the work and start living the life that God had designed for me. Not the one that I thought would satisfy me. What I discovered was that the life that God had laid out for me was abundant, lavish, extravagant, and above and beyond anything that I would have ever imagined for myself.

13

NINETY DAYS AT THE RANCH

After my five-day evaluation in the detox unit, I was transferred to one of the houses at the Ranch. I was put in a dual-diagnosis house, which means that the people in that house have a substance abuse disorder and a mental health diagnosis. I did not have a mental health diagnosis (other than alcoholism), but that is where they put me. I lived in a house with seven to eight other men. There were a few men there who did not even have a substance abuse disorder and were there for severe depression or anxiety disorders. We were responsible for our meals, ordering groceries (although the staff went out and got them), and were assigned a night each week where we would cook dinner for the entire house. The men ranged in age from early twenties through late sixties. Some of them were single; some were married and had families like myself. Some had been through several treatment centers, and one even had come to the Ranch a year earlier. He was still sober but was struggling with life on life's terms, and another round of rehab did a tremendous job of restoring him and setting him on a fabulous life path.

The opposite of addiction is connection/community.

Looking back, living in this house with these other men was critical for my recovery. Those of us with substance abuse disorders had been isolating ourselves for so long from any real emotional human connection with another male. By living together, we were forced into community to make connections with other people that we would have not otherwise chosen to do. I came to like, love, admire, and respect most of the men in our house. There were those that I was not fond of, but learning to deal with difficult personalities and people I do not like is necessary for living successfully. Although I did not like everyone who came into the house, I learned that I must love (serve, help, and tolerate) all of them to keep harmony throughout the house and keep my peace and serenity. We all had one thing in common. We had reached a crisis point in our lives and were there to effect some kind of change to live a better life.

This is a life skill that people generally do not gravitate toward. We generally seek to be around people who are just like us. People who look like us, act like us, have similar interests. The Big Book states,

> We are average Americans. All sections of this country and many of its occupations are represented, as well as many political, economic, social, and religious backgrounds. We are people who normally would not mix. But there exists among us a fellowship, a friendliness, and an understanding which is indescribably wonderful. (*Alcoholics Anonymous*, 4th ed., 17)

I have found that to be true, not just in twelve-step recovery, but also in my Christian journey. I have become close to and come to rely on people that I previously would have had not associated with. That, I have realized, is a tremendous disservice to me and society at large. We are quick to write people off because of one thing or another, but the fact of the matter is that every human being on the face of the earth is connected. We are all in relationship.

The first sentence I wrote in the first notebook I ever had at the Ranch was this: "Humility is the key to sobriety."

It is one of the spiritual principles of the twelve steps. It is what Jesus represented. Jesus was God, with all power, knowledge, and wisdom, but came down to earth and humbled himself into the likeness of man to give us the example of how to live and to have the ability to relate to our human experience.

Pride is my most glaring character defect, as it is for most humans, and almost all alcoholics. Pride was also the primary sin of the devil, who wanted to be God because he had been gifted with so many positive attributes.

I had not been very humble in my thirty-nine years of life. I had been given a myriad of gifts and talents that led me to believe that my life carried more value than the majority of people I came in contact with. Those gifts and talents led me to believe that my success in the world was a result of all my own efforts, and I was just better than everyone else at many things.

The reality is that I had been given many gifts and talents. But those things were not something that I can take credit for. The Bible states, "From everyone who has been given much, much will be demanded; and from the one who has been entrusted with much, much more will be asked" (Luke 12:48 NIV). I had been given so much but used it all for my own glory and advancement, rather than using my gifts and talents for the glory of God.

One definition of humility is to know and believe that every human life has the exact same value. This is how God views every human being on earth. All equally tremendously valuable. So valuable because of His love for us, in fact, that God gave His only begotten son to die for us to reconcile our relationship with Him.

Pride is believing that my life has a greater value than another person.

Shame is believing that my life has a lesser value than another person.

Living in this house with all these different men was a great tool to teach me humility. By the world's standards, being an orthopedic spine surgeon, a lot of people would view me as having greater worth than my fellows. The truth is that we are all created equal. Developing relationships with these men taught me that.

Going to twelve-step meetings is also another act of humility that I will continue for the rest of my earthly life. Merely by going into an AA meeting, I am admitting that I have a problem with alcohol and that I have the desire to stop drinking, to improve myself. The same needs to be true for the motivation in going to church. The purpose of going to church is not to demonstrate to people that I am a morally upright person. The acceptance of Jesus as my savior is an admission that I have a sin nature, a depraved heart, and am incapable of producing anything selfless with my own will. I thoroughly enjoy going to church, and the primary reason I attend is to help me seek God through Jesus so that he can transform my heart and renew my mind.

When I started rehab, I attacked recovery like I had approached everything else in my life up to that point. I needed to be recovered as quickly as possible, even though I was going to be there for ninety days. In addition to all our meetings, counseling sessions, and classes, I started reading as many books as I could on recovery. This was no different to me than the many classes I took in college and medical school. I felt that the more knowledge I would obtain, the better off I would be. God has gifted me with a tremendous work ethic, and it was in full force.

After about three weeks, I had read at least twelve books. I read the AA book. The NA book. *The Power of Now* by Eckhart Tolle. *The Sermon on the Mount* by Emmet Fox. *The Four Agreements* by Don Miguel Ruiz. *The Search for Significance* (and did the workbook) by Robert McGee. *The Purpose Driven Life: What on Earth Am I Here For?* (and did the study guide) by Rick Warren. The list goes on and on. I had gained tremendous knowledge about addiction, various recovery tools, and spiritual guidance.

I met once a week with my Christian counselor. The third week, I told her how many books I had been reading and how much information I was getting out of it. I was so proud of myself. Still being driven by performance and appearance, I was certain she was going to give me more books to read to keep my recovery going strong.

"You need to stop reading," she said.

I was so astonished at this. I do not even remember having a verbal response. I just had that head tilt, like my dog gets when he's trying to figure out whether or not I'm going to give him a treat.

She explained to me that, although beneficial, all the reading I was doing was not giving God enough room in my life to work. I knew the steps of AA, so I knew that it would only be by God's power that I would have the ability to stay sober. Yet I was still trying to play God and control my recovery. All the head knowledge in the world will not keep an alcoholic sober. A power greater than ourselves must work in an alcoholic's life to effect change.

I was so busy with all our meetings, group and individual counseling sessions, and chores, filling up any extra time with additional reading, that I still was not praying. I was still a "human doing," not a "human being." Every minute of my days was filled with some sort of activity to propel me to my goal of being recovered as quickly as possible.

She suggested that not only did I need to start praying, I needed to be still and listen to God. I had never done that before. "Be still, and know that I am God" (Psalm 46:10). The command is right there in the Scripture, and very clear, yet it had never occurred to me to actually do it. The only way I could access the power of God to keep me sober was by seeking and knowing Him.

I agreed to take her suggestion. Every morning, my routine was to walk up and down the driveway to the house we stayed in to get my cardiovascular exercise. I was waking up at 5:00 AM to exercise and read. I decided that I would take the first ten minutes of that time to pray, be still, and listen to God.

The house I stayed in was called Overlook. It was on the top of a hill, and from the front yard, there was a beautiful rolling hill with trees. In the morning, the sun would rise over those trees, and it was a truly beautiful sight. During my walks, I could appreciate God, the artist, and His creation in this.

That next morning at five o'clock, I grabbed a chair and my cup of coffee and sat down in front of the house at the top of the hill. I sipped my coffee, set it down, then set my watch for ten minutes. Ten minutes is not a long period in a twenty-four-hour day. I folded my hands together and started praying. My prayers at this point were a conversation with God, thanking Him for my life and various things and acknowledging Him as our Creator and heavenly Father. I finished my prayer and sat in silence to listen.

After what surely felt like ten minutes to me, I decided to look at my watch because I knew the time was almost up. Two MINUTES

HAD PASSED! ONLY TWO MINUTES! *Holy cow*, I thought to myself. I could not even sit still for more than two minutes before I needed to DO something else and move on. I was so uncomfortable just "being" with God. This realization was earth shattering to me. This exercise made it obvious to me that I was not allowing God enough room in my life to do the miraculous things that only He can.

Having no idea to pray, the Big Book gave me specific, explicit instructions to do each morning that helped me. Many sponsors (including mine) tell their sponsees to read pages 86–88 every morning and every night when early in sobriety.

> On awakening let us think about the twenty-four hours ahead. We consider our plans for the day. Before we begin, we ask God to direct our thinking, especially asking that it be divorced from self-pity, dishonest, or self-seeking motives. Under these conditions we can employ our mental faculties with assurance, for after all God gave us brains to use. Our thought-life will be placed on a much higher plane when our thinking is cleared of wrong motives. (*Alcoholics Anonymous*, 4th ed., 86)

I kept working on this each and every morning. Gradually, I was able to pray and be still in the presence of God for ten minutes, and my watch would signify the end of the time, rather than me stopping it. I was growing spiritually. God was maturing me and forging my faith in Him, little by little, but I needed to be still long enough to allow Him to do so. Even now, after many years of practicing this, I cannot say that I am good at it. It requires constant intention. When at meetings or other times when I am required to sit, I practice being still. Then I can allow more of God in me and less of me in myself.

14

FIRST SPIRITUAL AWAKENING

I distinctly remember what I would consider my first spiritual awakening. Once a week, we would have an adventure day. It usually consisted on some physical activity teaching us the importance of asking for help and relying on others. The adventure activities were naturally designed to be outdoors.

One adventure day, about a month into my stay at the Ranch, it was raining. They brought all of us men (most activities separate the men and women) into a large room and told us what the activity would be for that day. They told us that we were going to pair up. One man would tell the other man "his story" for fifty-five minutes, then the other man would do the same back to the first. We all looked at each other thinking, *What man talks for fifty-five straight minutes?* Also, *What man listens to another person for fifty-five straight minutes?* I did not remember a time when I talked for that long without interruption to another person.

I went first. My partner was a young man, about early twenties, who was a resident of my same house, Outlook. I knew him fairly well, and I trusted him. We had already spent a month living together and participated in various counseling groups and activities with each other. I started at the beginning, much in the same way I started this book. I talked, and I kept on talking. Without even realizing it, I kept going. I went into parts of my story that were things I was ashamed of. But they just came out. One after the other. I told him things that I previously swore I would take to my grave. Things I never wanted to reveal to another person. Things that I thought would hurt me somehow if anyone else knew about them.

Secrets keep us sick.

He just sat there. Listening intently. He would nod at times. I could tell he was paying attention. Looking back, this is a picture of God. Always there. Always listening. Interested in my life. What I have been through. How I felt. Willing to help. He was helping just by listening. God speaks to me through relationships. We are all created in the image of God, and when His spirit is present in our lives, that is how we reflect Him to others and how He reveals Himself to us.

I kept talking, chronologically through my story. The good, the bad, the ugly. All of it. To the best of my ability in that moment, I do not think I left anything out. All my secrets. All the things I was going to take to the grave. Every despicable, repulsive, detestable thing I had ever done.

Time was up. Fifty-five minutes. He nodded, and the first thing he said to me was "That's it? That's all you've done?" He shrugged his shoulders, and I could tell that he did not think anything I did was all that bad. Like I was not the only person on earth who had done these things. That it was normal.

In that moment, I felt a thousand-pound weight lifted off my shoulders. I had no secrets. I had nothing that someone on earth did not know about my story. And there was no judgment. Not an ounce. There was an understanding. Compassion. Something I had never felt before from another person. It was amazing. Bewildering. Spectacular. A reflection of God. Totally accepted. Completely forgiven.

In that moment, in my mind, there was nothing anyone could find out about me that could make me feel shame. In fact, the manner in which he responded actually made me feel like I was pretty noble. That is the paradox of keeping secrets. The very things that we think we need not tell anyone for fear of judgment and condemnation are the very things that if brought to light will make us look good. Why does this happen? Because God is there. When honesty comes forth, God reveals His presence; and we look good because we are making Him look good, reflecting His true nature.

Where honesty exists, grace and mercy abound. Grace (undeserved favor) and mercy (not receiving the punishment that is deserved) cannot be granted if we present ourselves as if we are morally superior by hiding our faults and failures. Only when the truth about us is known can grace and mercy be given from God, in and through other people. It is the light of Jesus and of almighty God.

I know for a fact that the ability for me to tell my entire story without leaving anything out was not something I was capable of. The Holy Spirit led me in that conversation and gave me the courage to do that. It was not forced. It just happened.

I was free.

People are drawn to other people and organizations where honesty exists. In sermons, my church's pastors and leadership are very forthcoming about their faults and failures. Our church is growing by leaps and bounds. The highest level of honesty I have ever found has been in twelve-step recovery meetings. There is safety in the rooms of twelve-step meetings because we all know what is said there stays there. The fellowship keeps growing and growing. Churches where the leadership and members present themselves as blameless and holy, divide and die. The only way we Christians can advance the kingdom of God is to be vulnerable and transparent.

Without knowing it, I had just completed my fifth step: "Admitted to God, to ourselves, and another human being the exact nature of our wrongs."

In my ninety days of rehab, I did that one other time, this time intentionally, with my Christian counselor who was walking me through the steps. The second time was easier. I did not hesitate. I knew what I was going to say beforehand because I had prepared. The feeling of relief after the second time was not as great as the first, but I did feel more freedom after that.

Every person needs another person to know everything about them. Freedom can only occur when this happens. God speaks in many ways, but one of the primary ways He speaks is through relationships. To this day, my AA sponsor knows everything about me. He has never said, "I can't believe you did that," to anything I have ever said. I feel acceptance, nonjudgment, forgiveness, and love from him; and that is how God reveals Himself to me on a continual basis.

A spouse cannot be this person. Although my wife knows just about everything about me and what I have done in my past, she does not know all of it. Nor is it any of her business. The actions and behaviors of my past predate our relationship. I am growing and evolving daily. In Christ, I am a new creation. The old is gone; the new has come. In addition, my wife, although almost perfect, is occasionally a source of some of my frustrations. I can talk about those with my sponsor, process them, and come to her with them in a constructive way. There are things that I just cannot process with her because they are about her.

Although I received a lot of counseling, had different experiential therapies, went to different anonymous fellowship meetings, and listened to various lectures, the most impactful time that I had there was every night when the men in our house would gather and do a group tenth step. In the Big Book of AA (4th ed.), on page 86, there is a list of questions that we are to answer to "constructively review our day."

Were we resentful, selfish, dishonest, or afraid?

Do we owe an apology?

Have we kept something to ourselves which should be discussed with another person at once?

Were we kind and loving toward all?

What could we have done better?

Were we thinking of ourselves most of the time?

Or were we thinking of what we could do for others, of what we could pack into the stream of life?

Every night, one of the residents who had been there the longest would lead our group of eight or so men, and we would go around the room and answer these questions to each other, one by one. Processing the events of our day, our feelings, faults, and failures together taught me so much about them and myself. It was a demonstration of the true nature of God. Accepting. Forgiving. Nonjudgmental. Loving. Kind. Compassionate. Helpful. By sharing our struggles together, helping each other, we grew. And started recovering. But this process requires rigorous honesty. If I had left anything out and not honestly answered my questions, there would be no benefit. Secrets really do keep me sick. Bringing them to light lets God bring healing.

15

ME AND GOD

No one comes into rehab on a winning streak. There were indicators in my life that would make me believe that, even though it was a lie. Financially, I was doing well. I was respected at work by my patients and staff. I was more humble toward the staff, for whatever reason, and I always took good care of my patients. Many of my partners did not respect me, due to my arrogance and self-centeredness toward them. My home life was a complete disaster. As you can imagine, I was not a good husband or father to my children, even though I believed myself to be because I was physically home more than other people in my profession. However, I was not emotionally or spiritually present with them, just like my father was with me. Different from my father, though, I was frequently drunk when I was at home because I was "relaxing," which obviously made me even less present with them, even though I was physically there.

When I entered rehab, there was a lot of uncertainty about my marriage. My wife was not pleased with me, and thoughts of divorce entered her mind. This drove a lot of shame and guilt within me that I could possibly be divorced again, for the second time. I was sad and shameful thinking that I would be that much of a failure in two different marriages. Thinking about dividing our three children up for parenting time, in addition to juggling my parenting time with my first daughter, was overwhelming for me. I felt a lot of fear about losing these things at this time.

Every physician who was in recovery and doing well told me that I did not have anything to worry about in regard to my job. If

I stayed sober and followed instructions and suggestions, I would be fine returning to work. Even though I heard this over and over, it was still hard for me to believe. I had concerns over being suddenly completely absent from work for ninety days, then returning to my practice. Would my successful practice recover? Would my reputation be tarnished because of this? Would I be able to remain sober once I returned to normal life and practice?

These thoughts—loss of my wife and family, loss or reduction in my job resulting in lower income, damaged reputation—were present in my mind. I had to come to grips with the fact that all these things could possibly happen to me. On top of this, I was in rehab, completely cut off from the outside world. I had absolutely no control over anything happening in the outside world. I could only talk to my wife for very short periods a couple of times a week. As far as work, my group was handling everything, so I had no control but also did not have any idea about how they were even managing it. I did not know what patients or the staff at the office or hospital were being told. I was going to disappear from my entire life for ninety days, and there was nothing I could do about it.

The first five days in rehab starts the forging process for faith in God because of the isolation. This process continued throughout my stay in rehab. My choices were to either trust God that He would take care of me and my life in the outside world or go insane trying to find out what was going on and then desperately try to figure out a way for me to influence anyone or anything outside of rehab. I had to truly learn the meaning of "Let go and let God."

Fortunately, I had a good foundational understanding of the nature of God from my journey to Jesus. I understood that God's nature was perfectly loving, forgiving, accepting, and protecting. Even though I had head knowledge of these characteristics, I now had to take steps to move them into my heart to fully trust that.

I spent a lot of time in meditation and prayer imagining my life without anything that I had previously valued. I envisioned myself completely alone with God in a room, and nothing else. My wife and kids had left me. I was no longer an orthopedic spine surgeon with no specific career or path professionally. I was just myself. Alone with God. Would I be okay?

Slowly, I came to believe and realize that I would be okay. I had been given many talents and gifts from God, and He would ensure that I would have something to do to provide financially. Even if my wife was gone and I had no access to my children, I could have peace and comfort knowing that they were taken care of somewhere and that He would be taking care of them. I would be okay, and they would be okay. If all I had left was God, my life would be fulfilling and satisfying, and I could be comfortable with myself and my life.

This revelation was not immediate. I spent a lot of time envisioning this and working through it. I think this process is the cornerstone of the abundant life I have today. He was all I needed. As I continued my journey, close communion with him is all I really want. Everything else is a bonus. The paradox of this is that as I grow closer to God, He provides all that I would ever want, and abundantly above and beyond what I would think that I would want. I believe that this process is CRITICAL for any person in recovery and/or Christian in their journey in order to unlock the extravagant life that God has planned for us.

Delight yourself in the Lord, and He will
give you the desires of your heart. (Psalm 37:4)

There it is. Right there in the Scripture. Even though I had read that before, it never sank in until I have now actually experienced it. Now, almost five years into my recovery and walk with Christ, everything I had ever been worried about losing has not only been restored, but I have above and beyond what I could have ever imagined when I first entered rehab.

Today, I delight myself in Him. I pursue God with all my mind, heart, strength, and spirit. I live my purpose of being of maximum service to God and the people about me. In return, not only am I sober, I live in eternal life (heaven) EVERY DAY. I consistently seek to know God's will and choose the next right action that will please

Him in any given situation. In doing so, I am rewarded with peace, serenity, comfort, and far more than that.

I do not desire what my heart desired before this relationship with God through Jesus. I have been given a new heart. The Bible states that the heart is wicked and evil, and that is the heart I had before this relationship with God through Jesus. My heart's desires are for godly things now, not worldly things. I have been transformed.

> I will give you a new heart and put a new
> spirit in you;
> I will remove from you your heart of stone
> and give you a heart of flesh. (Ezekiel 36:26 NIV)

16

TRAUMA THERAPY?

I grew up in a home where there was very little conflict. There was no physical abuse from my father toward me or my mother. Prior to rehab, I would have told you that I had the perfect childhood. There was no chaos. I played many sports and had fun playing with my friends. I went to school like everyone else. It was always calm in my house, and I never had fear of physical harm throughout my childhood.

In rehab, I signed up for some specific groups like Christian groups, but some of my counselors and groups were assigned based on the answers I provided on my intake form. In my first few weeks, I was assigned to a trauma counselor. *A trauma counselor*, I thought. *Why in the world would I need to be seeing a trauma counselor?*

For my first meeting with him, we went through the usual riga-marole of a counseling session. Tell me about yourself. Tell me about your childhood. Usual stuff. He listened and took notes without interjecting anything, and I went through my story.

I got to about college, talking about the things I said above about no chaos or trauma in my home; and I finally got the nerve to ask him, "This is a trauma session. You are a trauma counselor. Why in the world am I seeing a trauma counselor?"

He said, "Well, both of your parents worked, right?"

"Right," I replied.

"So you were a latchkey kid?" he asked.

"Yes," I said, dripping with indignation, nonverbally asking what his point was.

"So when you came home, your parents didn't come home for a few hours. Who did you talk to about your problems?" he inquired.

"No one. I just handled it," I stated emphatically.

"Exactly," he said. "You never had anyone to talk to about your problems. If something hurtful happened to you at school, you did not have anyone you could talk to about it, and you just stuffed whatever bad feelings you had deep down and tried not to feel them. You were eleven years old. You didn't have the capacity or tools to process your emotions properly and had no one to guide you through that. That's called neglect, and that's a trauma. It's the hardest trauma to identify because it's not there. Physical and emotional trauma is easily identifiable, but you can't even recognize this because this trauma is the absence of emotional support and teaching of life skills."

Damn! He was right! This made so much sense to me. Prior to this conversation, I would have never thought that I was neglected. My parents were home every night. All my physical needs were taken care of. Looking from the outside, as the world would view my parents and their care of me, it did not have the faintest hint of neglect. But emotional and spiritual neglect was there. I had no one to rely on. No one to talk to about my problems.

It is important to talk about feelings. I used to say, "You made me feel ——." This is not a true statement. No one can make me feel anything. If a negative emotion arises in me, it is because that negative emotion already exists in me. Whatever the other person said merely uncovered that feeling. For instance, if my wife says, "You have not bought me flowers in a long time," I would say or think, *You made me feel bad, like I am not a good husband.* That is not what she said. She only said that I have neglected to get her flowers. What I heard is that I am not good enough and am not expressing my love for her well, which makes me feel inadequate. She did not make me feel inadequate. That was already part of my core beliefs, and she simply uncovered it.

The statement, "I feel —— when you ——" is a communication tool that is widely taught by therapists. In making this statement, I can express how I felt about the situation and then make the true statement of what the other person did. In this manner, I am not shaming that person about their behavior; I am simply stating what happened and how I felt about it.

I realized that in my almost forty years of life, I could not ever remember starting a sentence with the words "I feel."

When I would voice a problem to my parents, they would tell me to just not let it bother me. That is about the worst thing you can say to a child. It is bothering them. By saying to not let it bother me, pathologic defense mechanisms were forming in me to not feel what I was actually feeling in that moment. Rather than processing the hurt in a healthy way, I was told to just not feel it. This led me to feel as though there was something wrong with me if I could not get negative emotions to go away—that I was defective.

When negative emotions get stuffed deep inside, they will eventually explode at some point, usually in an unhealthy manner. It is akin to taking a beach ball and holding it underwater. You cannot hold it underwater forever. As some point, it is going to burst to the surface and be expelled into the air in an explosion.

That is exactly what happened with me and my alcoholism. I found alcohol would numb the negative emotions and stuff them deep away. However, when I sobered up, the negative feelings were still present; and I would have more negative feelings of guilt and shame because of what I had done. It got to the point where I could not get drunk enough to make those feelings go away, and I would drink and drink and drink until really bad things would happen. The alcohol did not work anymore. I was not getting relief and just inflicting more and more pain upon myself and everyone around me.

The insane part of this thinking was that my life was absolutely wonderful from the outside looking in. I had a beautiful wife and children. I was successful in my career. I was vibrant and healthy. What I could not do was process any negative emotions in a healthy way, so I dealt with them the only way I knew how—by stuffing them deep down and drinking to try to make them go away.

My parents did a lot of things right, however. They educated me; they provided for all my physical and material needs. They ensured that I had a well-rounded childhood with sports and activities and friends. I did not have as much to overcome as many other people who struggle with alcoholism and addiction. My heart grieves for people who have endured so much trauma at the hands of their parents and others because I know that it will take a lot more work to recover from that. I think the reason why I drifted toward the extreme of alcoholism/addiction is due to the extreme nature of my personality coupled with the lack of spiritual guidance and emotional and spiritual neglect in my youth.

Once I entered rehab and recovery, since I did not have as much to recover from, I have not relapsed yet. I have tremendous compassion for people who continually relapse because I am certain that the wounds of their past are far greater than mine. My prayer is that I can be of benefit and service to them to lead them to the abundant life that God designed for them. I understand that I have had it easier than most, but that does not make my impact any less significant to those who are willing to receive my help.

This defense mechanism of disallowing emotion to come to my consciousness and affect my actions is one of my attributes that enable me to be a good surgeon. When unexpected things happen in surgery, I do not panic. I can methodically think through the situation and address it appropriately because I have been trained to not allow emotion to cloud my judgment in surgery. The fact that I do not allow myself to feel an emotion in a given moment and perform without it affecting me was something that I had previously considered an asset. And it is an asset—when I am operating. This asset, however, is dangerous to my life when applied outside of the operating room. Even when I handle a scary situation in the operating room, the negative emotions from that experience still live inside of me. Unless I can properly process and address it, it festers in my soul and was another reason why my alcoholism progressed.

Today, I am certain my parents did the best they could. They had no spiritual program of action and no spiritual teaching given to them that they could pass on to me.

For they disciplined us for a short time *as it seemed best to them*, but he disciplines us for our

good, that we may share his holiness." (Hebrews
12:10 ESV; italics mine)

"As it seemed best to them," it says. They did a great job, and
they did parent me as seemed best to them. They parented me based
on what their parents did, and what they learned about parenting,
and what they saw other parents do that they thought would be beneficial. But this scripture makes it clear to me that God is the ultimate father and KNOWS what is best. Each and every parent, including myself, has faults and shortcomings that God must ultimately
make up for. If parents do not direct their children to the one true
God, there will be repercussions in that child's life that will echo
into adulthood. Even with the best direction and modeling of Christ
as parents, because we live in a fallen world, there are still negative
unintended consequences that will occur as people grow into adulthood. But with proper spiritual guidance, mentoring, and, most
importantly, modeling, the consequences will be far less than they
would be without that spiritual direction.

**Train up a child in the way he should go,
but be sure you are going that way yourself.
(Charles Spurgeon)**

This brings me to my final point of this section. Teaching without modeling is just as damaging as not teaching our children about
God. It would be far better to never mention God or Jesus in a home
if the parents are not living out their faith daily. The disconnect
between parents making their children go to church and not practicing what they preach is just as detrimental, if not more so, than never
talking about God or Jesus.
More is caught than taught.
It is of critical importance that we instruct our children in the
truth, be present in their lives, and live what we teach. That is the
greatest gift parents can give to their children. It will form and shape
that child for their entire earthly life and set the stage for ultimate
abundant life or utter destruction. I pray that all my readers feel the

weight of this responsibility and are humbled by it. I pray they realize that they are not alone and can go to God for direction and guidance. I pray that parents who are separated from their children for whatever reason read this and it resonates in their heart and soul and they reconnect with their children. It is NEVER too late to enter his child's life and begin the process of redemption. But it cannot be done well or properly without complete submission and surrender to God and His ultimate direction.

17

LASER FOCUS

While I was in rehab, I had the privilege of being able to attend special meetings (called Caduceus) that are designed for medical health professionals who have alcoholism and/or addiction disorders. The TMF oversees these process groups throughout Tennessee because they recognize that there are issues in a medical professional's life that he/she may not be able to discuss in an AA or other anonymous fellowship meeting. In addition, there will almost always be another professional who has dealt with a similar situation and will have useful feedback. These meetings do not substitute for regular AA meetings, but they provide a safe place for us to discuss professional matters that have an emotional impact on us.

Since I went to a rehab near Nashville, I was able to attend the Caduceus meeting there. My practice was about thirty minutes from the city of Nashville. When I went to my first Caduceus meeting, I was pleasantly surprised to see other physicians that I knew. They were sober, succeeding in their job, and living fulfilling, satisfying lives. This helped fuel my faith in AA by establishing confidence in things unseen yet to me.

Whenever there is a newcomer to a Caduceus meeting, everyone introduces themselves before the newcomer. Then the newcomer has the opportunity to tell everyone about themselves, how they got there, and anything else they wish to disclose. After everyone else went, I started to tell them my story. Most of it was the two years leading up to my entry into rehab. I talked about how most of my drinking was on vacation and at home on weekends and how most people at work probably would not know about my drinking escapades.

After I finished, there was a pharmacist from Nashville who said, "Most people don't know about your drinking? Hell, I've been hearing about your drinking for the past two years!"

What? I thought. How in the world would this pharmacist know about my drinking? I was never drunk in public locally. I thought I was adept at hiding it from everyone except my family. My immediate reaction was that I was going to talk to him after the meeting and find out where he heard it from. I needed to know! I needed to know everyone and anyone who knew anything about how I was living.

As the meeting progressed, however, I came to realize that none of that mattered. What he heard, who he heard it from, what he knew was all irrelevant to me now. The fact was that he did know something and that I was not good at hiding my alcoholism. That was a truth I needed to hear. What I needed now was to know how to be relieved of my alcoholism so this would not happen again. It turns out that he is close friends with another physician in Murfreesboro who has close connections to my ex-wife, and that is how he had information. I did not discover this until well after I had left rehab. I did not confront him after the meeting.

This was another act of surrender. I could not change what I had done in the past. I had no control over what was said or what other people thought of me. There would be no purpose to any kind of interrogation I would subject him to. The only thing I could control at that point was my next action. I could control what I would do with this information and how I would use it to help my recovery.

I experienced another spiritual awakening in a later meeting. There was another physician who is in almost the same specialty of medicine as me whose practice was in Nashville. Spine surgery is a small world, and we pretty much all know each other to some degree, whether it be personally or professionally. We hear about each other through the operating room staff or patients who may see both of us for second opinions or subsequent care. He was a physician who was solid in his recovery, highly successful, and someone I respected. I had seen some of his patients that he had operated on years ago for another problem, and I knew he was an excellent physician and surgeon. At least from my view before rehab, he had what I wanted, and now I knew he had sobriety, so that was even more reason for me to respect him and listen to what he said.

One day he said to me during a meeting, "Listen, I know you and I know what kind of physician and surgeon you are. I know you do excellent work, and you take great care of your patients. You have a laser focus on what you do, and you do it very well. There is no doubt in my mind that you will be successful in your recovery. If you put that same laser focus on recovery that you do on your practice and spine surgery, there is no chance that you will fail."

Wow. I felt completely humbled. It was great to know that I had the respect of another physician who does what I do. I had only met him maybe once before in the nine years that I was in practice, so I knew his knowledge of my practice and skills did not come from anything I told him. He was absolutely right. Anything in my past that I had put my mind to, I was able to accomplish. This characteristic is one of the reasons why I did not believe in God for so long. If I worked hard enough, I could accomplish what I had envisioned professionally. I felt as though I was self-made and did not need God's assistance, even though the truth is that God was helping me all along. Again, more faith stirred inside of me.

As my recovery has progressed, and as I have been successful in it so far, I have come to realize that my laser focus is not really on the process of recovery, but on God. The basis of solid recovery is God (or higher power), turning our will and our lives over to the care of God. In putting my laser focus on God, my recovery has also flourished.

And so has my ENTIRE life. The process of me mentally eliminating everything in my life except God and being comfortable and at peace with that and that alone has allowed me to be absolutely certain that God needs to be the central focus of everything and anything I do. The serenity I feel knowing that God is my only true need enables me to live happy, joyous, and free, completely surrendered to His will.

In *Knowledge of the Holy*, A. W. Tozer writes about how God, by His very being, needs nothing. Because if He needed something, his being would be limited by whatever He needed. He created all things, was before all things, and is above all things. He is supported by nothing. He is the only being that can be truly termed "self-sufficient." Previous to recovery and my relationship with God, I would have said that I was "self-made" or "self-sufficient." What a grand delusion that is! I, by my very nature of being a human being, have been created and dependent on all sorts of people in my life, my parents to start, and many others. Therefore, I am in desperate need, and there is no other that I need to be dependent on other than God. God, being everything, and I together complete my entire being such that I am in need of nothing else. However, the great reward of being in close, conscious contact with God is that *all* of my needs are supplied by Him in gracious measure, beyond what I would attempt to construct for myself. How truly humbling and extravagant is that?

18

MIRACLES (IS THAT ODD, OR IS THAT GOD?)

One of the assignments I had in rehab was to observe any miracles that happened day to day. One definition of miracle is an effect or extraordinary event in the physical world that surpasses all known human or natural powers and is ascribed to a supernatural cause. Another definition is a surprising and welcome event that is not explicable by natural or scientific laws and is therefore considered to be the work of a divine agency.

Now that I was not drinking and my mind was clearing up, I started to notice these little coincidences that happened that could not be explained any other way. I started to notice how little things would line up just right through circumstances and events beyond my control.

One miracle I noticed was that I was able to use the exercise area twice per week, every week even though our schedule did not always accommodate that. In rehab, we had no control and were told our schedule throughout our stay. Twice a week, our house would be able to use the exercise room. Working out is very important to me. I enjoy it, and it provides therapy for me to challenge myself. Although my workout routine was nothing like it had been outside of rehab, I still sought to maintain my fitness level during my stay.

There were certain weeks when for one reason or another, our house was not allowed to use the exercise room during our assigned time. This would frustrate me because I knew going only once per week would be barely sufficient for me to maintain my physique.

Interestingly enough, however, I would ask our house advisors if there would possibly be a time during the week when I could go. The vast majority of the time, I was allowed to exercise for a second time that week. Sometimes I did not even have to ask, and it was offered to me without any effort on my part.

Who was in control of allowing me permission to work out? I definitely was not. Rehab is very structured, and we were told where we needed to go and when almost all the time. The fact that I got my way in this regard demonstrated to me that someone was looking out for me. Someone who knew what I desired and was willing to give it to me if I did what I was supposed to do. This is a miracle to me to be given this gift and special privilege even though I did nothing to deserve it other than just doing the next right thing.

Some of you reading this may think that this is hardly a miracle. I disagree. It was a welcome and surprising event that was not explicable by natural or scientific laws and therefore ascribed to a divine agency. The laws of rehab dictate that the residents are to do what they are told. If the schedule changes, then the schedule changes, and we missed out on whatever it was. Yet somehow, through divine intervention, I got what I wanted even though I never forced it or sought it out.

I use the word "miracle" on a daily basis. I am certain there are people who think that I am crazy. But throughout this process, I had a spiritual awakening on what is considered a miracle. A person's definition of a miracle is merely a matter of perspective.

Let me explain. I am a physician. I spent countless hours reading, studying, and in lecture about the body's processes and how it works. From anatomy to physiology to biochemistry to the molecular level, I have acquired a great deal of knowledge on the science of the human body. The textbooks that I read each weighed at least several pounds, and there were many. I was taught by PhDs who wrote books and did extensive research on the human body. I felt as though I had tremendous knowledge on the medical science of the human body.

However, today, I realize that the fact that I can even get up in the morning, move my body to get around, speak, eat, or any other mundane activity is a miracle. When one learns about all the chemical reactions, nerve impulses, and signals that result in contractions and coordinated movements, if one is truly honest with oneself, one must realize that we do not even have a fraction of a percentage of that explained with current medical science. There are so many intricate feedback loops and mechanisms. The brain must process stimuli and signals from all the senses in a delicate fashion and subsequently respond to that. The speed with which the brain does that is incalculable. No human machine or computer has anywhere close to the capability of what the human body can do with such precision.

Going back to the definition of a miracle—surprising and welcome event that is not explicable by natural or scientific laws and is therefore considered to be the work of a divine agency. ANY human activity, even sleep, cannot be explained by the current natural or scientific laws. How can it be explained then? I mean REALLY explained? Down to every last molecular reaction and ion moving across each membrane. The answer is that it cannot. We think we are so evolved and learned that we are close to explaining this. As a physician, with many years of postgraduate studies, I assure you that we are not even close. Not even one-millionth of one percent close to explaining this.

As my recovery has progressed, I notice miracles daily. I thank God for them. They are events and circumstances beyond any human control. In sobriety, I now have the ability to recognize them for what they are. They remind me daily of who is really in control. I feel great peace knowing that the one who is in control has a perfect plan for my life and everyone's life on this earth.

We know that all things work together for
the good of those who love God: those who are
called according to his purpose. (Romans 8:28)

That is the truth. Praise the Lord. Thankful I love God today.

19

GOD DOING FOR ME WHAT
I CANNOT DO FOR MYSELF

Another assignment I had in rehab (we had a lot of assignments) was to look back on my life and see where God was taking care of me. Times in my life where I may not have made the best decisions, yet everything turned out in my favor. I was also to record instances where I did not get what I wanted, yet the result turned out so much better than what I could have imagined than if I actually did get what I wanted in that moment.

This exercise was obvious for many things. The times where I was driving drunk yet somehow never got a DUI or got into an accident. The many times in Miami where I had been partying with alcohol and drugs and never got into trouble with the police. There were other times in my life where these revelations were not as evident. But as the assignment progressed, as I sought help from God, many more came to surface and revealed to me the power and goodness of God in my life.

This is the greatest example to me of how God loves me no matter what and how His plan is much better than my plan for my life. When I applied to medical school, being the arrogant, egotistical person I was, there was no doubt in my mind that I would be going to a prestigious medical school like Harvard or Johns Hopkins. A student of my caliber would certainly have to attend a medical school that was recognized throughout the world as one of the best. My grades were superb, and my Medical College Admission Test (MCAT) score was top-notch. In evaluating the top medical schools, I discovered that my MCAT score matched that of the average Harvard med student. Naturally, I felt as though I was entitled to go there.

In my overconfidence, I did not apply as soon as the application period opened. I figured I had time, and I would submit it with enough time to spare. I applied to Harvard (obviously), Johns Hopkins, Northwestern, Washington University, and University of Illinois at Chicago (UIC). My grades and MCAT scores were at least the average of those schools and mostly above. Coupled with my outstanding personality and compassion for people would certainly get me into at least one of those schools, if not all, was the delusion that existed in my mind.

What I did not know when I applied was that medical school admissions were rolling. That means that the schools evaluate applicants as the applications come in and accept them accordingly. Statistically, one has a better chance of being accepted applying early because as the process progresses, there are less spots available. I cannot state with certainty that affected my acceptance, but it would stand to reason that it played a role.

I sent my application materials in and eagerly awaited their positive response. The first response was from Johns Hopkins. Not accepted. Then Northwestern. Not accepted. I could not believe it. What were they thinking? Then the rest came in. Harvard—"We regret to inform you that you have not been accepted." The only school I got into was UIC. A state school? AGH! Are you kidding me! My only option was a state school? Not some prestigious recognizable private institution? And to make matters worse, I did not get admitted to the Chicago campus of the UIC system. UIC has campuses in Rockford, Peoria, and Urbana. The campuses in Peoria and Rockford were created in the hopes that the graduates would enter family medicine or primary care and then go to work in underserved parts of Illinois. The Rockford campus had the Rural Medical Education (RMED) Program, which was specifically designed for this purpose. The campus that I was assigned to was Rockford.

I was indignant. Insulted. In disbelief. There must have been a mistake. Didn't these people know what my grades and MCAT scores were? Didn't they know that they were passing on the most outstanding candidate they had ever considered?

The answer is they obviously knew what all my credentials were. After their thorough and fair evaluation process, I was not accepted as a student at all those private schools. My only option was UIC-Rockford. I wanted to be a doctor, so that was my only choice. Defeated and humiliated in my mind, I had to surrender to that decision and attend a state school geared toward training family practice doctors, not some high-powered, prestigious, world-renowned, recognized institution. I would still become a medical doctor, but in my delusional mind, my chances at a successful career and future accolades were going to be limited. Or so I thought...

I went to Urbana the first year because that is where all the basic science classes are due to the undergraduate University of Illinois being there. My second year, I moved up to Rockford for my remaining three years. The second year is another year of basic science classes. Third and fourth years are called clinical years where students are in the hospitals and clinics, working with clinicians, learning the real-life practice of medicine.

I entered my third year thinking that I might be a family practice doctor after all. I did care about people and enjoyed seeing multiple members of the family from babies to octogenarians, treating the whole gamut of medical conditions. My first rotation as a third-year student was obstetrics/gynecology. During this rotation, I found that I thoroughly enjoyed being in the operating room. I liked the immediate results of surgery. Being fairly athletic and coordinated, I liked and was proficient at performing surgery as opposed to diagnosing and prescribing medicine. It was at that point I decided to be a surgeon. Orthopedic surgery seemed like the best fit for me because of my athletic background. I also liked the fact that orthopedic surgeons operate to relieve pain. It is one of the most gratifying feelings in the world when a patient comes to see me with tremendous pain, I perform surgery, and when they are healed (by God), they are able to return to their life activities and athletics again.

During my surgery rotation that year, I was allowed to do a couple of weeks of a surgical subspecialty, and I chose orthopedics.

There were several community surgeons who participated in teaching the medical students. As it so happened (odd or God?), one of those surgeons was a man named Brian Bear, a hand surgeon. He was about two years into practice, not far removed from college and medical school. He had gone to Northwestern as an undergraduate student, and not only that, he was in the same fraternity (ATO) that I had been in! He was and is an outstanding person and really took me under his wing and helped me. He spoke highly of me to his partners, and I was able to scrub in with them for all kinds of orthopedic surgeries.

At academic medical centers like Harvard and Johns Hopkins, there are fellows and residents in every specialty. Residents are people who have graduated from medical school and are now in residency for a medical specialty, like orthopedics. Fellows are past residents and in training for a subspecialty of that medical specialty, like orthopedic spine surgery. The attendings are the medical doctors who have completed training and are the ones ultimately teaching and instructing on how to do surgery. At these medical centers, during a surgery, the attending is at the operating room table performing and overseeing the surgery. Standing across from the attending is the fellow and/or resident. Most of the time it is the fellow, and the resident is standing next to the fellow, possibly using suction to help or not even doing anything at all, but just observing. The medical student in these situations is possibly scrubbed in to the surgery but may not even have a chance to do anything and may even have a hard time seeing what is even going on.

At UIC-Rockford, there are no fellows or residents in surgery. For every surgery I scrubbed in to as a medical student, it was the attending and me, and only me. I was the first assistant, and as my experience grew, I was able to do more and more of the surgery under the attending's supervision. I was highly motivated. Dr. Bear and his partners knew I desired to be an orthopedic surgeon, and they wanted to help me. If I was done with whatever my responsibilities were for that day, I ensured they knew I was available. They were more than willing to call me for cases and have me scrub in and assist and teach me.

Because I was at UIC-Rockford, I was able to scrub in and actually perform a lot of these orthopedic surgeries (supervised, of course), an experience that would not have been possible at Harvard or Johns Hopkins. When I had finished medical school, I had almost the same level of experience with orthopedic surgery as a second-year resident. Even though I was indignant about going to what I perceived to be a subpar state school, it turned out to be the greatest education I could have ever received to reach my ultimate position as a spine surgeon.

Dr. Bear did his residency at the Hospital for Special Surgery (HSS) in New York City. HSS is one of the top orthopedic surgery residency programs in the country. The attendings there are all widely known and write many articles and textbooks. As such, the graduates of HSS naturally follow suit and disperse throughout the country, taking leading roles in various academic institutions across the country.

Since Dr. Bear and I had a good relationship; he saw firsthand my drive, knowledge, and skill; and we had the connection from ATO at Northwestern, he bent over backward to help me. During my fourth year, I was allowed to do away rotations at other hospitals. Because of Dr. Bear's connections, I rotated at HSS and Rush University Medical Center with one of his classmates at HSS, Brian Cole, who was a young burgeoning sports medicine doctor prodigiously making a name for himself in the world of sports medicine. These are opportunities that are not easy to come by. I was positioned perfectly to garner great experience and connect with these well-known and highly respected physicians, even though I was in Rockford, Illinois. This enabled me to obtain outstanding letters of recommendation from very well-known people that catapulted me to the top of the residency application lists.

Orthopedic surgery is very competitive, if not the most competitive specialty to be accepted into. All the candidates applying to orthopedic surgery residency are top of the class. Now, not only did I have those credentials, I had the support of physicians who were known and respected. I am certain all of these factors enabled me to get into residency at University of Miami-Jackson Memorial

Hospital, one of the best orthopedic residency programs in the country. From little ole Rockford.

Who made the decision for me to go to UIC-Rockford instead of Harvard? It surely was not me. It was in no way, shape, or form what I wanted for my life in that moment. Had I got what I wanted in that moment, my life's trajectory would be radically different. It may still have been a good path for my life, but I cannot fathom a life better than what I have today. Because of this, I understand that God makes better decisions for my life than what I think is best for me or what I would want. I am very careful these days when there is something that I desperately want or don't want. If the desire for that thing stems from my own ego and pride, it will end in destruction. In keeping conscious contact with God, I am better able today to submit to His will for my life with much better results.

Looking back, there were so many situations and circumstances that positioned me perfectly to enter my career as an orthopedic spine surgeon. What I thought was best for me was to go to a prestigious private medical school. Had that happened, I would have never met Brian Bear, and it is extremely unlikely I would have had such a close personal connection with someone like that being from the same fraternity at the same university. The chances are slim that I would have acquainted myself with someone like him who had just trained at a well-known institution with many connections in orthopedic surgery throughout the United States. And there is no possible way I could have gained the same experience in surgery as I did at a different institution with many residents and fellows.

> "For I know the plans I have for you," declares the Lord, "plans to prosper you and not to harm you, plans to give you hope and a future." (Jeremiah 29:11 NIV)

That is the truth. Praise the Lord.

To top this amazing miracle off, this was at a time in my life where not only did I not believe in God, I would fight and ridicule people for their belief in God. I was not a quiet atheist. I was extremely egotistical and intelligent, and I would make sure you knew how much smarter I was than you were. I would scoff at people who believed in God and insult them as if they were kindergarteners or hopeful daydreamers rubbing a lamp to get the genie out. At that time, I did not take any effort to investigate God or Jesus. Being god of my own kingdom, I did not have any reason to consider God because of my unwavering belief in myself.

Confidence in one's ability is one thing; arrogance is another. There is nothing wrong with being confident of the God-given talents and abilities that one has been given. Michael Jordan is very confident in his basketball abilities, and no one would ever argue that. However, arrogance is an exaggeration of one's abilities or the improper attribution of those gifts to oneself, dismissing any support or help in attaining those gifts. I was extremely arrogant back then. I thought everything I did, everything I had accomplished, everything I achieved, was a direct result of what I had done with no acknowledgment of anyone else or God. Today, I am confident in my abilities as a spine surgeon, but I recognize that where I am at today is the result of not only my own efforts, but countless others who have supported me along the way, the most important of which is God. God is the one who gave me the talents and provided the people in my path that has enabled me to get where I am today.

Realizing all this today demonstrates to me the unconditional love that God has for me and all His children. Even though I rejected Him and outright ridiculed Him and His followers, He ensured that I received everything I would need for me to become a spine surgeon. This reminds me of Jesus marching to the cross, with me spitting in His face, placing a crown of thorns on His head, and flogging Him on the back, all the while loving me and sacrificing for me to have abundant life. Loving me while I am knowingly and intentionally abusing Him! There is no greater love than that. That is very clear to me. It also gives me the confidence that I am completely forgiven for all my sins, past, present, and future because His love for me endured direct antagonistic action against God. This fuels my drive to please God out of my gratitude to Him for all that He has done for me. I do not serve God to gain anything else in this life. God is all I need.

I serve God today because my whole heart seeks to please Him out of thankfulness for His extravagant grace and mercy.

> But God proves His own love for us in that
> while we were still sinners Christ died for us!
> (Romans 5:8)

That is the truth. Praise the Lord.

20

CUNNING, BAFFLING, POWERFUL

> Remember that we deal with alcohol-cunning, baffling, powerful. Without help, it is too much for us. But there is one who has all power-that One is God. May you find Him now! (*Alcoholics Anonymous*, 4th ed., 59)

Those three words—cunning, baffling, and powerful—accurately described how I felt about alcohol before I entered rehab. I could not understand my complete and utter powerlessness over being able to control how much I drank once I had just one in my system. I had a great deal of perceived willpower I had in so many other areas of my life. God knowingly and lovingly used the massive hammer of alcoholism to force me to look at myself in truth and ultimately surrender to Him.

Toward the end of rehab, I was allowed to attend an Ed Sheeran concert with my then eight-year-old daughter that I had previously planned to go to before entering rehab. The same daughter who was so scared on that last vacation that she was rescued by one of her mother's friends. I most definitely wanted to go outside of rehab and participate in the world. This was about seventy days into my stay in rehab. I was feeling very good in my sobriety and had a lot of confidence that I would not have any issues going to the concert venue. My mom (the same mom who helped me drive the van back from Florida seventy days earlier) was going to go with my daughter and me.

Rehab is a sheltered environment. There are very few opportunities to even be able to go out and get alcohol to drink. If someone in rehab really wants to get alcohol and drugs, they are really going to have to put forth some major effort to do so. We were randomly drug and alcohol tested every week also. This environment creates a somewhat false sense of security in one's sobriety, if one is not aware that it will be much harder to avoid alcohol in the outside world. I have a tremendous amount of respect for people who get sober while living their lives and attending AA meetings and working the AA program. God knew that I did not have that kind of discipline when it came to alcohol. He knew I had to be forcibly removed from my entire life for ninety days. I was confined and sheltered from alcohol because He knows what I need better than I ever could.

Since I was going with my mom and my eight-year-old daughter, and I also knew that I would be alcohol tested when I returned from the concert, I felt pretty good about being able to not drink and not even have the desire to drink. They picked me up, and we headed for Bridgestone Arena. I had been to many concerts there, none of them sober. This would be the first time that I ever went to a concert where I did not drink anything. I had worked through step 6 at this point, had many counseling groups and therapy sessions, and felt that I was in good shape to handle this environment.

We parked and headed inside. Immediately, huge, MASSIVE signs for Bud Light, Tito's Vodka, and Mike's Hard Lemonade immediately came into my view. Even after all those days in rehab and treatment I received, I STILL had the desire to drink. I was in an environment where I had never been any other way before. I used the tools I learned, and I did not drink that night, but the desire to drink was strong and real to me. I thoroughly enjoyed the concert and was very grateful to experience it with my daughter and mom. The music was more crisp than what I ever remembered from a concert before. I could actually remember the whole concert! What a gift!

Cunning, baffling, powerful. Those words resonated in my head about that night. After all the pain that alcohol had caused me, why in the world would I EVER want to induce that pain on myself again? Why wasn't I "cured" of this obsession after all the treatment I had in rehab? The Big Book of AA has a story about a person who enjoys jaywalking. He starts casually, and as time goes on, he gets hit by cars more and more, and his injuries become increasingly severe. Yet he keeps going back to jaywalking because he cannot help himself to stop. Anyone would agree that this person would be considered insane. However, this is the EXACT same insanity of alcoholism. This was a revelation to me that my thinking regarding alcohol was insane.

What most people who are in Christ miss is that we are ALL insane in regard to our thinking and actions. Paul describes this insanity in Romans.

> For I do not understand what I am doing,
> because I do not practice what I want to do, but
> I do what I hate. (Romans 7:15 CSB)

Paul would be considered by most to be the greatest Christian missionary of all time. He wrote about one-half of the New Testament. Yet he does not do what he knows is the right thing to do and wants to do and, to the contrary, does what he hates! This is insanity. It is the insanity of sin. It is a human being's natural tendency to rebel against God and disobey Him. We are born children of wrath. I am not talking about the big sins of murder and adultery. Most people have enough moral compass to not do those on a regular basis. I am talking about most people consider "little" sins like lying, worry, overeating, getting angry, lustful fantasy, etc. To us, those are "lesser" sins. To God, they are all equal.

Anger for one millisecond is equal to murder. Looking lustfully at another man's wife is equal to a full-blown affair. That is how I know that it is impossible for us to keep the law. It also stupefies me how Jesus lived a perfect life and kept all the laws His entire stay on earth. Not one thought of lust? The woman the Pharisees brought to Jesus was a prostitute and was naked. Being fully God but also fully man, He did not have even one nanosecond of lust for her? I know that is not humanly possible and therefore reinforces my belief that He was fully God in human form.

I am overwhelmingly thankful God blessed me with the disease of alcoholism, as opposed to other sins. While this may seem like a strange belief, please let me explain. The earthly consequences of drunkenness are harsh and severe. They are readily identifiable by everyone, except the alcoholic himself when in active addiction. The intense and unrelenting consequences of my actions as my disease progressed forced me to realize that I was powerless over alcohol. I seemingly had power over other temptations, but alcohol was a foe that I could not defeat. If my main affliction was a lesser, more socially acceptable sin like gluttony, worry, or laziness, I may have never come to realize that I was not the one in control of life. If I was given a sin that the world is conforming to, I could easily see myself continuing in the delusion that my actions were not sin and that it is the world to blame for any negative emotions that would arise out of my personal sin. Fortunately for me, the world and God agree that drunkenness is a sin. No rational human being believes that it is appropriate to drive drunk or believes that a person could be justified in that behavior.

Every human being struggles with something. There is a sin in every person's life that creates more powerful urges than others. God uses that struggle to demonstrate His sovereign power IF that individual can eventually recognize and confront that sin and choose to combat it. The issue today is that so much sin is either socially acceptable or even condoned and celebrated by society. "If it feels right to you and it feels good, go ahead and do it. You are not hurting anyone else" is the mantra of today. The pride of man is powerful and convincing. People caught in sin will seek out others to support themselves in a vain attempt to prove themselves right.

God is a majority all by Himself. The truth is that He alone determines what is right and wrong spiritually. Human beings created in the image of almighty God Himself call this our conscience. Our conscience proves that we have some innate sense of right and wrong imparted to us. It is how we intuitively know in our hearts that it is wrong for an adult male to sexually assault a child, even if no one had ever told us that it was wrong. We intuitively know that in our hearts. Where does that come from? It comes from almighty God. The "lesser" sins that we deem inconsequential can be more easily dismissed and suppressed within our hearts. Yet the damage to our spirit will be present.

That is why I am eternally grateful that God used the disease of alcoholism to reveal Himself fully to me. It is my daily reminder that I am dependent on Him to stay sober, but also for every other facet of my life and existence. The miracle today is that I do not drink because I do not WANT to. When people ask me why I do not drink alcohol these days, my response is not because I am an alcoholic, although that is true. My response is that I feel so good today that a drink cannot make me feel better. I have happiness, joy, serenity, peace, and freedom so overwhelming; and an alcoholic beverage cannot improve that in any way.

Serenity is not compatible with struggle.

It is not a struggle. I do not have to fight that temptation anymore. When I see a drink today, all I see is pain. I no longer have that desire. I thank and acknowledge God every day for giving me His power to overcome that desire and change it. To transform my heart. That transformation was not possible under my own power, as I experienced.

Since I know that alcoholism is a chronic, progressive, fatal disease requiring daily treatment, I am also aware that I can never relent on my spiritual program of action. The extraordinary gift of this is with what I have learned and practiced in AA coupled with my walk with Jesus, I continue to seek God, enabling me to stay sober, but also granting me the gift of abundant life in all areas.

Therefore, so that I would not exalt myself, a thorn in the flesh was given to me, a messenger of Satan to torment me so I would not exalt myself. Concerning this, I pleaded with the Lord three times to take it away from me. But He said to me, "My grace is sufficient for you, for my power is perfected in weakness." Therefore, I will most gladly boast all the more about my weaknesses, so that Christ's power may reside in me. (2 Corinthians 12:7–9 HCSB)

That's the truth. Praise the Lord for my weaknesses!

21

REENTRY (LEAVING REHAB)

After finishing treatment and being removed from my life for ninety days, all of a sudden I returned to life again. I returned home to my wife and four children. I returned to work. There was a lot of fear inside of me about many things. Would my wife still want to stay married to me? Would my practice return to its flourishing state? Would I be able to stay sober? What are people going to say to me? What are people going to think about my sudden and prolonged absence?

I had been reassured by many physicians in recovery that not only would my life return to some state of normalcy, if I kept working the AA program one day at a time, not only would my life be restored, it would be a life that I had not dreamed of and could not imagine. This assurance fueled my faith and drove my actions to continue to follow the suggestions that were given to me.

The suggestions that I followed when leaving treatment were to

1. go to ninety AA meetings in ninety days,
2. go to intensive outpatient treatment,
3. see a therapist,
4. get a sponsor,
5. work the steps of the AA program,
6. attend the Caduceus process group for medical professionals, and
7. check in every day for the next five years for random alcohol/drug urine screenings.

Fortunately, upon my return to my practice, I was not as busy as I was before I entered rehab. My schedule allowed me to attend an AA meeting every day. Just as everyone had told me, no one asked me ANYTHING about where I had been. It was as if it never happened. A lot of people were glad to see me and told me they were happy I was back. But NO ONE asked where I had been.

The truth is that the great majority of people are so wrapped up in their own lives that they had not given one thought to where I might have been or what happened. It did not matter to them. It did not affect them, or if it did, they just found a way to deal with it. Many of my patients had seen some of my partners, but the majority of them returned to me when I got back, no questions asked. They were grateful that I was back, and there was no judgment about why I was gone. It was none of their business anyways. What was their business, however, was that I was back and doing what I was created to do. Now, I had the spiritual gift of being able to do it under God's direction and will.

This is an example of how people really do not care or remember what had happened to me. About a year after rehab, I received a bottle of wine from a patient as a Christmas gift. It had been dropped off when I was in clinic and was sitting on my desk in my office. When I walked into my office, I thought, *Oh great. Just what I need. All my partners seeing a bottle of wine on my desk and thinking about why I have a bottle of wine on my desk.* I had no desire to drink it at this point and saw one of my partners coming down the hall. I asked him if he liked wine and if he wanted it. He said, "Yes. I love wine. You don't drink?" I chuckled and said no, and he gratefully took it. All my partners knew I went to rehab for alcoholism, and he was one of the ones directly affected by seeing some of my patients while I was gone, yet he totally forgot. It is amazing the self-centeredness of alcoholics and how we are concerned about what everyone is thinking about us. The truth is what everyone is thinking about us is not much.

Even as my practice grew again, I purposefully limited my work hours. I remembered what the psychologist said to me my first week of treatment. Sobriety had to be the number one priority in my life or nothing else mattered. I made sure I attended my suggested meetings and started to find a sponsor.

A sponsor is someone who has worked the twelve steps of AA and has at least a year of sobriety. The purpose of a sponsor is to teach me (the sponsee) about the program of AA, work steps with me, and essentially teach me how to stay sober through his experience, strength, and hope. When a person gets a sponsor, it is suggested that the sponsee call the sponsor daily. When I finally found my sponsor, I did exactly that. Sometimes I did not even know why I was calling him, nor did I have anything to talk about. But I did what was suggested.

It is suggested that a sponsee is to call a sponsor every single day. That is how God designed a relationship to be formed. We were created to TALK to each other. God did not design us to send text messages to other human beings as our primary form of communication. I can hide my feelings and my demeanor in a text. God gave us mouths to communicate, not thumbs.

If I talk to my sponsor daily, even if I have nothing to talk about, somehow, we will find something to talk about, even just for a few minutes. Trust is built. Judgment is eliminated. That built the confidence in me that I had another human being on this earth to rely on. Someone who wanted nothing from me. His sole purpose in agreeing to be my sponsor was and is to help me stay sober.

I was assigned a temporary physician sponsor upon leaving treatment. Physicians make the worst sponsors. We are too busy with work and our families to be readily available. In early sobriety, an alcoholic may need to talk to someone at a moment's notice to prevent them from going to the liquor store. Most physicians just do not have that kind of availability. The relationship with my temporary sponsor was not working out.

God revealed my sponsor to me at an AA meeting. As I progress in the program of AA, I continually improve my conscious contact with God and my awareness of His will. Wise decisions enter my mind more readily. He stated in his share one fateful day, "I'm the type of guy who would rather climb to the top of a pole and tell you a lie rather than stand right in front of you and tell you the truth." I thought, *That is the guy.*

I found his name on the AA home group phone list, called, and asked him to be my sponsor. He has been my sponsor for four years now. He has a sponsor that he has had for over twenty years. That is how it works. Passed down from generation to generation. As God so would have it, the similarities that he and I share not only in our alcoholism, but in our relationship choices, and other facets of our lives is truly astounding. He is in his sixties, and I am in my early forties. We come from very different backgrounds, yet we are so similar in our decision-making I can have no other explanation than God on how this was arranged.

Remember it was agreed at the beginning WE WOULD GO TO ANY LENGTHS FOR VICTORY OVER ALCOHOL. (*Alcoholics Anonymous*, 4th ed., 76)

That was what I was willing to go to. ANY LENGTHS. Sobriety was my only option. I knew I would lose everything I cherished on this earth if I could not stay sober. As suggested, I went to ninety meetings in ninety days, not including the required weekly Caduceus meeting. As suggested, I started seeing a therapist every week. The best recovery therapists were an hour from where I worked and lived. That meant a three-hour commitment every week for eighteen months to learn about myself and techniques to handle life on life's terms. As suggested, I did intensive outpatient treatment for the first three months, which was another six hours each week. As suggested, I called my sponsor daily, and we sat down for an hour each week, going through the Big Book and working steps. In all, not including talking to my sponsor every day, that is eight hours of AA meetings and Caduceus, three hours for therapy, six hours of intensive outpatient therapy, and a one-hour meeting with my sponsor for a total of eighteen hours each week dedicated to my recovery. Few have the blessing of everything that was offered to me, and even fewer actually follow through and do it all. I am convinced that my laser-focused dedication has contributed greatly to my sobriety and continual seeking of God leading to abundant life.

I cannot think my way into right acting. I must act my way into right thinking.

The Big Book says that we alcoholics who have recovered have had "vital spiritual experiences." In the chapter "There Is a Solution," Dr. Jung, a doctor who treated alcoholics at the time, states,

> Here and there, once in a while, alcoholics have had what are called vital spiritual experiences. To me these occurrences are phenomena. They appear to be in the nature of huge emotional displacements and arrangements. Ideas, emotions, and attitudes which were once the guiding forces of the lives of these men are suddenly cast to one side, and a completely new set of conceptions and motives begin to dominate them. (*Alcoholics Anonymous,* 4th ed., 27)

How do these vital spiritual experiences come about? It is not a matter of wishing or willing it to happen. No amount of meditation and prayer by itself will cause this to come about, although those components are important. Getting baptized, chanting, or merely attending AA meetings or church will not cause them to happen

It takes action. Intentional work. Following suggestions. As many of them as an individual is willing to take at a time. I did not follow all the suggestions perfectly, and I still do not. No one does. But I had the willingness to go to any lengths necessary for victory over alcohol. The results have been outstanding, not only keeping me sober, but giving me an amazing new life.

> We have found much of heaven and we have been rocketed into a fourth dimension of existence of which we had not even dreamed. (*Alcoholics Anonymous,* 4th ed., 25)

It does not say, "We were waiting to go to heaven." It does not say, "We were looking for heaven." It does not say, "We wanted to go to heaven." It says, emphatically and powerfully, "We have FOUND much of heaven." Not just sobriety from alcohol, but heaven, and that is what I have found and continue to live in today.

All these actions are necessary.

This is how God reveals His true nature to us. How does this happen?

My sponsor, although he is not God (even though he may think it at times), demonstrates characteristics of God to me. He is almost always available (omnipresence). He has no expectation of repayment for the time spent helping me (love). I have shared every shameful act I have ever done, and he has never judged me (no condemnation). When I share with him such things, I receive understanding and guidance (compassion). He has the knowledge of how to stay sober, which is what I seek from him (wisdom). If I am in desperate need of something, he will go out of his way to do whatever he can to help me…if I ask. I have to come to him, just as we have to come to God. He will not intrude or interfere in my life, if I do not ask for his help (patience).

God reveals Himself to us in AA meetings. Attending an AA meeting is an act of humility and vulnerability. Merely by walking through the door, a person is admitting that they have a problem with alcohol to the others present. AA is the only place on earth an alcoholic can go where they are completely destroying their entire lives and everyone else's around them; and they are welcomed with open arms, hugs, and love. It is the only place where the more a person screws up, the happier people are to see them coming back because we know they could be dead if they did not.

The rules of engagement at an AA meeting are that we are only to share our own personal experience, strength, and hope and not comment on what anyone else has said. If someone is going through an issue, we do not give advice. For if advice worked, none of us would be there. We share what we may have learned from our experience if we have gone through a similar situation. In this manner, there is no judgment. We are not telling a person what he/she should or should not do. Attending AA meetings and hearing others share their story reveals to us that we are not alone. In fact, we are eerily similar. I can find similarities in myself to almost everyone I have ever heard at a meeting, although by outward appearance, I would never guess that.

No person has ever had their first drink thinking that he/she would become an alcoholic. No one ever. My drinking started as something I wanted to do. Then it became a habit. Then it became something I had to do, although for me, it was not a daily endeavor.

In order to relieve my alcoholism, that pattern had to be worked in reverse. The suggestion of starting with ninety meetings in ninety days is intentional and purposeful. I was required to do this by the TMF. Over this period, it then became a habit. After a while, and still today, it is something I want to do. I enjoy going to AA meetings. Every time I leave an AA meeting, I feel better than when I entered. The rooms of AA are filled with my friends who know me intimately, yet I may not have intermingled with them in any other setting than an AA meeting. I have the privilege and opportunity of being vulnerable without judgment and commiserating with people who have had the same or similar experiences and who think like me. We have camaraderie. We have fellowship. We have understanding. We have love for each other. I do not like everyone in the rooms of AA, but I love them all. No matter my personal opinion of any of them, I would never want to hear of one of them going back out and drinking again. I am interested and integral to their success, as they are to mine.

This feeling I now have about AA meetings is not the feeling I had when I first started going to them. The action had to be forced at times. It had to be required of me by an outside authority. Thankfully, I had enough willingness and surrender that I complied with the suggestion. Over time, that mandated action became habit and finally joy. That is how I was able to act my way into right thinking.

In the rooms of AA, we learn, over time, that what we have is not a drinking problem; we have a thinking problem. Alcoholism is a spiritual sickness that manifests itself in the inability to control one's consumption of alcohol. That overindulgence is a coping mechanism to deal with life on life's terms to dull the negative emotions that life brings. We alcoholics/addicts all share the same coping mechanism for life, and that is where the feeling of fellowship and togetherness arises.

The thinking problem that we discover is that we are all selfish, self-centered, controlling human beings who run our lives on self-will to get what we want, when we want. When that does not happen, we drink to excess, and the consequences mount. The program of AA leads us through steps and processes that enable us to undergo spiritual awakenings that transform us and our way of thinking. It changes our desires. I no longer have the desire to pick up a drink. Not in the slightest. But the program also teaches us that all we have is a daily reprieve from this desire. The suggestions of AA must continually be followed daily or that desire to drink will return, and the results are always more disastrous than they were the previous time. The disease of alcoholism/addiction progresses like any chronic disease despite being treated appropriately. Continued action is necessary for victory of alcohol.

The biblical principle that the AA program demonstrates is stated in Romans 12:2 (ESV):

> Do not be conformed to the pattern of this world, but be transformed by the renewal of your mind, that by testing you may discern what is the will of God, what is good and acceptable and perfect.

Although I had come to faith in Jesus Christ years earlier, I did not know how this process would occur. I did not have any idea of how to go about causing this to happen. The program of AA and the twelve steps gave me the necessary and efficient blueprint as to HOW this was to happen. Merely praying, meditating, thinking about God, and reading my Bible did not get me to the vital spiritual experiences that I had once I started and continued the program of AA. From my observation, I see many Christians going through this process of meandering their way in search of God, without clear direction or instruction, which ultimately delays their ultimate satisfaction in Christ and abundant life that Jesus has promised. It is my prayer that this book reveals to those with and without addiction or substance abuse disorders to see the value that the twelve steps and program of AA may play a role in their life to be happy, joyous, and free in Christ.

22

SPIRITUAL FITNESS

We human beings can readily understand phenomena that are in the physical realm. I enjoy working out. I started lifting weights at age fifteen, have competed in bodybuilding competitions, continue to exercise regularly, and eat a healthy diet. Except after the times I had back surgeries, I have worked out at least once a week for thirty years. God has gifted me with tenacious perseverance, a trait that I received from my earthly father. This regimen has visible effects on my physical body.

Spiritual fitness in seeking God is no different. However, the outward physical appearance of a person does not change as higher levels of spirituality are reached. Spiritual growth is unseen.

> As we look not to the things that are seen
> but to the things that are unseen. For the things
> that are seen are transient, but the things that are
> unseen are eternal. (2 Corinthians 4:18 ESV)

My physical body deteriorates rapidly if I am not perseverant in my dedication to my routine. Similarly, my spirituality declines just as quickly if I do not adhere to my spiritual program of action. The parallels between physical and spiritual fitness are apparent. **Better than yesterday. Worse than tomorrow.**

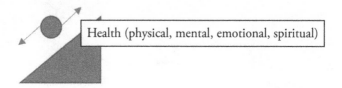

Health (physical, mental, emotional, spiritual)

All health (physical, mental, emotional, spiritual) is on an incline. We are either getting better or getting worse in this life. To stand still is to go backward. This is readily demonstrated physically. Each day, my body ages. There is no amount of wishful thinking that reverses this process. To believe that my body is not deteriorating is a delusion. Therefore, I must do something every day to improve my physical health. This is also true of mental, emotional, and spiritual health. If I am not actively doing something to strengthen those areas, I am going backward.

We are either working on recovery or we are working on relapse.

When a person begins a physical fitness regimen, it is usually not enjoyable at first. The person does not know how to begin. Muscles become very sore and painful and need to recover. That person may feel judged or intimidated by others at the gym, leading them to not want to come back. Without proper instruction and guidance, progress is slow and can actually be dangerous and cause harm to that person. Even with daily diligence in a workout routine, the body does not change rapidly, which can lead to frustration and disappointment. Without faith that the regimen is working, people are prone to quit and go back to their natural physical state, which is not vibrant, healthy, or desirable.

If a person stays consistent with their physical fitness routine, positive changes occur slowly over time. The person must be dedicated and unwavering in mindset to achieve the ultimate objective of peak physicality. Muscle soreness is not painful and is, in fact, a welcome feeling. As the changes occur slowly through daily action, faith grows. As they reach their goals, the process becomes more pleasant and worthwhile. Excitement and joy build as the end is approached and their adherence to their routine is no longer burdensome, but systematic. It is no longer a forced action. It is a new way of living. As peak physical condition is attained, the work required to maintain that physique is less than when the program was started. Usually, the person becomes so enthused about their progress that they feel the need to share their program and its benefits with others.

The path of spiritual fitness is the same. When commencing, the person does not know exactly how to seek God. Without proper guidance and instruction, the process is frustrating and can be exceedingly damaging if not guided in truth. The actions must be forced at first as they are unusual and uncomfortable, sometimes outright painful. The growth is slow. The changes in emotions and feelings leading to joy and happiness are hard to detect. The daily repetitive actions are cumbersome, and if no progress is appreciated, the person will likely abandon their program and God altogether and find alternative methods to feel better emotionally and spiritually.

However, if the person is diligent and dedicated in their spiritual program of action, results come slowly over extended periods. The amount of progress is not directly proportional to the degree of effort, but there is a correlation there. There are peaks of spiritual awakenings that enliven the soul and spurn the individual to continued daily action. Once routine, the work required to maintain their heightened spiritual condition and connection to God is reduced, but never eliminated. Peace, freedom, and joy start to become realized; and the person's desire to continue becomes greater. It is no longer a routine that is onerous, but one that is eagerly anticipated. It becomes enticing. It becomes a new way of life. The happiness, joy, and freedom experienced lead that person to want to share those with others. It becomes a driving force in that person's life to enrich the lives of others.

Don't quit before the miracle happens.

This corollary between physical and spiritual fitness helps me to understand my journey and continued path to God. After accepting Jesus as savior and the existence of God, I had no direction or path. Guidance was available, but there was no clear program to seek God to achieve abundant, eternal life. I followed a few suggestions, going to church, joining a small group, and volunteering in the preschool ministry; but my effort was forced and nominal at best. My spiritual fitness was so poor after five years of doing this that I ended up spiritually dead and in rehab for alcoholism.

One can imagine that if a person goes to the gym once per week, little to no gains will be achieved. If that person's effort is suboptimal at the gym, the results will be even worse. If diet is not monitored, then all effort will be for naught. All components are necessary to achieve optimal physical health.

And yet that is exactly how I approached my journey with Jesus to God after accepting him as my savior. I went through the motions, not completely giving myself to him. I surrendered what was convenient and comfortable for me. I did not realize that following Jesus is a program of action, not merely learning and memorizing.

The Bible does state very clearly that Jesus came not to be part of my life, but to be my abundant life (John 10:10). However, I never had "ears to hear" that until I entered rehab and read this sentence in the Big Book of AA.

Half measures availed us nothing. (*Alcoholics Anonymous*, 4th ed., 59)

Achieving sobriety for an alcoholic/addict and obtaining abundant life with Jesus require full surrender and commitment to a program of action. Half measures are even worse than not trying at all because one has some knowledge of the benefits of what one is supposed to be doing yet is continually frustrated that there is no progress because of lack of full adherence.

The long hours of continuous work I did when exiting rehab have laid the foundation for my spiritual fitness level today. It is akin to a rigorous boot camp for physical fitness with every facet of physical health addressed and adjusted appropriately. My spiritual program of action is now attractive to me, and something I enjoy. And obviously, with the writing of this book, I want to share this path with others to be happy, joyous, and free. I have been on both sides of the coin—atheist and Christian. Therefore, I have firsthand knowledge of the emptiness of life without relationship with God through

Jesus. It is my heart's desire that others commence their own road to happy destiny as a result of this work.

Because I am prone to return to my previous selfish nature of performance, appearance, and control, I must be careful that physical fitness does not become an idol in my life. When I competed in bodybuilding and when modeling in Miami, my image was one of my gods. My workout routine and diet were rigid and obsessive. It was consuming to me to the exclusion of others in my life.

In order to balance my physical and spiritual fitness today, I ensure that my time spent seeking God each week is at least as much as my time spent in the gym. I work out six hours or less per week. That is enough at this point in my life to maintain my health and physique. No longer do I have aspirations of being on the cover of *Men's Health* or winning a bodybuilding show because for me, those pursuits ended up being meaningless. I just want to maintain the way I look and feel for personal enjoyment, not the praise or adoration of anyone else.

In my spiritual program of action, I ensure that I meet or exceed six hours per week. Jesus said, "Where your treasure is, there your heart will be also" (Matthew 6:21 NIV). My most precious commodity today is time. Therefore, by ensuring my time (treasure) is spent seeking God, I demonstrate, at least to myself, that my heart is aligned under God.

I spend one hour a week at church, one hour leading a men's discipleship group, three hours in AA meetings, and at least one hour reading or listening to the Bible, Christian literature, or spiritual material. Those represent the designated times that I am seeking God; but with prayer and various discussions about God and Jesus in many places, I pursue God with all my heart, strength, mind, and spirit as continuously as I can throughout the week. This is not a burden to me. This is where abundant life, happiness, joy, and freedom are found.

Stillness benefits the mind. Movement benefits the body.

Do not be discouraged if your spiritual program of action does not look like mine. Everyone has a different journey. The important fact to remember is that it is all about progress, not perfection. I am not perfect each week in these endeavors, and there is no shame in falling short. God's love is infinite and unconditional. All he asks is that we seek Him, and He will change the desires of our hearts and cause us to want to know Him more.

I want to encourage my reader to continue seeking God in truth. Whatever you are doing, keep doing it. Be steadfast and unwavering in your commitment. Find people who have the peace, joy, and serenity you want and then be willing to go to any lengths to get it also. Follow their suggestions and ask them questions. If they are truly seeking God themselves, they will be happy to help you. The truth of God will be revealed to you, and you will not be disappointed.

> For the training of the body has a limited
> benefit, but godliness is beneficial in every way,
> since it holds promise for the present life and also
> for the life to come. (1 Timothy 4:8 CSB)

Training to improve my physique and to get a 500 lbs. bench press was of limited benefit; but seeking God with all my heart, soul, strength, and mind benefits me in how many ways? EVERY way, as stated above. That is the truth. Praise the Lord.

23

THE RESURRECTION
OF JESUS CHRIST

The resurrection of Jesus Christ is the most powerful demonstration of God's infinite power in history. Either it is the biggest, most elaborate hoax that carries on for two thousand years or it is the absolute truth. After investigating the evidence for this event and analyzing and entertaining all other alternative theories and explanations, the evidence is overwhelmingly in favor of the bodily resurrection of Jesus as the only plausible, reasonable theory that rationally explains what happened and the subsequent explosion of the church thereafter. It reveals how nothing, absolutely nothing, is impossible with God (Luke 1:37). The power by which Jesus as a human being was able to be bodily raised from the dead by God was because He lived a life of perfect submission to God. The way Jesus in human form was able to access His own infinite power as God was in His complete and total surrender to God in every single, solitary moment throughout His earthly life.

God, by His very nature, is not dependent on anything. God was never created. God has always existed. By its very nature, any created being or entity must be, by definition, dependent on whatever created it. Jesus is coequal to God and has always existed as God has. Jesus was God in the flesh. Jesus is one with God and, at the same time, taking human form, separate from God. Our feeble human minds cannot fully understand this concept.

We know that Jesus was fully God because of Colossians 2:9 (ESV):

> For in him the whole fullness of deity dwells bodily, and you have been filled in him, who is the head of all rule and authority.

Also in John:

> In the beginning was the Word, and the Word was with God, and the Word was God. (John 1:1 ESV)

> And the Word became flesh and dwelt among us, and we have seen his glory, glory as of the only Son from the Father, full of grace and truth. (John 1:14 ESV)

> I and the Father are one. (John 10:30 ESV)

Therefore, there is no question that Jesus was God. It is hard for me to understand how these verses, particularly the last one, can be interpreted in any other way.

However, Jesus as a human being lived in a physical body. He was dependent on Mary for His birth. He was dependent on His parents for raising Him. He was dependent on food and water for His earthly life. He was dependent on His disciples for companionship and fellowship. Jesus, the man, knew these things; but He also knew that the only thing He was completely and totally dependent on was His father, God. God provided for Jesus the man everything He would need on this earth, just as God does for us. But Jesus, also being a human being, had needs and desires just like all human beings do. He suffered life on this earth willingly. Jesus felt every emotion, temptation, and pain, physical and emotional, as we do. As a man, He surrendered His desires perfectly in order to fulfill God's plan of salvation for mankind.

When we casually say that Jesus was God, I think we miss some important points that can help us in our earthly life. Jesus had feelings and emotions. When He got cut, He would bleed. When He got hungry, He wanted to eat. When He was falsely accused, He wanted to defend Himself. When He was beaten, He wanted to fight back. All these feelings are natural human emotions that Jesus experienced.

We forget that Jesus had choices when we dismissively say that Jesus was God. Twice He said that He did not come on His own accord, but it was God who sent Him (John 7:28, 8:42). When Jesus fasted for forty days and forty nights, He had the choice to eat at any time, yet He did not. When Jesus was falsely accused, He had the choice to defend Himself, yet He said nothing. When He was beaten and spit on, Jesus had the choice to fight back yet did not. When Jesus was nailed to the cross and died, He had the choice to send angels to rescue Him and let Him live, yet He willingly let Himself die on the cross.

Jesus suffered. A lot. In every way. He can relate to our suffering like no one who ever lived can. He experienced it. He felt it.

Jesus, the man, died to His desires and needs to perfectly submit to God's plan for His life. If we are to "live like Jesus," I can see how the Christian life does not seem very appealing to us. When we are hungry, we want to eat. When we are falsely accused, we want to defend ourselves. When we are beaten, we want to fight back. When we are about to physically die, we want to physically live.

Jesus CHOSE to suppress all His human desires, feelings, and emotions in order to fulfill God's plan to rescue everyone in the world. I think we miss the feelings Jesus had after He said, "It is finished!" on the cross. The feelings He must have had of joy, satisfaction, contentment, and happiness that He had just saved everyone who ever lived are impossible to comprehend. His feelings of worthiness, achievement, and importance that He had just completely pleased God, the Father, must have been astronomical. He had ultimate peace at that point. He would suffer no more. Physical death, now that He had fulfilled God's will for His life being obedient to death, even death on a cross, was desirable.

These are the same feelings that we as Christians can have toward physical death. We are not seeking physical death; but when death comes, provided that we have sought God and executed His will, we can have peace knowing that we will also no longer suffer. Death is no longer something to be feared, but to be embraced. In this manner, we can live without fear of death. It has no sting. It is not the end.

The action we need to take to attain these feelings is we surrender our lives, EVERYTHING about our lives, to God. This surrender often does not feel good or comfortable in the moment. We get hungry, we get tired, we get offended, we get hurt. Love, service to another person not expecting anything in return, is often inconvenient and uncomfortable. Yet we must die to these feelings to surrender to God's plan for us and for His ultimate plan of salvation for mankind.

When we say that Jesus lived a perfect life, we most often think about how Jesus had perfect behavior. That misses the point. What Jesus did perfectly was that **He was completely and totally surrendered to God.** Perfect surrender leads to perfect obedience and perfect behavior, not the other way around. When we are told to "live like Jesus," our limited human minds lead us to think we need to aim for a life of perfect behavior. Our futile efforts to try to live this way end up with frustration and despair because as children of wrath, we do not have the power to do this on our own. We need to strive for a life of perfect surrender, not perfect behavior. Our behavior will follow this surrender as we realize and come to understand God and His love for us. In *The Sermon on the Mount* by Emmet Fox, he states, "Spiritual attainment and the highest standards of moral conduct must go hand in hand. Unless both are there, neither is there."

To endeavor to "live like Jesus," we must strive to live a life of perfect surrender to God. We often think of "good" or "mature" Christians as those who follow the rules well. That is not the only mark of spiritual maturity and deep relationship with God and Jesus. The criminal on the cross lived a life of little good behavior, but at the end of his life, just before he died, he had complete surrender to Jesus. Jesus assured him that he would be in paradise that day. Our ultimate goal needs to be total surrender, not perfect behavior. Our behaviors improve as we follow Jesus and seek God, but behavior does not fully indicate the condition of a person's heart. The Pharisees exemplified good behavior, and Jesus called them a "brood of vipers."

In Matthew 7:21–23 (ESV), Jesus says,

> Not everyone who says to me, "Lord, Lord" will enter the kingdom of heaven, but the one who does the will of my Father who is in heaven. On that day many will say to me, "Lord, Lord, did we not prophesy in your name, and cast out demons in your name and do many mighty works in your name?" And then I will declare to them, "I never knew you; depart from me, you workers of lawlessness."

The important phrase here is "the one who does the will of my Father." Jesus emphatically states that entrance to the kingdom of heaven is dependent on action. The action of doing the will of God, His father. Not thinking about it. Not learning about it. Not talking about it. Doing it.

In order to do God's will, we must seek Him. We must love Him above all created things. We must know His word because if we do not know God's Word, we cannot do God's will. The rewards that God grants when we surrender to His will allow us to have abundant life and find heaven on earth and for eternity.

In examining the suffering that Jesus experienced on the cross, we tend to think of the physical pain. However, the greatest suffering, the most agony, the utmost excruciating pain that Jesus felt was emotional pain.

When He was falsely accused, whipped and flogged, nailed to the cross, and a crown of thorns was pressed into His head, He never said a word. He was able to endure that physical pain that He most definitely felt being fully God in human flesh. When Jesus cried out, "My God, My God, why have you forsaken me?" that was the moment at which the pain was so great that He almost could not bear it. Another word for forsake is "abandon." When Jesus made that statement, all the sin of mankind was laid on Jesus. Sin separates us from God. Therefore, it was in that moment that Jesus, the Son, was separated from God, the Father. The mere thought of that pain was so intense that it caused Him to sweat drops of blood in the garden of Gethsemane. The pain and suffering of that separation and loss of that relationship was so excruciating that Jesus could not help but cry out, "Father, why have you abandoned me?"

It was not Jesus Himself that God was abandoning for God cannot abandon Himself. It was the incarnation of all the sin of humanity in the human being of Jesus that God forsook.

That pain was emotional. Relational. It was the pain felt in the separation of the Father and the Son. The severity of pain in breaking a relationship is directly proportional to the intimacy of that relationship. Jesus valued His relationship with God, the Father, more than anyone or anything on the earth; and that is why the loss of that relationship was the most painful reality that Jesus, the human being, could experience on earth. He willingly bore that pain for us so that we can also have what He cherished so greatly, a relationship with God, the Father, through Jesus Christ, His son.

When Jesus wept right before He resurrected Lazarus, He was not weeping because He was sad about Lazarus. Why would He weep when He knew He was going to see Lazarus alive in just a few minutes? Jesus was weeping for every lost soul of mankind who chooses with their own free will to be separated from God. He was weeping for all the Pharisees and other people in attendance who were about to watch Him raise Lazarus from the dead, after being dead four days, and still not believe that Jesus was God. And the many after that who, using the free will that God had given them, continue to deny this fact in the face of overwhelming evidence.

We must feel like Jesus in order to act like Him. While we are called to act like Jesus, our hearts must be transformed to feel like Jesus having compassion for those blinded to the truth. It is only in this manner that our actions will reflect our hearts. Feeling like Jesus means losing focus on ourselves and gaining interest in others as Jesus never sought to fulfill one of His earthly desires and only sought to serve others and be obedient to God, the Father. We must strive to do as He did, doing the work of emptying ourselves and our selfishness and filling our hearts and minds with God. Then our compassion will lead to action, which is service, loving our neighbors.

This teaches me that the greatest pain in life is not physical, but emotional. It is separation from God, the Father. Relating this to the human experience, it also demonstrates to me that the greatest pain a human being can experience is abandonment by their earthly father. We see this playing out in the world today. Society is becoming more and more chaotic. Love and tolerance are decreasing, not increasing, as mankind continues to sell our brand of it, and not God's. Violence, hatred, oppression, sex trafficking, addiction, and suicide continue to grow. Education, legislation, science, and medicine have little effect on these problems. We need an entity or being bigger and more powerful than the US government to solve these problems.

If you do not have peace on the inside, you will not have peace on the outside. (Joel Osteen)

Are we as a society really better off today with less and less people believing in the one true God? As long as we continue to value our intellect, image, material possessions, wealth, earthly relationships, status, power, hobbies, sports, substances, food, or any created thing above our relationship with God, we will continue to live in conflict. We cannot live in right relationship with each other without proper relationship with God.

Since prayer was removed from schools in 1962, how are we doing? When the shooting at Columbine happened in 1999, people kept asking, "Where is God in all this?" The answer is simple. We asked Him to leave schools. God forces Himself on no one, and if we ask Him to go, He will leave along with His care and protection. If we do not learn from history, we are doomed to repeat it. How many times did Israel turn its back on God, and God allowed them to continue to suffer? Then how many times did God redeem Israel when they turned their hearts back toward Him? God will allow us to suffer as long as we wish while turned away from Him, and He will always be there for us to redeem and restore us when we are willing to return to Him.

The strength of a nation lies in the homes of its people. (Abraham Lincoln)

Although tolerance is a virtuous target to aim for, it is better to strive for understanding. Jesus did not merely tolerate us human beings; He understood our human experience. That allowed Him to have empathy for our situation and compel Him to action in saving it. If we only pursue tolerance for others and we miss, we will end up with hate. If we seek understanding and fall short, we will still be able to land on tolerance. If we reach understanding, then we can truly experience empathy and compassion, which will lead us to the action of love, serving others with no expectation.

The greatest pain and suffering on this earth comes from broken relationships, with each other and with God. Jesus came to reconcile all things back to God and all of us to each other. The only hope we have for peace today is God through Jesus. We cannot reconcile this on human power. Human power is what got us here in the first place.

24

WHAT THE CHURCH CAN LEARN FROM ALCOHOLICS ANONYMOUS (AA)

Most people do not know that Alcoholics Anonymous was originally founded by Bill Wilson through his experience with the Oxford Group, a mostly nonalcoholic Christian fellowship that emphasized universal spiritual values in daily living. The group was founded by Dr. Franklin Nathaniel Daniel Buchman who was an American Christian missionary from England. The group's philosophy was stated in six sentences.

1. "All people are sinners."
2. "All sinners can be changed."
3. "Confession is a prerequisite to change."
4. "The change can access God directly."
5. "Miracles are again possible."
6. "The change must change others."

The standard of morality of the Oxford Group was the Four Absolutes, which is a summary of the teachings of the Sermon on the Mount.

1. Absolute honesty
2. Absolute purity

3. Absolute unselfishness
4. Absolute love

Oxford Group meetings were similar to the AA meetings of today. Their focus was not just on the disease and sin of alcoholism, but any sin. Sin was considered as a disease, a spiritual sickness that every human is born into. In order to relieve the disease of sin and alcoholism, the focus of these meetings followed the principles set above. In 1955, Bill Wilson wrote, "The early AA got its ideas of self-examination, acknowledgment of character defects, restitution for harm done, and working with others straight from the Oxford Group and directly from Sam Shoemaker, their former leader in America, and from nowhere else."

Bill Wilson formulated AA from the foundation of the Oxford Group, which was rooted in Christianity. He broke off from the Oxford Group and founded AA because he believed that the bondage of an addictive disease cannot be ever completely cured, while the Oxford Group emphasized the possibility of complete victory over sin. Bill Wilson continued to make God (as we understood Him) to be the focus of AA but removed any mention of Jesus. I believe he did this because his life became a mission to save alcoholics, and many people have preconceived notions about Jesus that may have repelled them from the program of AA. I know I did when I was atheist. Alcoholics particularly are destitute, full of shame and guilt, and oftentimes, their experience with the church is that of judgment. Bill Wilson did not want that to color a person's perception of AA and wanted any alcoholic to feel comfortable coming into the AA fellowship. Starting with a belief in a "higher power" is a nonjudgmental way of starting an individual's process to constructing a proper concept of God.

Since the program was founded in Christian principles, it stands to reason that the program would be an effective way to follow Christ. I believe that the Big Book was divinely inspired. I regard the truths in that book in the same manner that I revere the truths of the Bible. For me, the book *Alcoholics Anonymous* (a.k.a. the Big Book) is a practical, effective, efficient way for me to grow my faith.

It is written in a language that is easier for me to understand than that of the Bible. The truths and promises I find in the Big Book can all be traced back to specific scriptures in the Bible that validate them as truth.

There are specific suggestions for the newcomer to ensure success in the program. If applied to the Christian newcomer, I believe these things could be transformational and lead many more people to their destiny in an efficient way, which will further the kingdom of God.

One suggestion is to get a sponsor. The sponsor-sponsee relationship has been previously discussed. The way the steps are worked is variable between sponsors, usually passed down from generation to generation. That is how God exerts His will in the steps. Every person is different and has variable needs. God knows what that person needs, and that is why there is no specific workbook for this process. The general principles for working the steps, however, are delineated in the Big Book of AA.

Rigorous honesty is a cornerstone of the program of AA. This honesty is with others, but most importantly, with oneself. It is difficult for me to identify my selfishness or character defects at times. Who wants to admit to themselves that they are inherently flawed? However, this honest self-appraisal is necessary for spiritual growth. Honest self-examination is impossible for a human being in isolation. As my sponsor has the most intimate knowledge of my life and my thinking, truth about myself is revealed to me that I may not have otherwise identified.

The unexamined life is not worth living.
(Socrates)

How different would the Christian church be if when a person puts their faith in Jesus Christ, they would find a more mature Christian of the same sex who has read the Bible and has studied the Bible with a spiritual mentor themselves and continues to do so then calls that person every single day? There were times when I would be calling my sponsor and would think I had nothing to talk about or nothing specific bothering me or going on. I would call my sponsor anyways. This is important because that is how relationships are built. I do not need a specific reason to call my sponsor. It is about the relationship. If I am only calling my sponsor when I need something, then I am using that person and not developing a real human relationship with him. I am just looking for what I need out of that person. If a Christian called another more mature Christian every day, not needing anything but just to talk, then a Christ-based relationship forms and becomes stronger. Then when life happens and things get hard, it is not as hard to pick up the phone and ask for some godly advice.

In the Christian church, we call this discipleship. It is the Great Command from Jesus Himself. Jesus did not say, "Go and make confessing Christians." He did not say, "Go to church." He did not say, "Read your Bible." All of those things are necessary and important, but THE most important instruction that Jesus gave was "Go and make disciples." It is critical in order to access and experience abundant life.

I believe this single action would strengthen the Christian church immeasurably. This was never suggested to me. The reason why the sponsor-sponsee relationship is so important is overcoming alcoholism can be a matter of physical life and death. But how much more important is it for spiritual life and death? For the two are deeply interconnected. Alcoholism is a medical disease with a spiritual solution. Human life is the spiritual disease of sin with the spiritual solution of faith in Jesus Christ. Telling me to just have faith and follow Jesus was about as useful as dunking me in water and rubbing a Bible on my head. I needed more specific instructions, and that is what I found when I started working the program of AA.

Later in my journey, I did have the privilege of being discipled by the senior pastor in our church, Brady Cooper. God revealed to me that I needed a Christian mentor, and I texted him asking if he knew of anyone who would be willing to disciple me. As God always does, He came through for me beyond what I asked or expected. The senior pastor of our church of six thousand-plus members came back and said that he would do it. He was the one who first got my attention and the first person that I heard from who told me that Jesus was an actual person. This was something my wife had been praying for fervently. She also was blown away that I had been given this incredible gift, beyond what she expected as well.

We agreed to meet once a week, and he led me through several studies and a twenty-five-week curriculum on the teachings of Jesus. I am an orthopedic spine surgeon with four children, and life is busy. However, I set my full intention on meeting each and every week, and so did he. That kind of commitment is necessary to obtain the maximum spiritual progress in seeking God. It is so easy to make excuses today in our culture. I could have easily said many times that I had something else I needed to do, like take care of a patient or our children. But I did not.

I have learned when I say that "I don't have time" for something, I must substitute the words, "It's not important." We make time for what is important. When I say, "I do not have time," that is not being rigorously honest with myself. By saying "It's not important," I can check my motive; and if it is truly something that is important, then it uncovers my selfishness and self-centeredness in seeking my will and not God's. The only way I can truly know what God's will is and not mine is by maintaining conscious contact with God.

I preserved that time because it was more precious than gold. Because of this dedication, my Christian walk was rocketed into the fourth dimension. I am eternally grateful for his sacrifice as he was as intentional as I was in discipling me. He has at least as many commitments and obligations as I do. What he found, and what I find, however, is that being the person who is teaching and leading the discipling is as impactful and effective in furthering our faith, if not more so, than the one receiving it.

> **If you want happiness for an hour, take a nap. If you want happiness for a day, go fishing. If you want happiness for year, inherit a fortune.**
>
> **If you want happiness for a lifetime, help someone else. (Chinese proverb)**

We have an abundance of retired people who have a tremendous amount of experience, strength, and hope who could mentor the youth who are in desperate need of wisdom. Unfortunately, many retired people live in the delusion that they have really "made it" and can now enjoy their lives by pursuing their hobbies with unlimited time. The sad truth about this is that fullness of life and abundant joy would actually come from serving and mentoring others. Many retired people, especially men, become despondent and dissatisfied quickly because the career that gave them fulfillment and satisfaction in helping others has now been left behind. I pray that the retired people who receive this message are encouraged and empowered by this awakening. I pray they realize what a gift they are to the next generation and can use their gifts and abilities to help save others. The paradoxical truth that they will find is they find abundant joy in living their purpose of being of maximum service to God and the people about them. We all will be better off because of it.

The spiritual life is not a theory. WE HAVE
TO LIVE IT. (*Alcoholics Anonymous*, 4th ed., 83)

In AA, it is stressed to the newcomer that it is a program of ACTION. One of the chapters in the Big Book is called "Into Action." Not "Into Thinking." Not "Into Reading." Not "Into Pontificating and Discussing the Program." ACTION. The program of AA does not work without action. The actions are getting, working with and calling a sponsor, going to meetings, and helping other alcoholics. It is just that simple. It is not easy, but it is simple.

The Christian life, similarly, takes ACTION. It is not enough to be Christian. We must LIVE Christian. Stepping into one's destiny and leading the abundant life Jesus promised necessitates action. Merely going to church once a week or less alone, although important, does little to renew a person's mind and effect transformation to one's heart. The old adage of going to church does not make one a Christian any more than sitting in a garage makes one a car rings true. The actions that I learned following the AA program profoundly deepened my faith in Christ and led me to the rich, true life that God has ordained for me.

At the end of our AA meetings, after we say the Lord's Prayer for all who care to participate, we say, "Keep coming back. It works if you work it." "Keep coming back" is a phrase that we say over and over again to the newcomer and to anyone who may have left the rooms. To everyone really. It is vitally important to attend meetings on a regular basis. "It works if you work it" is self-evident. Some will add, "You die if you don't." Macabre, but true.

The AA responsibility pledge states, "I am responsible. When anyone, anywhere, reaches out for help, I want the hand of AA always to be there. And for that: I am responsible." How different would the Christian church be if each believer stated that daily after one claims Jesus as savior? To be responsible to help someone in need who reaches out. Jesus instructed us to love our neighbor at all times, but this statement is much more clear and direct to me.

When my phone rings today, I almost always answer it. Because of my experience as an alcoholic, I know it could be another alcoholic who may be on the brink of a horrendous disaster. It is my responsibility to take action and be available. This concept has bled into my journey as a Christian as I must be available to anyone who has a situation in which I may be able to help.

Buddhism has a concept called "noble friends, noble conversation." Noble friends do not imply that the Buddhists who are together for this purpose are being prideful, nor do it state that they have some kind of royalty or moral superiority to another person. Noble friends mean people who are congregating who have their minds fixed on noble thoughts rather than normal mundane day-to-day musings. Their thoughts are fixed on a higher plane and purpose of life for this time of gathering. Noble conversation entails discussion of these thoughts by the people present. The repetitive action of people gathering in smaller groups to discuss noble ideas and thoughts transforms a person's mind in a positive way.

This concept is exhibited in twelve-step meetings. Most alcoholics who attend twelve-step meetings would not consider themselves "noble." However, by attending meetings, that alcoholic has his/her mind fixed on the higher purpose of achieving sobriety. Those new to the program do not know that this will entail many spiritual awakenings that will improve their life in a myriad of ways, but that is eventually what happens through this process. In meetings, we then have "noble conversation" because our discussion is about the solution to alcoholism—the program of AA. Everyone shares their experience, strength, and hope, of their own situation, to instill faith and hope into someone else. You never know when you might hear something that can have a profound impact on your life, which is why it is so important to keep coming back on a consistent basis. God will provide the exact information at the exact time that could change the trajectory of an alcoholic's life forever, for the better.

Every meeting is composed of different people at different points in their journey. The people are never exactly the same as any other meeting that has ever happened or will happen. This variety demonstrates God's will. Rather than we alcoholics choosing what people we are going to congregate with, by not choosing a specific group of alcoholics for a meeting, we are allowing God's will to be done and allowing Him to provide the people and information that are necessary for our recoveries.

AA emphasizes the critical importance that the members attending each meeting are to remain anonymous. This means that whoever is seen and whatever is said is not discussed with anyone once leaving the meeting. This provides a safe environment for all in attendance. We can be completely vulnerable, discuss our worst actions and feelings of guilt and shame about those, and not feel any judgment, nor fear that this information will be shared outside the meeting. This level of vulnerability to other human beings is essential to bring about healing. It is how God's attributes of love, nonjudgment, and noncondemnation are revealed to us. When I talk about a problem or issue that is particularly troubling or shameful to me, it takes the power out of that situation because God is there to heal it. I can do so without fear because I know that it will not leave that room. Almost always, there is another alcoholic who has gone through a similar situation as I have, and I do not feel alone. That person may share their own experience, strength, and hope about that situation, which helps me navigate life when I leave. **Two of the most powerful, healing words in the English language are, "Me, too."**

In the Christian church, this same concept is attempted in small groups. I was encouraged to join a small group, of my choice, to discuss and study the Bible. The problems I encountered were many. The first of which is that my small group would meet only once per week. That is four times a month, and if a situation arose where the meeting was cancelled, or I could not attend, the frequency was even less. Sin is a daily spiritual disease. It needs daily spiritual treatment, not just with prayer and reading the Bible. Having a mature Christian mentor to call every day helps with this daily walk, but having groups of Christians meeting discussing the truths of the Bible would help even more.

Gossip is rampant in the Christian church and drives hordes of people away. In my small group, I never felt safe sharing my most vulnerable feelings and issues for fear that they would be discussed outside of that group. I know many people feel the same way. The Christian church can learn the concept of being anonymous. Whatever is discussed in a Christian small group needs to be kept in that group. As I have matured in my faith, I do not have fear anymore about discussing my deepest, most vulnerable issues, hence the reason I am able to write this book. However, in the beginning, I needed comfort and safety knowing I could discuss my issues and feelings while having the security that whatever I said would not be repeated. This is what I found in the rooms. At the end of every AA meeting, we state, "Whoever you see here, whatever you hear here, let it stay here. Here, here!"

It would help the Christian church immeasurably if the church leaders and members humbled themselves and attended some open AA meetings. The level of humility and honesty in these meetings is unparalleled. It is at this intersection of humility, honesty, and truth where God provides healing, in a safe environment devoid of judgment with others who truly love one another and desire success for all.

"Noble friends, noble conversation" does not have to only happen at an AA meeting or a church small group. This activity is not limited by space and time because God is not limited by those things. For me today, it happens anytime, anywhere I go.

The church is not a building where people go to worship. The church is the bride of Christ. In contemplating the concept of this, a bride is beautiful, radiant, ravishing, irresistible, and overwhelmingly desirable. Church has become a repulsive word in our culture because of people lukewarm to the gospel. We must rid ourselves of this concept as Jesus stated, "So, because you are lukewarm, and neither hot nor cold, I will spit you out of my mouth" (Revelation 3:17 ESV). For me as a follower of Christ, the last thing on earth I want is to be spit out of Jesus's mouth.

Years after I accepted Jesus as my savior, after finally receiving the gift of the gospel with a transformed heart through the twelve steps of AA, God revealed to me that I was now in full-time ministry. I carry church with me wherever I go. Church is when I am enjoying a meal with other people talking about God and Jesus. Church is when we listen to and discuss a book of the Bible in my operating room each week. Church is every night at Bible story with my family and children. Church is a conversation with my wife about God and Jesus. Church is when I am at an AA meeting, and we are discussing the spiritual solution to alcoholism and seeking God. The word "Jesus" does not have to be stated for it to be church. It is about the spirit of Jesus alive within us, spurning us to noble conversation and heart transformation.

We must have an upheaval of our mindset of the word "church." It is not a building. It is not just on Sunday. It is the Holy Spirit alive in us today through Jesus Christ connecting us to our almighty God who is omnipresent.

I have a new employer. I work for God. Every hour. Every minute. Every second. Throughout the day, I pray and try to maintain conscious contact with God. My awareness of the Holy Spirit is much better today. When I sense people are interested in seeking God, we can discuss Him and have "noble conversation." God relates to everything and anything and can be introduced into every conversation. Maintaining my conscious contact with God throughout the day and talking about Him keeps me in His presence, I know Him more, and heaven is found.

Some reading this may term me "very religious." Religion is a set of doctrines and practices related to specific beliefs about moral or spiritual matters. Religion divides. Jesus reconciles. I would not use the term "religious" to describe myself. Although I go to a Baptist church, I would not claim to be Baptist. God has protected me from knowledge of the different practices between Christian denominations. There is only one truth that must be agreed upon—that Jesus was the perfect son of God, died on the cross, and rose from the dead three days later. There is only one denomination—the denomination of Jesus Christ. Christianity is not a religion. It is a fact of human history. I live in His spirit and follow Him with my heart. It is all about God, Jesus, and the Holy Spirit. Spirituality.

Religion is for people who're afraid of going to hell.
Spirituality is for people who've already been there. (Vine Deloria Jr.)

25

LOVE

When I was in rehab, God revealed to me that although I have extensive education, I did not know the true meaning of many words I used every day. This is a humbling revelation. I could explain what a spondylolisthesis was; but simple words like "love," "humility," and "sarcasm," I could not define. In AA meetings, some members will pull out the dictionary to look up the actual definition of words in the Big Book. This technique is extraordinarily helpful for me, and I continue to do this today when I am not certain of the exact meaning of a word in the Bible or Big Book or anywhere. Instead of assuming I know what a word means, I search for truth.

Love is a word that I heard and used throughout my life. It is a word that everybody uses.

I love my wife.

I love my kids.

I love my parents.

I love my patients.

I love my dogs.

I love pizza.

I love working out.

All those statements use the word "love," yet the meaning of love in each of them is completely different. I love all those people or things, yet it is obvious I do not love each of them in the same manner. In stating that I love my dogs, pizza, and working out, this demonstrates the transactional affection that most of the world understands. I "love" each of those things because I get something in return from them. My dogs give me affection, pizza gives me a pleasurable eating experience, and working out gives me a release and helps my physical body. If they did not provide from me what I expected of them, then I would no longer say I love those things.

This is not what human relational love is. This created confusion for me on what love actually means when commanded to "love my neighbor" by Jesus. It was not until I was in rehab at age forty that I developed the correct, working definition of human relational love meant by Jesus.

Love is service to another person, expecting nothing in return.

This is unconditional love. In truth, the term "unconditional love" as applied to human relations is redundant. If love is conditional, then it is not truly love. It is transactional affection. It is defined by man and not by God. It is devoid of truth. It is how most of the world views "love." We have turned people into objects. The world's delusion of "love" that is transactional affection is serving or caring for another person with the expectation that it will be returned by that person. Not having the proper definition of human relational love in a marriage inevitably leads to dissatisfaction, destruction, and divorce.

The sad fact is without a true understanding of God and His love for us, most people are devoid of human relational love and are searching for it in another person. When in a real relationship with God through Jesus, my heart is now overflowing with love such that I can pour it out onto others with no expectation of reciprocation. I do not wake up each day looking for my wife or anyone else to love me. I wake up each day to love them as properly defined in human relations because God loved me first.

One of my partners who had a major impact on my life was the great O. Tom Johns. He grew up in Murfreesboro and was passionate about sports. He became a sports medicine physician and practiced in Murfreesboro for forty-two years and served as the team physician for Middle Tennessee State University for forty years. Every coach and most parents in town had his cell phone number, and he was willing to help anyone at any time. He lived a life of maximum service to God and those about him and absolutely loved every minute of it. It was also clear that he had been transformed and loved God and Jesus with all his heart, soul, strength, and mind.

He was the only man in my life who regularly told me, "I love you." In truth, he told everyone he knew that he loved them. And he meant it. You could palpably feel it. Being atheist at the time, and not having the proper definition of love, I thought this was quite strange; but it did not change my respect for him. When he would tell me this, I would tell him that I loved him too, but I did not know what that truthfully meant at the time.

Today, through my journey to God through Jesus and after working the twelve steps of AA, I know EXACTLY what this means. Dr. Johns was an outstanding physician, loved by everyone. The reason that everyone loved him is he loved them first. Just as God does with us. At his funeral, they asked everyone who had ever been told by Dr. Johns that he loved them. The whole room raised their hands.

I strive to do the same today. When I started telling people that I love them, it was awkward and uncomfortable. It still is today sometimes. I do not tell every single person every day that I love them, but when the situation arises and I am guided by the Holy Spirit, I do. There is never a sexual connotation involved when I say this. I am not looking for anything in return from that other person. I simply want that other person to know that I truly love them and will help them in any way I can. It grieves my heart to know that there are many, many people who go through their days without a single person telling them that they are loved.

It is the spirit of Jesus alive in me today that allows me to do this. For most of my life, I never received the love of God nor understood it, so I lived the transactional love that the world taught me. My heart was not full of love, and therefore, I had none to give.

I rarely say to people, "Jesus loves you," unless they are at that point on their spiritual journey. While this is undeniably true, it is impersonal. When I was atheist and people told me that Jesus loved me, that meant nothing to me. In fact, it drove me further from the gospel. I did not know He existed.

Another one of my partners, Rick Rogers, demonstrated the love of Jesus to me and had an impact on my journey. One day when I was going through my divorce, he stopped me in the hall at the office. We talked for a few minutes. He gave me a coffee mug with his church's logo and said, "This is where I go to church. I wanted you to have this mug, and if you ever wanted to come join me sometime, I would love that." I thanked him for the gift and told him I appreciated it. Atheist at the time, I thought thanks, but no thanks. However, that gesture did touch my heart. I felt his love in that moment. He saw that I was struggling, even though outwardly I would not admit that. He knew I was living in the delusion of the lies of the world because I was getting divorced and showed his love, not judgment. He never mentioned Jesus. He sought to walk with me rather than preach at me.

The love of the spirit of Jesus must first be expressed through me because it is in me where Jesus exists in the world today. It then must be felt by the other person before I introduce them to the historical Jesus. As Christians, we are called to share love and truth. Love must come before the truth. If truth is shared before love, it does not work. When people live in the delusion of the lies of the world as I did when I was atheist, sharing truth first causes defensiveness and drives people further from the gospel.

No one cares how much you know until they know how much you care.

Jesus is not here in the flesh today. Jesus lives inside of me. He has commanded me to love everybody. When he said everybody, he meant everybody. Therefore, it is incumbent on me to love everybody, which means serving them and not expecting anything in return. My actions follow my words. By verbalizing to another person "I love you," my mind renews and my heart transforms and my actions follow. My thoughts do not bless anyone. My words, and more importantly, my actions, do.

The blessing does not flow to us; it flows through us.

Human beings all desire to do good works and be kind to others. However, if our natural inclination was toward this end, then the law would never have to have been written down. If being kind and loving was inherent to our being, it would not have to be taught. A bird does not need to be taught to fly. It just flies. It is a bird's nature. Even though we want to do good works, because we are innately selfish, there is always an expectation that we will be repaid, unless our hearts have been transformed. Other religions teach that our good works must outweigh our bad in order to get to heaven. There still exists a transaction with this mindset. The individual with those beliefs expects something in return from God for their actions on this earth. Even in Buddhism where there is no belief in God, there is an expectation in the law of Karma that positive energy, intention, and action will be returned by the universe to that individual.

This is the beautiful truth about the gospel of Jesus Christ. There is no transaction. I expect nothing when serving others because I need nothing. I already have everything. I have God through Jesus. Anything I have on this earth beyond my relationship with God is extravagance. I am not doing good works to earn my place in heaven. I am already there. I do not have to perform well for God to love me. I am already loved by God. Through Jesus's crucifixion and resurrection, Jesus has earned my place in heaven through His good works, not mine. He perfectly served God and mankind and expected nothing in return. I freely accept this gift of heaven; and I now love, give, and serve with no expectation of repayment from God or any person. My service is out of gratitude, not obligation. I can freely love other people without being forced. It is a joy instead of a burden.

You have not lived today until you have done something for someone who can never repay you. (John Bunyan)

Being a physician, I lived in the delusion that I was a loving, caring person because performing surgery on patients and helping them regain their lives looked like service to me. If I am getting paid for my work, it is not service. It is my job. My love for my patients goes beyond that. I understand that today. It is in this service to others where the joy of Christ is found.

It is easy to love someone who loves me. Or someone who is similar to me. It is hard to love someone who has hurt me or my family. Who has lied to me. Who has stolen from me. Who has actively and intentionally tried to cause me harm. Who hates me. How do I serve that person and not expect anything in return? This is impossible for a human being. It is not natural or instinctive. That tells me the only way this is possible is through a supernatural power that must exist outside of me. The ability to truly love everybody can only come from the one true God through Jesus.

26

STEPS

1. We admitted we were powerless over alcohol—that our lives had become unmanageable.
2. Came to believe that a Power greater than ourselves could restore us to sanity.
3. Made a decision to turn our will and our lives over to the care of God as we understood Him.
4. Made a searching and fearless moral inventory of ourselves.
5. Admitted to God, to ourselves, and to another human being the exact nature of our wrongs.
6. Were entirely ready to have God remove all these defects of character.
7. Humbly asked Him to remove our shortcomings.
8. Made a list of all persons we had harmed and became willing to make amends to them all.
9. Made direct amends to such people wherever possible, except when to do so would injure them or others.
10. Continued to take personal inventory and, when we were wrong, promptly admitted it.
11. Sought through prayer and meditation to improve our conscious contact with God as we understood Him, praying only for knowledge of His will for us and the power to carry that out.
12. Having had a spiritual awakening as the result of these steps, we tried to carry this message to alcoholics and to practice these principles in all our affairs.

The twelve steps of AA are the pathway to healing, peace, happiness, joy, freedom, and abundant life, not just sobriety. Everyone who comes to AA does not expect nor even want those things when they enter. We just want to stop drinking. A lot of people who come to AA do not even want to necessarily stop drinking. They just want the negative consequences of their drinking to stop. However, in working the steps and the AA program, even if a person just wants to get out of trouble but not stop drinking, he/she will undergo a change of his/her desires, and a significant portion of him/her will end up sober. It is the ACTION of doing the program that changes the heart and its desires.

Tradition 3 states, "The only requirement for membership is a desire to stop drinking." One does not even have to admit or claim that one is an alcoholic. All that one must have is a desire to stop drinking.

There are many stories of people who are sentenced to drug court where they are mandated to attend AA meetings for a period, usually years. Many of them have no intention of quitting drinking or using drugs. They just need to fulfill their legal obligation. But many of them end up sober and begin to lead the lives that God has for them because of the tremendous effectiveness and efficiency of the spiritual change that occurs inside them. They find happiness. They find joy. They find peace. They find freedom. They find serenity. And once that is found, no human being in their right mind wants to let that go.

When I came to rehab and learned of "working the steps," I thought that was the dumbest thing I had ever heard. What does it mean to "work a step"? I can read. I read them all. I can read them out loud. I had no concept of what "working a step" meant.

"Working a step" means a million different things. The steps and basic instructions of how to work the steps are delineated in the Big Book of AA, but how they are actually worked varies from sponsor to sponsor, just as all God's people are created individual and unique. There are no specific, detailed instructions on how to work each step because that would eliminate God's will and effect on them.

Because there are no specific instructions on how to work a step, each sponsor-sponsee allows God to direct them. What is important is for a sponsee to find someone who the steps and program has actually worked for because that demonstrates the fact that it has been effective for that person. This is why it is suggested to find a sponsor who has been sober for a year or more. That sponsor has what the sponsee wants—sobriety. The sponsee needs to be willing to go to any lengths to get it.

Much of the "work" in working a step involves writing, either answering questions on a worksheet related to that step or simply journaling one's thoughts and emotions related to that step. There is magical healing that happens when putting pen to paper. By writing, I do not mean typing. I mean taking a pen and writing, by hand, on paper. This is something I cannot explain as it is ultimately from God how this happens. From my observation and that of many alcoholics, we can attest to its effectiveness and power.

Specific prayer for each step is also part of this process. There are specific prayers for each step in the Big Book. As we progress through the steps, each prayer develops stronger faith in God/higher power as we seek Him. Having specific prayers that we can follow helps us renew our minds and incrementally surrender.

The steps are in order for a reason. They cannot be taken out of order or they will not be effective. The first three steps identify and develop a relationship with God or higher power. Steps 4 through 7 establish a relationship with oneself. A person cannot have a proper relationship with oneself until one possesses an appropriate understanding and relationship with God or higher power. Steps 8 through 12 foster relationship with others. The steps do not work if taken out of order.

These groupings can be also simply labeled as such: Trust God. Clean house. Help others.

I had effectively worked steps 1 through 3 when I came to faith in Christ. I had not, however, surrendered to all the concepts in those steps. I knew I was powerless over alcohol, but I did not believe my life was unmanageable. I believed I was managing my life very well because I had success in work. My success in work was lauded by the world and its values, and therefore, I felt validated that my life was manageable. What I failed to see was that I was destroying my family, and although I was aware that I was doing that with my drinking, the phrase "life was unmanageable" did not resonate with me. God revealed to me how unmanageable my life was when He arranged the circumstances and situations that forced me into treatment against my will. This was absolutely necessary in order for me to admit this unmanageability. I am thankful that I had enough willingness to submit to God's will when this happened.

In steps 2 and 3, I had come to believe in God (a power greater than myself), and I had made a decision to turn my life and my will over to Him. I did not believe that I was insane. God gave me the disease of alcoholism because once I became willing to seek God fully with my heart and mind, the insanity of alcoholism is obvious.

Insanity is doing the same thing over and over and expecting a different result.

As my alcoholism progressed, each time I drank, the negative consequences would get worse and worse. There were times when I would not have negative consequences, which led my limited mind to believe that I could drink successfully. However, the general trend over the two years leading me to rehab was a steady increase in the frequency and severity of those negative consequences. Yet I still continued to drink, even though I did not want to.

This is the same insanity of sin that Paul talks about in Romans 7:15 (ESV): "For I do not understand my own actions. For I do not do what I want, but I do the very thing I hate." I am thankful for the disease of alcoholism because the negative consequences are not subtle. They are blatantly obvious. God gave me no choice but to turn to Him. Other sins, which people consider lesser sins, but God considers equal, do not have such drastic negative earthly consequences. Unfortunately, because of that, many people are blind to their sin and never discover their insanity in it. This leads to the belief that one can manage life on their own and eliminates their need for salvation.

From my observation, most Christians do not go through the cleaning-house process. This process is uncomfortable and messy. It is where a person must become the most vulnerable to other people. Steps 4 and 5 are probably the most difficult steps to complete. Many alcoholics relapse while doing these steps because so many raw emotions and feelings are uncovered. No human being wants to make a fearless and searching moral inventory of oneself and then share that with another person. We alcoholics do it because we must, or we will drink again. There can be no secrets that we take to the grave. If an alcoholic leaves out one thing that he/she carries shame over on his/her step 4 inventory and subsequently fails to share it with another person, someday that person will drink again over that secret.

When we come to faith in Jesus Christ and accept Him as our savior, our sins are completely forgiven and washed away by God. Although this is instantaneous for God on His part, it is not so for us human beings on our end. Our hearts have been wounded and evil for many years, and cleansing them requires self-examination and work. It is a process. A journey with Christ. This requires effort. Steps 4 and 5 were the mechanism for me to be cleansed of my sins by Jesus. Merely accepting Him as savior and then dismissing my evil heart and the destruction of my past provided no healing or transformation of my heart.

The cleaning-house process is absolutely vital for abundant living and sobriety. The most healing occurs on the other side of it. God reveals His characteristics in many ways, but He does so powerfully in these steps. By sharing our deepest, darkest secrets with another person (sponsor, clergyman, trusted mentor), we experience understanding, love, forgiveness, nonjudgment, noncondemnation from that person. It is God revealing Himself to us. We find the no-matter-what-ness of God. That we are loved no matter what. That we are forgiven no matter what. That we are not judged no matter what. That we are not condemned no matter what. That there is nothing so shameful in our minds that we cannot reveal or be forgiven for. We cannot outsin God's grace. No matter what.

The sense of relief and peace I experienced after completing steps 4 and 5 was tremendous and intense. I felt as if I had no secrets anymore. I felt I had been washed clean, and I was starting anew with a fresh slate. I experienced the freedom of not carrying the shame of anything I had done before. That was my first spiritual awakening in AA, and I had no intention of doing it that day. My story just came out, warts and all, which demonstrates to me the effect of the Holy Spirit in my life.

Steps 4 and 5 cannot be done prior to steps 1 through 3 because an alcoholic must have an understanding of God/higher power who is able to provide the love, understanding, forgiveness, nonjudgment, noncondemnation that will provide healing in that moment. If an alcoholic's concept of God/higher power is insufficient, then feelings of fear, guilt, and shame will creep in; and that person will likely drink again. We must have a God/higher power big enough to handle all our problems before commencing steps 4 and 5.

My success in treatment and thus far in my recovery has been a result of me doing extensive work investigating God and establishing an appropriate understanding of God five years prior to rehab. I did not blindly accept God and Jesus Christ. With scientific scrutiny and investigation, I sought the evidence for Jesus's life, death, and resurrection and discovered the truth. As a result of that, I came to believe in God because without God, the resurrection would not be possible. Therefore, I had a strong concept of God and His characteristics before I entered recovery.

The spiritual concepts behind steps 6 and 7 are willingness and humility. The admission of powerlessness and acceptance of our character defects have been completed. In these steps, God reveals His sovereign power in His ability to help us remove these defects of character. We notice improvement in our behaviors and how we treat others. For years prior to this point for most alcoholics, we have tried to effect change in our lives through our own thinking and actions, and it never worked. We know that this transformation has not come from our will and our power. It must be coming from another source, and we develop more faith in our God/higher power as we observe the results.

Step 7 states, "Humbly asked Him to remove our shortcomings." When are our shortcomings removed? It is not when we go on to step 8. The humbling truth is that our shortcomings are never fully removed. This reminds me that praying to God to remove my pride, selfishness and self-centeredness is a daily ritual that must never end. Certainly, there is improvement in my character since my journey began, but I must never remit in my diligence to do this. It is progress, not perfection. I see many Christians praying for other people most of the time, and while that is very important, it is equally important to pray for oneself to allow Jesus to enter our hearts and minds and cleanse us daily.

In steps 8 and 9, we become willing and subsequently make amends to people we have harmed. No human being has the desire to do this. It is uncomfortable and frightening. In progressing through this process, we discover the infinite forgiveness of God. Most amends we make produce results we did not expect where the other party forgives our actions and the relationship is reconciled. There are times when this does not happen. However, in making the amends, we experience healing and peace knowing that we have done what is right in the eyes of our God/higher power. There are also times when restitution must be made. Part of making amends is asking the other party, "What can I do to make this right?" Most often we find the other party asks for nothing. But if there are instances when a request is made, we must be willing to follow through. Again, it is not between us and the other party. It is between us and God.

People are often unreasonable and self-centered. Forgive them anyway.

If you are kind, people may accuse you of ulterior motives. Be kind anyway.

If you are honest, people may cheat you. Be honest anyway.

If you find happiness, people may be jealous. Be happy anyway.

The good you do today may be forgotten tomorrow. Do good anyway.

Give the world the best you have and it may never be enough. Give your best anyway.

For you see, in the end it is between you and God.

**It was never between you and them any-
way. (Mother Teresa)**

Step 10 suggests continued daily perseverance in self-examination and reconciliation. Step 11 is my favorite step for continued
success in the program of AA.

Sought through prayer and meditation to improve our conscious contact with God as we understood Him, praying only for
knowledge of His will for us and the power to carry that out.

When I do not know how to pray, this step spells it out clearly
for me. Praying only for knowledge of His will for us and the power
to carry that out. One reservation I had with prayer when I was atheist was that I saw people praying to God and treating Him like a
magic genie. Praying for the things they wanted to have or to happen
and becoming upset when God did not follow through. I saw prayer
as a selfish act.

Prayer is not about asking God for what we want, although
there is nothing wrong with that. The Bible clearly states that we
are to make our requests to Him. What is important to us is also
important to Him, no matter what it is. The error is drawing con-
clusions about God and His characteristics based on the response to
our prayers.

God knows our hearts and our desires better than we do. He
wants us to willingly delight in Him and Him alone. Psalm 37:4
(ESV) says, "Delight yourself in the Lord and He will give you the
desires of your heart." We think we know what our heart really
desires, but we do not. Our intellect and vision is limited. God's is
not. He knows what our deepest desires and needs are. Seeking Him
makes that clear to us and aligns our will with His.

Alignment under God's will may sound to some like a burden.
It comes across as doing what He wants us to do, rather than what
we want to do. At the end of the day, the fact of the matter is that
God's will is going to happen, no matter what. As human beings, no
amount of manipulating, controlling, or fighting God's will is going
to change it. If it is going to rain, it is going to rain, and there is
nothing any human being can do about this. This is a simple phys-

ical example, but it holds true for everything in life. We are not in control. God is. COVID-19 has made that exceedingly clear. If you thought you had control of anything in your life before COVID-19, your perspective is probably different now after most everything in the world has shut down because a 100 nm (a nanometer is one-billionth of a meter) virus has changed everything.

The most miserable place to be in life is to be outside of and fighting God's will.

Prayer does not change God's will. Prayer changes my alignment under God and gives me the opportunity to ask Him to draw from His infinite power to have the ability to carry out my part in His plan. In doing this, our hearts are transformed; and we delight in Him as we see how He loves us, protects us, and provides far above and beyond what we could ever ask or expect.

As I started to practice prayer, I gained better insight into what God's will was for me. The choices I need to make wise decisions for my life come into my mind more quickly and with greater force than before. As an alcoholic/addict, I learned this spiritual principle:

First thought wrong.

My first thoughts regarding relationships, marriage, parenting, and life in general are almost always wrong. I lived in the delusion that I could make good decisions about these things because I made life-altering, critical, important decisions in my practice and in surgery daily; and I do that very well. However, there is no self-seeking motive in that. I can separate myself from those decisions. I choose to do what is best for the patient based on what I have been taught.

In life (relationships, marriage, parenting, etc.), my selfishness and self-centeredness are difficult to suppress. Whenever I have a decision to make in these life areas, most often, my first thought is selfish and therefore wrong. My brain will naturally immediately select the option that will benefit me, and only me, and disregard the other party. That is our natural instinct as human beings. We all have this characteristic inherent within us.

Through the program of AA, I have learned to pause and employ techniques such as prayer or calling my sponsor or another person that enable me to seek God and His will. In doing so, I am able to get to my second, third, fourth, or sometimes fifth thought to make a wise decision. A decision that is not selfish, serves God and mankind, and pleases God that in turn ultimately benefits me and my spirit, although it may not benefit me in the moment.

In step 11, "only" is the first key word, and "us" is the second: "Praying ONLY for knowledge of His will for US…" When I started, I improved quickly in discerning what God's will was for me. I did not progress as rapidly in discovering what God's will was for us, meaning every other person in my life and the world. Step 11 states the word "us" specifically for a reason. The Big Book teaches me that in my alcoholism/addiction, I am like a director trying to run the show. If people only did what I wanted them to do, the show would come off grand. However, in life, people do not always do what I want or expect them to do. Therefore, I must seek God to know what His will is for them also to prevent me from trying to control or manipulate other people.

The closest relationship I have in my life is my wife. Therefore, she is the person in my life that I had the hardest time with accepting the principle in this step. It took me years to learn to release my perceived control of her and relinquish it to God. In order to do this, I had to develop an unwavering trust in God to know and believe that He would do a better job than me of keeping her married to me. My biggest fear is that of being alone, and that is why I tried to exert my control over her and manipulate her to make her stay. That is not my responsibility. That is God's responsibility. It is not my job to make her happy. It is God's job to do that. Most every attempt I made to try to please her ended in frustration. By praying for knowledge of God's will for her, and accessing the power to carry that out, I have become able to let her be who God intended her to be and love her even more as she becomes His beautiful creation.

The problem with my delusional view of marriage in my first marriage and early in my second is that I understood marriage to be a contractual relationship. This is what marriage has been reduced to in the United States today. It is a financial contract between two individuals to share in assets and obtain benefits like health insurance from the other party. When one party is not satisfied with the contract, the contract gets broken in divorce. As human beings exert our authority over marriage, the failure rate is 50 percent. That is merely the divorce rate. The rate of dissatisfaction and discontent in marriage is much higher than that, but many couples remain married for other reasons, yet miserable with each other.

Dating compounds this problem. When we start dating another person, the primary driver for that relationship is how that person makes us feel. That person makes us happy. That person makes us feel fulfilled and important. We get what we want out of that person. The problem is that when we enter marriage, under the authority of the covenant of God, we must do a 180-degree shift in our mindset. Marriage has nothing to do with how the other person makes us feel. We must love and serve that person no matter what, as God loves us. However, when we enter marriage, there is now an expectation that the other person will continue to make us feel good and fulfill our needs. That expectation will inevitably fail at some point because we are all selfish in the absence of spiritual direction. When most people say, "For better or for worse," they just mean "For better."

Expectations are future resentments.

As the expectations are not met, the resentment grows, and couples "grow apart" from each other. "Irreconcilable differences" is what we call it. Those "differences" are that each spouse has a different expectation and vision for marriage because of our inherent selfishness and, if not aligned under God, will inevitably lead to separation. I pray that my children will find spouses who love God above anyone or anything else. For if their spouses truly believe in their heart what Jesus said, that "greater love has no one than this: to lay down one's life for one's friends" (John 15:13), they will have satisfying, fulfilling, happy marriages and avoid much of the pain of this world.

My heart grieves divorce and unsatisfying marriages because God did not design it this way. It took me many years to understand that the best way to "enjoy life with my wife" (Ecclesiastes 9:9 NIV) is to serve her and expect nothing in return. The world states that this is irrational and illogical, and under this mindset, the statistics speak for themselves.

It is insanity to think about this. When we first started dating, and finally married, she was her own individual, pursuing God and fulfilling her destiny that He ordained for her. Then all of a sudden, once we were married, I thought that being her husband, I had to "help" her become the wife and mother I thought she needed to be, rather than let God do that.

Helpfulness is the sunny side of control.

Why in the world would I want to change her from the person she was when we were dating? I fell in love with the person she was, and she was that person with ZERO input from me at that point. Somehow, in my limited human mind, I felt that I knew better than God how she needed to be as a wife and mother, and I would provide my input.

I had been divorced once already, and I did not want that to happen again. I would exert my will to try to prevent that. All of us have some level of fear that our spouse may leave for whatever reason. In my first marriage, my first wife was not being the wife and mother that I thought she needed to be. Having no belief in God, and in my selfishness, I decided to leave.

What I have learned needs to happen is for me to seek God's will for my life and allow my wife to seek God's will for her life. After all, isn't that what was happening when my wife and I were dating prior to being married when we fell in love with each other? I need to allow God to work in her life. I need to leave her alone in a lot of matters. I need to actively listen to her and seek to understand. Helping her is not making suggestions or telling her what to do in any situation, unless asked. Helping her is supporting and encouraging her, as she is seeking God's will, and providing what I can as her husband and serving her to fulfill God's will for her life.

This is difficult sometimes because God's will for her is not in alignment with what my will is for her or us. It sometimes puts me in a position where I do not get what I want in order for God's will to transpire. However, today, as a result of this work I have done with the twelve steps and therapy, I know and believe that God's will is best, and my role is to encourage and support that, rather than try to manipulate it into what I want it to be.

My wife was the first in our marriage to surrender to God's will in our lives. We were having difficulty getting pregnant and had to go through in vitro fertilization (IVF). IVF is extremely difficult to go through, physically and emotionally. The highs and lows are dramatic and intense. It is a very arduous process to go through for any woman, and any marriage.

After our first round, she was pregnant, and we were very excited. Two weeks later, after all those injections, and all that testing, she had miscarried. She was devastated, but since I was not the one going through all these treatments and not emotionally sensitive, I was not compassionate and just felt like we (she) would go through it again. She did not have the support from me that she needed, and that made the whole process a lot more difficult.

She is educated as a physician's assistant, which is how I met her. Since we were having difficulty getting pregnant and finally had to go through IVF, she knew that she could not bear the stress of working and IVF. She surrendered to God's will for our lives by quitting her job, which I came to realize was more difficult than I acknowledged at the time. She is a very independent woman and had career aspirations as I did. She put those aside to have our family, which was a sacrifice, putting our future family's needs ahead of her own.

When we were blessed enough to start having children, she continued to be a stay-at-home mom (SAHM as I have come to learn for short). Being a SAHM is the most underappreciated occupation in the world, yet one of the most important. Moms do not get paid and do not get appreciated enough, yet being a SAHM is a tremendous amount of work, physically, emotionally, and mentally. Children continually make the same mistakes over and over again, so the encouragement that moms get by seeing the fruits of their labor comes slowly over time, not daily. Most moms also do not have confidence in their abilities because they have never been trained or educated in being a mom and have never done it before. It is a humbling process with many failures and frustrations.

This was a world away from when my wife was a PA making a great deal of money, continually getting praised for her work, and having the confidence in her outstanding clinical and surgical skills.

She let all of that go, and died to her own desires and ego, to surrender to God's will for us to have a family. This certainly was not easy. She made this decision humbly and courageously to sacrifice her own desires in the moment, for the ultimate goal of us having children and raising them well. I am thankful for her knowledge of God's will for us at the time and the power she had to carry that out.

I, on the other hand, did not die to my own ego and desires during this process. I did not provide the compassion or support she needed to go through these extremely difficult processes. Of course, I did want her to be happy, but I did not understand what she really needed. In my delusional mind, I thought that what would make her happy would be for me to be very successful as a spine surgeon and generate a lot of money for expensive houses and extravagant vacations. In pursuing this goal, however, I was also feeding my own ego and seeking what I wanted in life at the time. I worked a lot of hours and continually collected among the top in my group. When the collection numbers came out each month, I felt a lot of satisfaction seeing mine at or near the top. Patients thanked me frequently, which fed my ego and made me feel like I was a very gracious doctor. I thought I was doing an outstanding job as a doctor and as a husband, providing for her and our family.

The truth is, I had no clue what my wife needed from me, and I was too selfish and egotistical to recognize it. My wife complained a lot that I worked all the time and only cared about myself. At that time, I took her complaining as criticism of me, which led me to feel like I was not good enough. I am not blaming her, but this drove a lot of my alcoholic drinking. This feeling of me not performing well as a husband led me to believe I was not good enough, and I would drink to numb that pain.

What I have learned is that often when my wife complains, she is actually telling me what she needs. The problem was not with her, but with me. My life was not in alignment with God's will for us. I was in agreement with her that I wanted children, and I also wanted a family, but I wanted a family on my terms, not on His. I wanted to be able to continue to be a busy spine surgeon working many hours and making a lot of money to feed my ego. Then I could have the beautiful picture of our wonderful life without any sacrifice on my end. I justified this by saying that I was just doing what I was supposed to do to provide for my family, but this was only a lie. The truth is it was all about my ego and pride.

The now-hilarious paradox I have discovered is that by letting go and letting God work, and then supporting and encouraging her in her path, our marriage is maximally fulfilling, joyous, and prosperous. By allowing her to fulfill her destiny that God has ordained, we have a mutual adoration and respect for each other. And all of this through without manipulation or suggestion from myself! God manages her life better than I ever thought I could, even though I tried for years. God truly knows what is best for us, and surrendering to that brings ultimate enjoyment of life. After all, He is the author of life, so who would know better what it takes to obtain the most satisfaction and happiness out of it?

A satisfying, fulfilling, enjoyable marriage is one of the most powerful ways in which God is revealed. It displays the no-matter-what-ness of God's love. When each partner loves, supports, encourages, and serves the other during times of pain and hardship, even times when that partner has actively done something to harm them, the power of God's unending love is displayed for all the world to see. That we, as God's children, can love, endure, and STAY WITH the other no matter what.

God loves and supports no matter what. Even when he is being actively rejected, He is omnipresent and immutable, patiently waiting for the time when a person discovers God's love and returns to him willingly. He does not impose His will upon us, for if He did that, then we would have no choice but to love Him. He has the option to do that yet does not. He chooses to let us have free will in our lives. When we become willing to come to Him and love Him, it is our heart's free choice, and that is genuine and real.

If each partner in a marriage acted the way God does, there would be a revival in the condition of marriage today, and many more people could experience satisfying, fulfilling, happy marriages. Each partner seeking God, leaving the other to seek God on his/her own, and then being present to love, support, serve, and encourage each other. That is how it starts with dating; but somehow, some way, when people get married, we think we know how the other person should act and attempt to impose our own will on them.

The grass is not greener on the other side.
The grass is greener where you water it.

It is my opinion that marriage counseling has very limited effect in marriage. It was a disaster for my wife and me. Marriage counseling is akin to hiring a mediator to address what is wrong with the other person. It is always the other person's fault, and it is the other person who has the problem. If only the other person would act right, then everything would be all right. This is a delusion.

Each person in a marriage is 50 percent of the problem. This is actually great news. If I am the problem, then I can work on the solution. If my spouse is the problem, then I have little effect on the solution. If each individual would address his/her own issues, then at least 50 percent of the marriage would be improved. Each partner in a marriage only has control of his/her own actions, so it is more effective for each person to work on themselves, prior to addressing the spouse. If each person directed their hearts toward God and sought Him, they grow closer together.

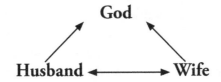

If I pray for only one thing, it is for "the knowledge of His will for us, and the power to carry that out." This eliminates "irreconcilable differences" because each spouse's target is close communion with God. Like all the steps, this is simple, but not easy.

After rehab, surrendering to God's will, the twelve steps of AA, and applying these principles to my Christian faith, my life looks a lot different today than I had envisioned, and for the better. One of the suggestions I received was to limit my work hours for a period when I left rehab. As I returned to practice, it took time to build back up again, so limiting my hours was easy at first. Now, five years later,

I continue to limit my work hours even though my ego and pride tell me otherwise.

In limiting my work hours, I am better able to submit to God's will for me to be a husband and father. I am able to be home earlier to spend time with them. I have the opportunity to drop the kids off and pick them up from school a couple of times each week. My relationship with my wife and kids is immeasurably better today because of this. However, the choice to limit my hours is not an easy one. I am constantly bombarded with patients trying to get in for surgery, and I must have clear boundaries to limit this. Also, when the collection numbers come out, I see my name dropping down the list. It is still more than enough. I do not feed my pride and ego by "beating" everyone else anymore. Until I had peace with God, my definition of "enough money" was "a little more than what I had."

My ego tells me, "Just add another surgery on. It will be okay for you to come home a little later. It will increase your collections, and you will be back on top again. And you are doing a good thing. You are helping those patients." The human mind is an incredible machine that justifies and rationalizes almost anything a human being desires. Surrendering to God's will for me is most often sacrificing my pride. It is making the choice that does not seem to give me fulfillment and satisfaction in the moment because I frequently seek to obtain the praise of other people, rather than from God.

In the book *The Top Five Regrets of the Dying*, a palliative care nurse named Bronnie Ware recorded the dying epiphanies of terminally ill patients in their last twelve weeks of life. Every male patient she nursed had the regret of "I wish I hadn't worked so hard." She writes, "This came from every male patient that I nursed. They missed their children's youth and their partner's companionship. Women also spoke of this regret, but as most were from an older generation, many of the female patients had not been breadwinners. All of the men I nurse deeply regretted spending so much time of their lives on the treadmill of a work existence."

Every. Single. Man.

If you only live for yourself, you will end up by yourself. (Brady Cooper)

Winning in life is not about having the biggest house, the fanciest car, or going on the most exotic vacations. Success in life is having satisfying, fulfilling, meaningful relationships. These relationships are cultivated by men by being servant leaders. That is not our natural tendency.

I am thankful that God snapped me on the neck in 2015 by sending me to rehab. This was His way of saying to me, "I desire a relationship with you." He took me off the treadmill of my work existence, away from the busyness of my life to give me the time to seek Him. In turn, as my relationship with God developed, my relationship with other people matured appropriately.

Today, I make decisions based on what I believe would please and honor God. I have found that in doing so, although I may not receive immediate gratification, recognition, and compliments from other people, my spirit is filled; and my heart rejoices as I feel satisfaction, happiness, joy, and freedom within. That is the blessing. For me, blessing is the ultimate peace, satisfaction, happiness, contentment, and freedom I feel from sacrificing my pride. This is something I never found in chasing the things of the world that promise these feelings yet come up empty.

Discerning God's will is not as hard as I make it out to be. For starters, even if I am unable to discern God's will in a given situation, I certainly know what God's will is not. God's will is not for me to have an affair. God's will is not for me to start drinking again. God's will is not for me to intentionally harm other people. We human beings have a way of making simple things complicated. The Bible has clear instructions that lead to abundant, extravagant life. We make it complicated because the majority of those instructions go against our ego and pride and do not fulfill our innate desire to satisfy ourselves in the moment. We are born separated from God and, therefore, enemies of God. What we want before our hearts are transformed naturally goes against God. The very gift of the magnificent brains that God has given us works against us to justify and rationalize our behavior, when in our hearts, we know deep down that what we are doing is wrong. The more I must explain my decision-making in a certain matter, the more I know that I am seeking my will and not God's.

I am married. Therefore, His will for my life is to be the best husband He created me to be. He has gifted me with four wonderful, beautiful children. Therefore, His will for my life is to be the best father He created me to be. Inherent in fulfilling those two destinies is the fact that I must be with them, physically, mentally, emotionally, and spiritually. I know and understand that today, leading me to live the abundant life He designed for me. That takes surrendering my ego and pride at times to step into that.

In my disease of alcoholism, I lived in the delusion that I had plenty of money. There was a lot of money coming in and going out of our checking account. What I failed to realize, however, was that I had drawn several lines of credit and was running balances on our credit cards. Even though there were large amounts of money coming in and going out, feeding my delusion that we were financially stable, I just paid the minimums on the lines of credit and credit cards, and those burdens were not decreasing.

This illustrates how the disease of alcoholism is not just a drinking problem, but a thinking problem. My thinking was delusional and disordered when it came to basic life skills. My thinking when not surrendered to God centers on myself and disregards others. On day 5 of rehab, I sat down at the computer and organized our finances because I had to give my wife the information to manage them for the next ninety days. The truth of our financial situation was revealed to me. I was in shock. I could not believe how blind I was to the truth. We were $220,000 in debt, and our checking account had $20,000 in it.

By surrendering my life and my will over to the care of God, not only have I cleared all that debt in five years, we were able to buy a beautiful farmhouse in the country, and even another vacation home within that time. This is not the result of me being a spine surgeon and making a lot of money. I made more money before I entered rehab, and I still had that debt. This is a result of surrendering to His will for my life by intentionally being a better husband and father and God rewarding me for that. I also surrender my finances to him, tithing appropriately; and just as the Bible promises, He provides beyond my needs and wants. I give joyfully, out of gratitude and not begrudgingly. This obedience is not easy or comfortable at times, but to obtain the peace of God that surpasses understanding (Philippians 4:7), it is always worth it.

> Bring the full tithe into the storehouse, that there may be food in my house. "Test me in this," says the Lord Almighty, "and see if I will not throw open the floodgates of heaven and pour out so much blessing that there will not be room enough to store it." (Malachi 3:10 NIV)

The only word I can use to describe that is a miracle. A miracle is defined as a surprising and welcome event that is not explicable by natural or scientific laws and is therefore considered to be the work of a divine agency. I witness miracles in my life every single day as a result of step 11, constantly improving my conscious contact with God, praying only for knowledge of His will for us and the power to carry that out. The power to carry that out is surrendering.

I work less hours and make almost the same amount of money. That does not seem mathematically possible, but it is true. God has made me more efficient. Even though I was never drunk at work, my productivity was affected. My clinical decision-making and surgical skills were unaffected by my alcoholism, but my life skills of organization and overall vision were. By praying for knowledge of God's will, I have found ways to make my practice more efficient and productive. Rather than just adding more patients and trying to work harder, He reveals to me ways in which I can work smarter. God is doing for me what I cannot do for myself, which enables me to fulfill my destiny as a spine surgeon, husband, and father the way He intended, providing ultimate satisfaction and happiness for me.

Step 12 states, "Having had a spiritual awakening as a result of these steps, we tried to carry this message to alcoholics and to practice these principles in all our affairs." Sobriety is the result of many spiritual awakenings that we have had along the way as we have worked these steps. The Big Book states that our purpose is to be of maximum service to God and the people about us. Every day, when I awake, I ask God to help me to be of maximum service to God and the people about me. Step 12 reminds me to carry out this purpose.

You can't keep what you have unless you give it back.

Helping and serving someone without expecting anything in return fills our spirit. We obtain peace, joy, satisfaction, and contentment as we draw closer to God. These things are not quantifiable or calculable. Therefore, with our limited human minds, we do not seek them like we do things that we can touch and feel like sex, money, and power. However, in seeking that which we can see and feel and trying to find ultimate satisfaction and enjoyment out of that, our lives end up in frustration and despair as our spirit dies by not following God's instructions for our lives. God wants us to enjoy those things that are done best under His parameters because He created those things for us. This is stated in 2 Corinthians 4:18 (ESV):

> As we look not to the things that are seen
> but to the things that are unseen. For the things
> that are seen are transient, but the things that are
> unseen are eternal.

The transient satisfaction we get from sex, money, and power feels good in the moment. But if not carried out and enjoyed under God's transcendent parameters, it will ultimately lead to dissatisfaction and discontent.

The power of step 12 is incredible. A friend of mine found twelve-step recovery first through Overeaters Anonymous over forty years ago. He subsequently transitioned to AA and, for the past over forty years, has been going to four to five meetings a week and helping other alcoholics and addicts get and stay sober through the AA book and program, working the steps with them. He has been able to maintain over a 100 lbs. weight loss over that time, remaining at his high school all-state football playing weight.

How is this possible through the program of AA and especially the twelfth step? The obesity epidemic is not much different than the opioid epidemic except for the substance and consequences. Addiction is defined as continued use in the face of adverse consequences. Obesity is an adverse consequence of repeatedly overeating. Overeating results from medicating unwanted negative feelings with the most widely available and accessible medicator, food. Food is the most widely abused antianxiety drug. Food addiction is the most challenging addiction to overcome because the medicator is ubiquitous and universally available, socially accepted and acknowledged as a medicator ("comfort food"), society has made a concerted effort to accept obesity as a desirable state, and a person cannot completely abstain from food as one can with drugs and alcohol. As it is necessary to moderate one's consumption of food, overcoming food addiction is much more difficult than other substances that can be eliminated.

Before my reader becomes offended, I will state that all human beings, no matter what size, are magnificent beings, wonderfully and beautifully created by God. We all have equal value and worth. I do not recognize beauty in a person by their weight.

Taking image out of the equation, I will speak to this issue on medical terms. I am not aware of any study that shows superior outcomes in people who are obese versus those of normal weight. Results of any kind of treatment for any medical condition or surgical treatment are always worse with higher body mass index (BMI). As a physician, if I fail to address obesity as a detriment to health, I am doing a disservice to my patients and endorsing behavior that will ultimately hasten their physical demise. On June 22, 2015, the *Journal of the American Medical Association* announced that the number of obese Americans (BMI over 30) outnumbered those that are overweight (BMI 25–30). The truth is food addiction is rampant, and the situation is not improving.

Although the media has attempted to convince the public that being overweight or obese is acceptable or even desirable, I have never seen a success story reported by the media as someone who gained over 100 lbs. Success, in terms of weight, is defined by loss of weight, not gaining of weight.

The solution to the obesity epidemic is not a diet. It is not exercise. It is not a pill. Obesity is akin to alcoholism in that it is a medical disease with a spiritual solution.

The root of the problem is a spiritual affliction that is most effectively treated with the program of AA. My friend is a resounding demonstration of that fact. For over forty years, he has been able to maintain more than a 100 lbs. weight loss. He does not yo-yo diet. He does not struggle when it comes to eating. He is happy, joyous, and free and enjoys food as it was intended. He continuously lives the AA way of life by going to meetings and helping others overcome their alcoholism and addictions, and because of that, he himself has complete freedom over a food addiction that previously crippled him.

I have seen this in my journey as well. As I continue to live the AA way of life, I have found that my self-control steadily improves when it comes to food and in all areas of my life. This is a sign of spiritual maturity. The fruits of the Spirit are love, joy, peace, patience, kindness, goodness, faithfulness, gentleness, and self-control (Galatians 5:22–23 NLT). Every word of the Bible is intentional, purposeful, and specific. The reason why self-control is the last fruit of the Spirit is it is the most challenging one to obtain. Surrendering one's life and will over to God is a daily endeavor, and my friend has continued that for over forty years, enabling him to live in the sunlight of the Spirit with extraordinary levels of self-control enabling him to maintain his high school weight.

Of the twelve steps, only two mention alcohol/alcoholic, and six mention God/power greater than ourselves. The first step states, "We admitted we were powerless over alcohol—that our lives had become unmanageable." Whatever substance or behavior you keep returning to that causes you physical or emotional pain can be substituted for alcohol in that first step. The more difficult ones to identify are worry/anxiety, work, and relationships. However, everyone has something or someone they just cannot quit. It is much harder to be rigorously honest with oneself that their life is unmanageable.

The message of Christianity is that we are powerless over everything. Control is an illusion. God is in control. We are not, despite our best efforts to continue in that delusion. For me, this is the reason why the twelve steps applied to my Christian faith have helped me tremendously in every single area of my life because of my awareness of my lack of control leading to trust in the true nature of God that He is in control.

One delusion that I lived under for many years was, because I am a doctor, I felt that I served people all day long. All day, every day at work, patients come to me with their spine problems; and I help them get better. Although this feels like service, this is not true service work. Anything I do and get paid for is not service. It is my occupation. A lot of physicians succumb to this delusion and do not serve their marital partners or children at all. They feel that they serve them by providing them with big houses and expensive vacations, but that leads to a lot of dissatisfied spouses and children with many problems growing up.

Education can make you look good on the outside, but it cannot transform you on the inside. (Robert Lewis)

We must remember that our children are our most important disciples. Our spouses are our most important earthly relationship. We must serve them above all others, and that means doing that without expecting anything in return. If everyone followed the instructions in this quote from Mother Teresa, the world would be an amazing place to be: **"If you want to bring happiness to the world, go home and love your family."**

Many people do the "one-twelve" program. Trust God, then help others, but not clean house. That does not work. The AA program clearly states that a spiritual awakening must occur before we are to help others.

I see this in the Christian church. Many people come to believe in God, and they are told to now go serve others. While serving others is important, in fact most important for Christians, without a proper examination of one's life and God, service to others does not produce the proper spiritual effect in a person's life. Serving others becomes a burden, rather than a joy. It is seen as an obligation, not a privilege. This, in turn, leads to discouragement and frustration, ultimately turning a person's heart away from God, rather than toward God.

27

PURPOSE

As it relates to human beings, the definition of purpose is the reason for which we exist. This is a concept that I did not contemplate much in my first thirty years of life. Growing up, I thought my purpose in life was to be "successful" in order to be happy. To that end, I basically had two purposes for how I spent my time. Either I did what I thought I needed to do to "get ahead" in life, or when I was not doing that, I would do whatever I felt would make me happy. I remember distinctly when I was a resident in orthopedics in Miami, I made a conscious decision about this. Since we were extremely busy and awake most nights when on call, I decided that if I was going to be up all night working some days, there would be other nights where I would be up all night partying. Work hard, play harder. There was no higher purpose to my life other than myself. My "success" and my happiness were the ultimate goals.

It was not until I was in rehab, almost forty years old, that I learned what my true purpose in life really was.

Our real purpose is to fit ourselves to be
of maximum service to God and the people
about us. (*Alcoholics Anonymous*, 4th ed., 77)

This sentence was a spiritual awakening to me. It has changed my entire life. It is the action of love.

This is not just the purpose of an alcoholic's life. It is the purpose for the life of every single human being that has ever existed.

That sentence is the most eloquent, understandable, and clear definition of a human being's purpose that I had ever come across.

This is what Jesus's life was all about. The purpose of His earthly life was to be of maximum service to God and every person who ever lived. He never sought to fulfill one earthly desire that He had as a human being and instead surrendered to God's will for His life to serve and save everyone. When I was instructed to follow Jesus, this is what I was being called to do. Putting it in this manner, being of maximum service to God and the people about us finally made my directive clear.

Today, I check my motive and purpose in any decision I make or any action I take. I ask myself, "Is this something that serves my purpose of being of maximum service to God and the people about me?" Certainly, being a limited human being, there are times when I must find rest and do something that does not necessarily serve others. However, I do not seek pleasure in and of itself for myself because I know that in the end, it will leave my spirit unsatisfied and discontent. I know that the ultimate pleasure comes from my relationship with God through Jesus Christ, and serving Him and other people is how this is accomplished.

I now have one singular purpose that encompasses my previous two purposes for my time. I can now "get ahead" and "have fun" at the same time. "Getting ahead" in life is not about any of the things that I thought it was. "Getting ahead" in life is drawing closer to God. I do seek to be happy. Everyone does. However, the things I do today to serve God and people give me joy. It is better than happiness. It is abundant joy. It is that indescribable feeling of my spirit being filled. Now, I can enjoy the journey. The way I use my time "gets me ahead" in life coming into closer conscious contact with God; and I obtain happiness, satisfaction, and joy along the way.

Life without purpose is punishment.
Life with purpose is passion.

The beauty of this purpose is that it is not contingent on education, physicality, specific talents, personality, social skills, or anything else. Every single person on earth has this specific purpose by virtue of the fact that they are a human being created in God's image. Every person has specific God-given talents, abilities, skills, and characteristics that are unique to that person that no one else in history has ever had. Any and all of those can be used to serve God and the people about them in that person's individual manner to further the kingdom of God. Each person has tremendous value and worth. All are equally important. It is my prayer that you seek and find your special talents and abilities to fulfill your purpose and destiny.

Growing up, all Bethany Hamilton wanted to become was a professional surfer. At age thirteen, she lost her left arm to a shark attack. Eventually, she was able to become a professional surfer after all, and her story is an inspiration to amputees and others throughout the world. From this seemingly senseless and random tragedy, she was able to fulfill her true purpose to God and mankind in not only becoming a professional surfer but also giving hope and inspiration to amputees and others that they can also fulfill their dreams despite their handicaps. She has found a joy and satisfaction with life above and beyond what may have been had she become a professional surfer with two arms. Her autobiography *Soul Surfer: A True Story of Faith, Family, and Fighting to Get Back on the Board* has inspired millions all over the world. Her willingness to reveal herself to the world, her struggles, and how she overcame them help and inspire others.

As a physician, when people call me, they frequently say, "Sorry to bother you." Even though I emphatically tell them that it is not a bother, just about every phone call starts this way. Reflecting the heart of Christ, my mindset must be that of service.

You are not an interruption to my day.

You are the reason for it.

This truth renews my mind and allows me to be present for people. It enables a spiritual shift in my feeling and thinking to listen more intently. I do not feel the pull of other obligations. It allows me to fulfill my purpose.

Comparison is the thief of joy.

There are many things that I eliminated in my life in applying my new purpose. I eliminated all social media (Facebook, Instagram). Pride is my most glaring character defect, and my ego is my worst enemy. Prior to entering rehab, in examining my motives for posting things on social media, it was almost always about my ego. Did I put that picture up of my family to share with everyone to bring them joy, or was it really to show off what a great father I think I am? Was that sleeveless shirt really one of my favorite shirts that I just wanted to show everyone, or did it show me in such a way that I would get a compliment? Was I really putting scripture up and a picture of my Bible to help someone, or did I want people to think that I was really being a "good" Christian?

This is the rigorous honesty that is necessary in my life today. The Big Book states that I must be capable of "grasping and developing a manner of living which demands rigorous honesty" (*Alcoholics Anonymous*, 58). This means with other people, but most importantly, rigorous honesty with myself. In checking my motive in everything I do, I must thoroughly examine myself and my intentions. Having a sponsor or other person seeking God to talk to about decisions I make helps me to be rigorously honest because there are times when I am so blinded by my ego that I cannot see what the truth really is.

Checking my motive and purpose for everything I do may sound exhausting, but I assure you it makes my life much easier.

The pain of discipline is less than the pain of regret.

Taking the time to go to God in everything I do enables me to make wise decisions that will help me avoid regret. Any action I take out of selfish desire is going to have physical, emotional, mental, and spiritual consequences. The physical consequences of a bad decision are the easiest to identify; but the emotional, mental, and spiritual consequences are not. That is where I need God's help and direction. He knows the story from beginning to end, and He has given instructions in the Bible as to how to avoid those consequences. Praying only for knowledge of His will and the power to carry that out is how I can avoid negative emotions in my life and live in the "peace of God that surpasses understanding" (Philippians 4:7 ESV).

I am not perfect in this manner of living, and I never will be. However, it is all about progress, not perfection. There are times when I fail in checking my motive, and there are amends to be made. I know that I am forgiven, but it is incumbent on me to take a daily personal inventory and see where I have wronged someone. If I do or if I was wrong, I promptly admit it and make amends. I do not wait. The toil it takes on my emotional and spiritual health is grave if I do not take corrective action immediately.

28

HOW DO I KNOW THAT JESUS IS ALIVE TODAY?

I am certain that Jesus lives inside of me today. I cannot fully explain this nor make anyone understand completely. I have seen the power and glory of God through Jesus Christ in my life, and I found that only after I entered the program of Alcoholics Anonymous. I have had many spiritual awakenings throughout this process, too numerous to list. However, there are three specific experiences that reveal to me that Jesus is alive today and that he lives in me.

I told the story earlier about the horrendous vacation that privileged me to spend ninety days in rehab. It is a memory that I need to have the ability to recall in order to stay sober. The Big Book states, "We are unable, at certain times, to bring into our consciousness with sufficient force the memory of the suffering and humiliation of even a week or a month ago." I am thankful that I can bring that memory into my consciousness when needed to prevent me from drinking alcohol again.

I told of my daughter who was eight at the time, who was so scared that she texted her mother who sent someone to come rescue her. She obviously had a tremendous amount of fear of me at that point. Trust was at a minimum. I had told her and many others, time and time again, how I would stop drinking; yet I could not. Our relationship at that point was at its absolute lowest.

Fast forward the story about two years into my recovery. We had taken her to counseling, and she had properly processed the emotional trauma of that event, which I believe is critically important. In medicine and as a society, we take great measures to address physical pain from an event. However, we minimize or ignore the emotional pain that a person endures as a result of that event. That emotional pain can wreak much more havoc in a person's life and severely damage them spiritually that they are emotionally crippled for the rest of their lives. We must begin to recognize the value of mental and emotional health in order to improve as a society.

Now that I was sober, our relationship had improved greatly; and I could be mentally, emotionally, and spiritually present in her life, not just physically. I had a spine surgery conference that I was obligated to attend in Las Vegas. I spent a lot of time in Vegas in my past, and it is not a place where I would choose to go anymore. However, I had a good reason to be there for this conference, and I was working my AA program to be spiritually fit enough to handle all the temptations I would encounter there.

A day or two before I was leaving for this conference, I was sitting alone with my daughter, who was now ten at the time. I was telling her that I needed to go and that she could be assured that I would not drink. She replied casually, "I know, Dad. I trust you."

Those six words entered my soul and invigorated my spirit like a tidal wave of joy into my heart. I was so overwhelmed with gratitude to God. The fact that she could emphatically say that she trusted me, after all I had put her through, almost made me cry tears of joy. I was so happy and grateful. I knew that I could not have produced this with my own power. I had tried to quit drinking for two years unsuccessfully. It was only until I surrendered to God that this was possible.

Jesus came to earth to reconcile everything, every relationship, back to God. When I finally allowed Jesus into my heart fully by surrendering to God, I could experience this ministry of reconciliation. This event proves to me that Jesus is working in my heart and in my life. My daughter was not seeing me and my selfishness anymore. She could see Jesus and the heart of a servant with integrity and truth that never changes and never fails.

The second example of Jesus being alive in me was displayed in my marriage. My pastor says in marriage counseling, he advises people that they know they can be ready to get married when they are ready to put their spouse's needs above their own. No one likes to hear that. Most people enter marriage because they like what they get from their spouse and want more of that. They want what they want and do not consider putting the other person's needs first. Again, a primary reason why many marriages fail. It is not pleasant sometimes, and it is definitely not easy a lot of times. However, it is crucial to a successful, satisfying, joyous marriage.

I rarely considered putting my wife's needs ahead of my own prior to us getting married and during our first few years of marriage. I was looking for her to meet my needs and "complete" me. That line in the movie Jerry Maguire that is so sweet—"You complete me"—is so destructive in marriage. Each partner needs to be complete on their own accord. The spouse complements the other person. Looking for "completion" of oneself in another broken human being is destined for disaster.

After rehab, growing in my spirituality and relationship with God and Jesus, my understanding of marriage became quite different. I came to realize that my role as a husband is to love, support, and encourage my wife; and in doing so, we enjoy each other. Previously, when I sought my will to get what I wanted or needed out of her in whatever circumstance, I would sometimes succeed; but it damaged our marriage each and every time. Today, I realize I must seek God's will for us, not mine, for success in marriage.

My wife was and still is an outstanding basketball player. She went to Kansas State on full athletic scholarship for basketball. To this day, she is still the third all-time leading three-point scorer in the entire Big 12 conference. If that does not impress you, I do not know what will. She is incredibly smart and analytical as well and is just as amazing a coach, if not more so, than she was basketball player. She began coaching as an assistant for one of the local high schools and eventually became the head coach of another high school. Because she understands life much better than I do, she had trepidation in taking a head coaching job because of the time demands and schedule. Wisely, she consulted with me, and we talked a lot about whether or not this was the right choice for our family. I knew she loved basketball and is extremely gifted in coaching. Fulfilling my role as a supportive and loving husband, I expressed my utmost support and encouragement.

When we met, I knew nothing about basketball. I never played basketball, nor did I ever have any desire to watch it. Being the egotistical maniac that I am, since I had never played and therefore was not good at it, it was not something that I would seek to watch. I went to Northwestern, a Big 10 school, with Big 10 athletics; and I never even went to a single game, men's or women's.

My wife started coaching, and she was gone a lot. Being in better conscious contact with God, I knew that the more time we spend together as a family was and is beneficial for us. Dying to my own desires, I would take the kids to almost all the games that she coached. I did this to support her. To encourage her. To love her. I also wanted our children to see her doing what she loves by observing her as a successful coach and not only their mother. From my preceding statements, obviously, this is not something I would have ever done before by choice. I would have much rather gone to the gym or worked on something that I was interested in or pursuing. But the heart of Jesus was alive in me, and I surrendered my wants and needs to fulfill my role as her husband.

It was not easy. Our children were toddlers at the time and could not pay attention to the game. I spent a lot of time chasing them down, making sure they did not fall down the bleacher stairs, trying to keep their hands clean after they would put them all over the floor before they would put them in their mouths, and constantly going to the concession stands to get snacks to keep them occupied. I could only watch maybe 25 percent of the actual game.

Our children and I became fixtures at all of her games. Everyone knew we would be coming, and we almost always did. Instead of being resentful at her, I began to enjoy everything about women's basketball. We are blessed in our county that we have many superb women's basketball players here. I would follow them and their careers as they entered college. I started to watch women's basketball on TV. Most of the time, I would tell my wife what women's game was coming on, and we would watch them together. I knew more about women's college basketball than she did at this point. And I loved it.

One day in the summer, she was complaining about how her office was so dirty and unorganized. I started to offer some suggestions about how she might go about cleaning it or hiring someone to do it. She replied to me, "Why don't you take a day off and clean it?"

WHAT?

My first thought (which is always wrong) was that I was a busy orthopedic spine surgeon. That makes absolutely no worldly sense for me to take a day off work, lose that revenue for our family, and clean her office. However, I did not react and thought about it. I prayed for knowledge of God's will for us and the power to carry that out. I came to the decision that I would, in fact, clean her office.

I hate cleaning. I hate getting dirty. I wash my hands forty times a day, so I hate it whenever there is any dust or anything on my hands. Her office was an old office in the school that had not been used in years. It was covered in dust and grime.

I started cleaning her office, begrudgingly, and just proceeded to do the next right action. I found myself repeating to myself over and over again, "The Son of Man came to serve, not to be served." Over and over again. That's all I said to myself. All day long.

I finished cleaning her office, and she finished practice. She said thank you and gave me a kiss. Although I was covered in dust and dirt, sweaty from working all day, I felt peace and satisfaction that I was able to fulfill God's will for us. It was not pleasant. It was not fun. It was not what I would choose to do. But I knew in my heart that I had pleased God and that He would reward me and our marriage from that action, continuing my surrender over time.

The ability for me to do this is not inherent to me. It did not come from my natural choices or desires. It was not on the list of the first one hundred things I would have liked to do that day. That ability came from Jesus. Him being alive in my heart and spurning me on to be like him was the only way I could have the power to do that.

God gave Adam a woman to be his "helper." The only other two people in the Bible that the word "helper" is used to describe are God Himself and the Holy Spirit. That is good company to be in.

In my first marriage and early in my second marriage before coming to understand God's design for marriage, I thought the word "helper" meant that my wife would help me build my kingdom. She would help me be successful in my career. She would help take care of the house and kids so I could make money to live the life we had envisioned. She would help me feel good about myself and fulfill my physical needs.

In thinking about God and the Holy Spirit being the only two other people in the Bible that the word "helper" is used to describe, God has revealed to me that my definition of the word "helper" is not what He intended.

My wife's purpose in being my "helper" is to help transform my heart and renew my mind to think and act like Jesus. She is helping me conform to His image. That is what "helper" means. My wife is a mirror that reflects my selfishness and exposes the parts of me that I want hidden from the world. The purpose of this is not to shame me but to allow God to work in my life to transform me to be more like Jesus.

The world would view my actions as noble. I was helping my wife. The fact that I took a day off to clean my wife's office demonstrates what kind of outstanding person I am, from the world's view. What a prideful delusion this really is. That was not what was happening at all.

My wife was helping me. She was revealing to me how a marriage aligned under God and Christ operates. Thankfully, I had enough conscious contact with God to surrender to His will and proceed with a Christlike action. I am not holy, and I did not appreciate my assignment that day. However, being close to God through Jesus and viewing life from God's lens showed me the privilege I have to serve and love her the way that God and Jesus love me. That action drew me closer to the presence of God, which gives me a glimpse of heaven on earth, the abundant life and the peace of God that surpasses understanding. The purpose of marriage is to make us holy.

Since this is God's design, in all marriages, even in marriages where people are not Christian, this plays out. Without a proper understanding of God's love of us through His son Jesus, no man willfully desires to become a humble servant to his wife. The world's design is for the husband to lead and dominate the wife. This conflict between God's will for us and the will of each person in the marriage leads to marital dissatisfaction and discontent and, ultimately, divorce in 50 percent of cases and misery in many others. This grieves my heart because the fallout from this conflict is damaging not just to the husband and wife, but also to the innocent children and other family members as each person seeks their own selfish will in the marriage.

This is the point. By surrendering to God's will for OUR lives, not just my own, my desires started to change. Her desires became my desires. OUR desires. God's will for OUR life. It is not that I did not have dreams or desires of my own, but I was willing to surrender some of my life to improve our life. To have the marriage that God intended us to have.

The paradox is that in doing something that I would not naturally choose to do in order to love my wife well, I am happier, more satisfied, and fulfilled in my marriage and in life. I became interested in something I never had any interest in before. This took action on my part to pray for knowledge of God's will for us and then use His power to carry that out. Since this is not my natural tendency, I am absolutely certain it can only be the Holy Spirit, given to me by God through Jesus, that this transformation was possible. This is how I discovered the abundant life, the pure joy and happiness in my marriage, that I could have when in relationship with God through Jesus.

The third example I have of Jesus being alive in me happened in 2018, three years into my recovery. The hospital where I operate opened in 2003. I started my spine practice there in 2006. I was the only spine surgeon working at that hospital, and the county it served did not have many spine surgeons in it. Therefore, my practice grew exponentially, and within six months of starting practice, I was as busy as I would ever want to be. Building a practice this quickly is distinctly uncommon in medicine. Today, I know that this was a gift from God at a time when I was actively renouncing Him.

Having no belief in God, and only belief in myself, I attributed this overwhelming success to me and my abilities. I felt tremendous power, value, and worth in my practice and myself. My ego was gargantuan. For whatever reason, I was not arrogant to the hospital staff and patients, and I had attained an excellent reputation.

HCA, the hospital's corporation, has an award that they give every year called the Frist Humanitarian Award. Thomas Frist, who founded HCA, exemplified the heart of a humble servant. Although I never knew him, I had heard of how caring and compassionate he was with everyone he encountered. He embodied the motto of HCA, which is "Committed to the care and improvement of human life." The award recognizes the physician, employee, and volunteer at each HCA hospital who demonstrates a level of commitment and caring that goes beyond everyday kindness. The recipients are selfless and dedicated to compassionate care of patients and everyone around them.

In my delusional mind, I felt that there was absolute certainty I would receive this award because of my success. God has gifted me with an enjoyable personality, and most people in the hospital liked and respected me, at least as far as I could tell. The great success of my practice in bringing many surgeries to the hospital made me feel as though I was very important. On top of this, I became active in hospital leadership, becoming chief of surgery and eventually chief of staff. I was positive that the success of my practice coupled with my activity in leadership of the medical staff would be recognized. It was just a matter of time before I would be given that award.

Time went by, and year after year, I was never even nominated for that award. I would not say that I was strongly affected by this, but I would feel disappointment on some level each year as it was given to someone else. In my delusional thinking, I could not understand how I could be so prominent in the hospital and so vital to its financial success yet not be given this award.

After rehab in 2015, I pretty much forgot about this award. I had to concentrate on my spiritual program of AA, rebuilding my practice, figuring out family life, and basically just doing the next right thing. I followed the suggestions I had been given from my treatment team and AA and went about my business. I went to AA meetings, called my sponsor almost every single day, did the AA step work, asked someone to disciple me in the church and met with him almost every single week, and did whatever else I could to live my purpose of being of maximum service to God and the people about me. One day at a time, I prayed for knowledge of God's will for us and the power to carry that out, and then surrendered to that, whatever it looked like for that day. I followed this truth:

The best preparation for tomorrow is to do today's work superbly well. (William Osler)

In 2017, I was shocked and surprised that I had been nominated for the Frist Humanitarian Award. I received an email notifying me of this. I remember being in disbelief. I was completely humbled that it had finally happened. That award had not even crossed my mind since 2015, and I spent no time nor effort in figuring out how I would get it. God revealed to me that, through no specific effort of my own, He would reward me if I continued to surrender to Him.

I received the Frist Humanitarian Award in 2017. I felt overjoyed, humbled, and fully satisfied. God did for me what I could not do for myself. What was surprising to me was that I felt that I was not much different in the hospital and in my care of patients. Mechanically, to me, from the outside, not much had changed about what I was doing and how I was acting in the way I treated other people. The person who nominated me wrote, "When I saw the list of the Frist Award recipients, I was surprised to see that Dr. S's name was not already on that list."

The difference now was that people could see Jesus alive in me, and that was recognized. This is how I know that Jesus is alive today. Jesus's spirit of love, compassion, service, gentleness, kindness, noncondemnation, and nonjudgment was being displayed in my actions. I know that I did not win that award because of myself and my abilities. It was God being glorified for His work in a life surrendered to Him. Jesus's spirit was shining brightly from me for everyone to see, and I felt affirmation of that when I received that award. I was truly thankful and humbled by that experience of God providing rewards for me that I could not attain on my own by continually surrendering to Him and His will for my life.

29

LANGUAGE

When God created everything, He spoke it into existence. He did not build it with His hands. He SPOKE, and everything that ever was or ever will be was formed. This demonstrates the massive power of words. Being created in God's image, our words, although not nearly that powerful, similarly have tremendous impact. People underestimate their power because they cannot see the physical effect of words on another person. However, the effect of our words on another person's spirit can change the entire trajectory of another person's life, positively or negatively. We never know when we might say something that will change someone's life forever.

For example, one day an engineer from a spine company that I work with flew in to observe one of my surgeries. He was in his early twenties and was struggling with some issues in his life. I was not aware of any of this at that time. In the operating room that day, I was talking about how focus equals feeling. It was just what I had been learning about and wanting to share that day. Whatever I focus on will affect the way that I feel. This concept was helpful to me, and it was on my mind.

Some months later, I had to fly to this spine company for a meeting with my rep, who is in the operating room with me for cases he is needed for. My rep told me at the end of that day that he had talked to that engineer earlier. The engineer told him that after that day in the operating room, he started to focus on the positive things in his life, and his life had improved dramatically. He told my rep that I was his spiritual teacher, at least that day. I do not take the credit for improving this young man's life. God was obviously direct-ing my speech that day, and He knew exactly what that engineer needed in the moment. I was not expecting my comments to have that kind of impact on someone else, but God had other plans. This is an amazing testimony to the power of words. This is the reason I continually seek conscious contact with God and talk about things related to Him that are on a higher plane of thinking. There are no greater ideas than those of God.

Great minds discuss ideas; average minds discuss events; small minds discuss people. (Eleanor Roosevelt)

The words we choose to say are critically important to how we feel and how we affect others' feelings. Language colors the perspective of a person's experience of life. For example, suppose a person watches a lion chase and kill a gazelle. If that persons says, "That was a great display of the power and domination by that magnificent lion," that person feels that experience from that per-spective. However, if another person says, "That gazelle was shred-ded to pieces, blood and guts coming from everywhere," that expe-rience feels quite different. Yet it was the same event that occurred. The words I choose to use are so vitally important. I have spent a lot of time and meditation on my use of language. It is something that I continually work on because of its importance to the way I feel and affect other people.

I try to never start a sentence with the words "To be honest." That implies that the other times I am talking, I am being dishonest. "To be honest" is a statement that is useless. I live a life of rigorous honesty today. The freedom I feel in that is incredibly wonderful. My pastor calls it "leading with weakness." Others sometimes say it is being transparent.

I am just telling the truth.

About what is going on in my life. About what I am struggling with. About what things I am learning from God that help me today. About how I feel. I can do this today because I have a close connection to God. What another human being thinks of me has little effect on my emotional or spiritual condition. It does not matter. With God, I am totally loved, accepted, and not judged in any way. Knowing and believing that in my heart gives me freedom.

> And you will know the truth, and the truth
> will set you free. (John 8:32 ESV)

Knowing the truth about God allows me to speak the truth, and that indeed sets me free.

One of my spiritual awakenings about language came as the result of a conversation with my sponsor. One day in early sobriety, I was on the phone with him ranting about something. He interrupted my diatribe and said, "Juris. I want you to try something. Try not using the word 'perfect.'"

I said, "Really? I did not realize I was using that word."

He said, "Yes, you were. About three times in the past minute." He suggested I try to find another way to say "perfect," and I agreed.

I decided instead of saying "perfect," I would say, "Everything is going to turn out exactly the way it's supposed to." This may seem like a minor point, but I assure you, it has massive implications for my emotional and spiritual health. I came to the realization that whenever I used the word "perfect," I meant what I considered to be perfect. Whatever the situation or circumstance was, it was only "perfect" if it the result was exactly what I wanted.

The problem with this manner of thinking and speaking is that I understand today that every situation and circumstance is perfect in God's will. The Bible tells us that God's will is "good, pleasing, and perfect" (Romans 12:2). That means everything that is happening in the world is "perfect." Even if it is something that I do not like, it is God's will and therefore perfect. Eliminating the word "perfect" from my vocabulary helps me realize this and then allows me to accept or even embrace it because I know and believe that God's intentions are for good, to prosper, and not harm. What seems to me was meant for evil, God will use for good. It prevents me from fighting it. My thinking comes into better alignment with God. God's will is going to happen whether I want it to or not. It is my acceptance of God's will that will affect my spiritual and emotional health.

> Do everything without complaining and arguing. (Philippians 2:14 NLT)

The Bible is not as hard to understand as I sometimes hear people say. This verse is clear. Complaining demonstrates a lack of acceptance of God's will. If I am complaining, I am stating that I know better than God what needs to be happening, and I am not accepting His will for us, which is "good, pleasing, and perfect." Through continually improving my conscious contact with God, I complain a lot less than I used to, which draws me closer to Him and allows me to have peace and serenity. Similarly, I strive to not argue with anyone (I am still not good at this—ask my wife) because my happiness in that moment depends on it.

Do I want to be right, or do I want to be happy?

I had been conditioned to speak simple phrases that would impact me emotionally and spiritually. For instance, if someone had done something to harm me, I had been conditioned to say, "That's okay." That is not a true statement. If the person that hurt me was in the wrong, then it is not okay. The offense was not justified and, therefore, not okay. It would cause me to stuff that negative emotion within me and find a way to avoid feeling it, which eventually exploded at some point.

My correct and truthful response for an event that truly hurt me is "You are forgiven." One useful definition for forgiveness for me is the following:

Forgiveness is releasing someone else's emotional control over me.

When I forgive someone, apology or not (I never expect anyone to apologize anymore for anything), their offense no longer has emotional control of my mind. Vengeance is not mine. It is God's. Knowing and believing that God is just and fair, I no longer feel the need to repay evil for evil. I am free. The truth is that the person who has hurt or offended me likely has no awareness that they have done so. They experience no disturbance to their spirit, and I do not need to either.

Forgiveness does not mean that the offense is something that I condone. It also means that I have no obligation to become friends and necessarily like the other person. It is true I must love that person, wanting the best for them and being willing to help and serve them if they are in need, but I do not have to force myself to be in relationship with them. If God so wills it, it will happen, but that is not my responsibility in forgiveness.

Sarcasm is another habit that I work on trying to eliminate. My entire life, up until I entered rehab, I thought that sarcasm was a good thing. I try to be a funny person, and I used sarcasm a lot to get a laugh. And it was quite effective. I spoke sarcastically quite frequently, and I received plenty of laughs. This, in turn, would fill that God-sized hole in my heart, leading me to believe that people thought I was funny and liked me. I did not feel completely loved by God, and therefore, I did what I could to entertain and make people laugh. Sarcasm was a big part of that.

Sarcasm is anger's evil twin.

The issue with sarcasm is that it is saying the opposite of what one actually means in order to make somebody laugh. This is the opposite of speaking the truth. The dictionary definition of sarcasm by the *Merriam-Webster* dictionary is "a sharp and often satirical or ironic utterance designed to cut or give pain."

When I read that, I thought, *Wow. Cut or give pain.* It was never my intention to cut or give pain to anyone. I just wanted people to laugh. The person that the sarcasm is directed at often laughs as well. However, internally there is a wound to that person's spirit. For example, if my son falls down on his bike while trying to show off a trick and I say, "Wow. That was a really good trick," that will likely generate a laugh from people; and he will also probably laugh. Deep down inside, he knows I do not really mean to hurt his feelings because I love him, but he will be hurt. I used to blow this off saying that this type of thing is no big deal, but today I believe that it is. The words I use are meant to encourage and inspire, not to cut or give pain, even if I think it is minor. Especially to the people I love, I NEVER want to say anything that will wound their spirits.

I was a master at self-deprecating sarcasm. This wounded my spirit. Self-deprecating sarcasm is a phenomenal technique to get people to laugh. Some comedians have made entire careers in comedy with it. However, the wound to their spirits and the fact that they never felt good enough, no matter how much money and fame they generated from that, have caused some of them to commit suicide. That is how damaging self-deprecating sarcasm is.

Today, I strive to speak solely in true statements. The acronym for THINK that helps me with my speech.

T-Is it true?
H-Is it helpful?
I-Is it inspiring?
N-Is it necessary?
K-Is it kind?

If what I am about to say does not fit the criteria delineated above, it is in my best interest to refrain from speaking. Most of the time I can pause long enough to stop myself if what I am saying does not. By consistently remembering this and reminding myself, this gradually becomes a working part of the mind. However, I still fail at this every single day.

Progress, not perfection.

If I speak in true statements, I find freedom. There is no guilt. No shame. No ill will toward myself or others.

I have been the grateful recipient of a lot of counseling. At the time, I would probably not have said that I was so thankful for it. Spending ninety days in rehab, taking time out of my schedule to drive and go through counseling was what I would say is less than convenient. However, those actions and that work I did as I was getting sober have laid a solid foundation for my recovery and walk with Jesus.

Most, if not all counselors, I have ever seen have told me that I need to remove the word "should" from my vocabulary. It's called "shoulding" on people. The Big Book of AA describes alcoholics as wanting to be directors, running the whole show. If only everyone did exactly what we think they should be doing, everything would be fine. Not only do we know what we should be doing, we think we have everyone else's best interests at heart and have strong opinions on what they should be doing so that their lives and our lives would be better. The fact, however, is that I never would have thought that the best thing that could happen to me would be that I would be gifted with the disease of alcoholism. Deep in my disease, without conscious contact with God, I did not know what was good for me or anyone else, for that matter.

This may seem like a minor detail, but I assure you, removing the word "should" from my speech has been revolutionary for me and the people in my life.

Everyone thinks of changing the world, but no one thinks of changing himself. (Leo Tolstoy)

The doctor-patient relationship is not a vertical relationship, as the world would lead us to believe. It is a horizontal relationship where I am a partner to my patient. My patient comes to me for help, and I have been educated and instructed with the tools to have the ability to help him. We share in the decision-making, the surgery, and postsurgical care. Therefore, when I tell patients what they need to do postoperatively to ensure the best results, I give them instructions. I offer suggestions and recommendations. But I am careful to never say what they should and should not do. I am not the authority over them, and I have learned many times over the years that I cannot make anyone do anything they are not willing to do. If a patient does not follow my postoperative instructions on what they need to do to obtain the best surgical results, that is God's will. I am powerless over that. I tell them what I recommend they need to do, based on my education, experience, and knowledge to heal and recover properly.

When I use the word "should," I am implying that I am God. This goes back to my primary daily struggle of remembering that there is a God and that I am not Him. It effectively states, "I know better than you how to run your life." It imparts a feeling of superiority and pride in me, and a feeling of shame and inferiority to the other party. The truth is, I do not know what God's will is for my life or for anyone else. Therefore, I do not know exactly what a person should or should not do in any situation. I do not know what God's outcome needs to be for that person. I can give advice, when asked, on what a person needs to do to stay sober or live in eternal life, based on my experience, strength, and hope, and also from the truth of the Bible. To say that I know what a person "should" do in a given situation implies that I know what their path is and where it is going. Sometimes God will allow a person to continue to burn their life to the ground because He is leading them to Him. Therefore, even if I think a person "should" do something to improve their situation, that may not be God's will for them in that moment.

You do not have to tell an alcoholic that they need to stop drinking. Even if that person states emphatically they do not have a problem when the obvious damaging consequences are mounting, deep in their heart, they KNOW they need to stop drinking. In the throes of my alcoholism, it was not necessary to tell me that I needed to stop drinking. I KNEW that. What I needed from someone at that point was love, understanding, compassion, and a willingness to help and walk alongside me. This is true of anyone who is deluded by any sin. A person enslaved to sin does not need a lecture, sermon, Bible verse, or verbal tirade. That person needs love. Sometimes love means leaving that person alone and letting God work in their heart, and sometimes that means allowing them to reach their bottom, as painful as that may be.

Jesus did not come to condemn the world (John 12:47). He came to save the world. Therefore, I also do my best not to condemn anyone. If I speak works of condemnation and judgment, then the spirit of Jesus is not alive in me at that moment. My Christian witness is damaging to non-Christians if I am judging and condemning others. I try to speak words of encouragement, just as the Bible instructs in Ephesians 4:29 (NLT): "Do not let any unwholesome talk come out of your mouths, but only what is helpful for building others up according to their needs, that it may benefit those who listen." This instruction is simple and does not need interpretation.

"Always" and "never" are two more words that I endeavor not to use. The only being where these words can be applied and be true is God. There is no "always" or "never" for human beings. In my past as an atheist and as an active alcoholic, I used those words frequently. The statements I made were not true, because again, there is nothing that is always or never for us. In using those words, those are also shaming statements, either about me or about the person I am talking about.

If I tell my wife, "You never hug me when I come home anymore," that is not a true statement. It may not be as frequently as I would like, but it is not "never." That statement also shames her by implying that she is not a good wife. My wife obviously loves me, and it is not her intention to not hug me when I come home. But there may be many things that had happened over the past several days leading up to this statement where for one reason or another, she did not. Making my request with kindness is direct communication to let her know what I need and not imply anything about her.

We human beings think that communication is intuitive. We learn to talk and then learn proper grammar in school, and therefore, we feel as though we have the tools necessary to communicate with others. However, we learn from other human beings (parents, teachers, coaches, counselors, etc.), and that experience is extremely limited. Adults teach children how to talk to other people, but it comes from their individual experiences.

The proper way to communicate with others is clearly delineated in the truth of the Bible. I was never exposed to that as a child. I do not ever remember hearing, "Treat other people the way you want to be treated" (Luke 6:31) as a child. Not once. Or the analogy of the tongue to the body being like the rudder of the ship (James 3:4–5). The rudder is small but directs the entire ship. Similarly, the words we use affect our entire being and those around us. Or how the tongue is akin to a tiny ember that sets ablaze a forest fire (James 3:6). If I had been taught these things and seen them demonstrated in others, my realization of the importance of my words may have helped me avoid a lot of emotional and spiritual pain in my life.

It is my prayer that sharing my current knowledge of language, its importance, and techniques I have accrued over time aid you in your speech and communication to conform to the language of God and Jesus and, therefore, love.

30

SEX

The pursuit of sex is the most powerful motivating force that exists in nature. Sigmund Freud, the great American psychologist, said that every action of a human being is in the pursuit of sex. Society supports this point as well. The total revenue from the porn industry is more than that of the NBA, NFL, and Major League Baseball COMBINED. Jesus said, "For where your treasure is, there your heart will be also" (Matthew 6:21).

We know where the treasure is, and that is where society's heart is as well. Therefore, I KNOW sex is important. Very important. EXTREMELY important. To every single human being. The person who is reading this with indignation, astonishment, and/or contempt is not being rigorously honest with him/herself. If any negative emotions are stirring inside of you, that is because you have been confronted with the truth. The truth has no emotion. Our reaction to the truth reveals our heart, and our view of sex.

Have you ever wondered why sex is so important to human beings? I admit I never contemplated why. I just knew it was important. Sex does not just feel good because it is necessary for propagation of the human race. I believe it is the greatest gift that God has given us, outside of holy communion with Him through Jesus.

The reason I believe that sex is so important to human beings is when experienced between a man and a woman inside of a marriage committed to God, it is the ultimate feeling of bliss that a person can experience on earth. Why, though? There are lots of things that make us feel good in the moment, but why is sex experienced in this way the best?

God is neither male nor female. As God is everything, God is both. Therefore, when a husband and wife are one flesh together while having sex, that is the closest a human being can get to being one with the Father. It is an act of male and female fully intertwined physically, mentally, emotionally, and spiritually. God intended for this act to produce this amazing, delightful, pleasurable feeling as we draw nearer to our Creator. It is the picture of Adam and Eve in paradise, together, when they were naked and felt no shame. When enjoyed as a husband and wife in Christ, there is safety in the knowledge that each partner is committed to the other alone, and no one else. There is the comfort in knowing that these sexual experiences will not be had with another person. Fear of judgment is eliminated having this security in the spouse because each partner knows that the other will not leave, no matter what.

But we human beings have perverted sex into something it was never designed for. Because the feeling of orgasm and sex is so pleasurable, we go to great lengths to seek it. And it can be sought in a million different ways outside of a husband and wife in marriage. We can reach orgasm on our own power, which leads us to believe that it is something we can and need to control. The spiritual consequences of having sex outside the parameters that God has ordained are not immediately identifiable. Since these consequences do not appear right away, our limited human minds convince ourselves that whatever we are doing is acceptable.

Having sex and reaching orgasm FEEL like we are drawing near to God because that is what God intended. God, being neither male nor female, is both; and that is what the act of sex is intended to feel like, heaven, being in His presence. Drawing close to Him. Knowing Him. The unfortunate fact is that when experienced outside of a marriage between a husband and wife, it is not as God intended and leads to negative spiritual consequences. Without the truth of God dwelling within our hearts, we are convinced that we will not suffer harm (emotionally or spiritually) from our actions. These spiritual wounds arise in our hearts, and we find ways to medicate ourselves with substances or behaviors to lessen those negative feelings that lead to destruction. Alternatively, we seek to justify and rationalize our behaviors trying to convince everyone around us that what we are doing is acceptable and then find difficulty reconciling that within the true nature of our hearts.

I know, from the truth of the Bible and from my own experience, that this is a lie. There is significant spiritual damage done to our hearts when we enjoy sex outside of God's parameters. The guilt and shame are not readily apparent and are buried deep within ourselves until it manifests in some other pathologic way that does not lead to abundant life. The fullness of life is dampened as we progress deeper and deeper into sexual immorality, until it leads to gates of insanity and spiritual death.

The beautiful truth about this, however, is that when sex is enjoyed between a husband and wife in a committed marriage under Christ, heaven is experienced here on earth, as God had intended. For me, there is no more pleasurable and satisfying feeling in the world. Because we live in a broken world, it is only but for a short period, but I imagine that this feeling is continual in the kingdom of heaven. I can only imagine what that must feel like to live in the constant perpetuity of that feeling. Until that day comes, I am thankful that I get to experience it here on earth, even if it is just for short moments.

Now having experienced sex in the way God has intended, I wish I had not had the previous sexual experiences that I did. There are residua in my mind that I cannot eradicate which affect me today. That is why I pray my children can learn and understand that sex is reserved for a husband and wife under the covenant of marriage because I believe that the experience could be even more pleasurable and satisfying if there had not been any previous encounters.

When I reentered the world after leaving rehab, my wife would barely touch me. Our relationship was at its absolute lowest point relationally and sexually. She would pull away when I touched her, and we went many months without having sex.

Through twelve-step recovery and my Christian walk, I continued to seek God one day at a time. As I matured spiritually, our relationship slowly started to improve. I am eternally grateful that she loves me the way that God does, no matter what, and that she decided to stay with me though I hurt her deeply. Instead of trying to make her happy, I began to see that I needed to love Him more than I loved her. Although this sounds illogical, the only chance I have of loving my wife properly is by seeking God and asking Him for help. When my wife is my higher power, that leads to frustration, disillusionment, and discontent for the both of us.

Today, ten years into marriage, we enjoy the most satisfying, fulfilling, pleasurable sex life that I have ever had with no expectation, asking, or coercion from me. I love and serve her without expectation, seek God, and my desires become fulfilled. I pray for God's will for us and the power to carry that out, and there is not a week now that goes by where we do not worship Him in this way. My pastor was right after all. God does want me to have sex. Praise the Lord!

31

FATHERS

I have never heard this story in the rooms of Alcoholics Anonymous:

> Growing up, I had the best dad in the world. He was always there for me and our family. He loved my mom, served and protected her constantly. They were always hugging and kissing each other, holding hands, and laughed together. There was no doubt in my mind that they would always be together. I never saw them argue, although I knew they did. They would just never argue in front of us kids. Every day, he told me he loved me. He came to almost all my activities, sporting events, plays, etc. Even when I failed though I was doing my best, he would encourage me and tell me that he was proud of me. It's not like he didn't discipline me, though. If I did something that I knew was wrong, I would get punished in some way. But he would always explain to me calmly why I needed to be disciplined and what I need to do to improve the next time. He always asked me how my day was, listened, and was interested in what I said. I felt like I could tell him about anything. I could always tell him if I was sad, mad, angry, happy, embarrassed, ashamed, excited, or whatever. Although

he corrected me, he never judged me for making the bad decisions I made. He helped me through them by talking to me. When he made mistakes, he would admit that he did something wrong and see what he could do to make it right. I knew he wasn't perfect, and he knew it too, and he was willing to admit when he was wrong and take corrective action. He prayed all the time. It did not matter if it was morning, night, before meals, in the car, wherever. If there ever was a problem he or our family faced, he would pray about it. He was the happiest person that I have ever known. He helped people all the time, even if it meant sometimes he was not able to do something he really wanted to do. He did work to provide for our family, but he was home as much as he could be and even picked us up and dropped us off at school sometimes. He was intimately involved and interested in my life. Even today, I know that I can call my dad anytime, and he is available to me. I always knew he would protect me if someone was threatening me, and that I was safe... then I became an alcoholic.

That is a story that just does not happen.

As we are growing up, our parents, but particularly our fathers, are our God templates. I pray that every male reading this feels the weight of this responsibility. This is not disrespectful to mothers. It is God's design. Mothers are extremely, extremely important, but God's design is for children to mostly form their concept of God on the ACTIONS of their fathers. Think about it. When we are children, our parents do everything that our heavenly Father does for us. Our parents feed us, hold us, nurture us, protect us, correct us, teach us, and make sure all our needs are met. Since we, as human beings, base our beliefs on our limited experience, our earthly fathers exemplify what God's nature is like. Our finite human minds can only assimilate the information presented in the moment; and that is why the concept of God, our heavenly Father, is primarily constructed from the image of our earthly father.

For example, in the absence of truthful spiritual guidance, if you grew up in a home where your father abused you, your concept of God is likely that He is always looking for you to get in trouble and punish you. If you grew up in without a father in your home, you think that God has abandoned you and is not interested in your life. Neither of these views of the one true God are even close to accurate.

I will share my experience about my father and how that has shaped my concept of God, before coming to know Him through recovery and the Bible. My father was home every night. He provided everything we needed for our family. I do not remember lacking anything that I really needed. He would eat dinner with us then go to the study to continue working. I never had one deep, emotional conversation with him. He taught me to do many things: algebra, ski, tennis, ice-skating, and hockey, to name a few. The only times he ever said "I love you" were when I performed well by making straight As, hitting home runs, etc. As far as I can remember, he never asked me how my day was or how I felt about anything. If I had a problem at school, he told me to just get over it and not let it bother me. If I was threatened at school, he never took any action to try to protect me.

Therefore, my concept of God was that He was always there, but not interested in how I felt or my life. That is why I never prayed when I first got saved because I did not feel like God was interested in my feelings and thoughts. He knew what they were, so why did I have to talk to Him about them? On top of that, if I did have a problem, I did not feel as though God would protect me or do anything to help me solve my problems. If I got in trouble, there were very few consequences. I do not struggle with worry because there was no chaos in our home, and I knew he would be home every night. He was always physically present, but emotionally absent. I do not worry also because everything I ever needed materially was always provided for. I felt that God's love was conditional. As long as I was performing for Him and doing well, He would love me. If I was not perfect or fell short in any area, I was no longer loved.

What I had to learn about God was that I was loved all the time as I am, not because of anything that I could do. It was unconditional. I previously believed the world's definition of love, which is conditional. God's is not. If I fail in any way, God's love is still ever-present in my life. I needed to learn that God WAS interested in everything and anything that I did. And not only that, God would solve my problems if I just came to Him and trusted Him. If I came into relationship with God, through Jesus, God had plans for me, not to harm me, but to give me a hope and a future (Jeremiah 29:11). I am thankful that my earthly father lived out many attributes of God, so I did not have to completely formulate my concept of God from the ground up. I grieve for those who grew up with no father or with abusive fathers, because I know that it takes a lot more work to construct God as He is. Unconditionally loving, totally accepting, completely forgiving, fully protecting His children.

Is it any wonder that 40 percent of children today are growing up in homes without fathers and we have a nation full of people who don't believe in God? And of the households that have a father in the home, how many of those fathers are intimately involved in their children's lives from an emotional or spiritual standpoint? In the book *Kingdom Man* by Tony Evans, he states that every societal malady and problem we have today is a result of fathers not being present and not aligned under God. If we are to get to the root cause of ANY problem we face today, it starts at home with the father.

One father is more than a hundred schoolmasters. (George Herbert)

This is my plea to fathers. If you have been blessed to have a child in this world, God's will is for you to be a father. Your highest calling in life is to be a godly father. The paradigm must shift.

Raising children is not "women's work." It is our primary responsibility. And not only to be a godly father, but continually point your children to the only perfect father, God. No father, not even Billy Graham, was or ever could be a perfect father. However, we have been presented with the Bible written by God and about God and His love for us. It is our responsibility not only to our own families but to society as a whole to continually seek God and His will for us and the power to carry that out.

No man can be considered a success in the world without first being a success at home.

In order to be a godly father, it is necessary to learn about God and what His characteristics are. Without God's Word, this is impossible. The Bible was written by God, about God. There is no better source for this information.

The most important attribute of God that fathers need to have is to genuinely desire and seek an intimate relationship with their children. From this, the other characteristics of God will be displayed in our actions. It is not enough to teach children about God. We must demonstrate as closely as we can the only perfect father in God.

I want my children to be nice to other people. Am I nice to other people? I want my children to pay attention to me when I am talking. Do I pay attention to them when they are talking? I want my children to stop complaining. Do I complain? I want my children to read their Bible. Do I read my Bible? I want my children to pray. Do I pray? I want my children to have wonderful marriages. Do I love my spouse well? I want my children to do well in school and always do their best. Do I do my best at work? Parenting is not as difficult as we make it out to be. The reason why it seems so difficult when not living in the truth is that it is a lot easier to say, "Do as I say, not as I do," and continue to live selfishly than to always strive to do the next right thing ourselves in every situation and die to our own natural, selfish desires.

Be the change that you wish to see in the world. (Mahatma Gandhi)

This is the reason that some doctors' children endure struggles in life. Growing up, these children hear from everyone else how caring and compassionate their fathers are. They hear how their fathers work long hours tirelessly to take care of their patients. Their experience, however, is that their fathers are rarely with them; and often, even if they are, they do not exert the same energy toward their children. This disconnect is confusing to children. Their concept of God is that He has vast capacity to care for other people but does not care for them.

We, first and foremost, must be present with our children. If we are physically not there, there is less chance that we can be emotionally and spiritually available. If work demands that we cannot be physically present, we must FaceTime, call, or verbally communicate in some fashion to let our children know we are intentionally seeking and desiring a relationship with them. In developing a relationship with another person, it is necessary to ask questions. We do not depend on their mothers or others to give us a report. It is our responsibility to continually get to know our children. Just because they were born of us, we cannot assume that we know their hearts.

Showing up for the game or the recital intermittently is not enough. Being a father is a daily endeavor that requires intention to pursue relationships with our children and our wives. Many times, I have taken them for granted because I "see" them every day. If I do not inquire about their lives, their feelings, their dreams, their aspirations, then I demonstrate to them that they are not significant. The time required for this is minimal, yet the rewards are eternal.

One day, I was talking to a physician friend of mine who has two daughters. He said, "I just can't play Barbies. I have such a hard time with it. But I do it." I laughed because I can relate to that. Many times, my children want to do activities that I would not choose to do in the moment. But I do them. I am present with them because I want to show them that I desire to have an intimate relationship with them. Satisfying myself in the moment and disregarding my children will lead them to destruction and me to dissatisfaction and an unfulfilling life. This requires conscious contact with God. The power for me to be able to do this is not of myself or my nature. It can only come from a supernatural force outside of myself.

When my eldest daughter became twelve, I took her on a date. I will continue to do this with all my daughters at least twice a year.

How are they supposed to know how a boy is supposed to treat them if I do not show them? From TV and movies? From social media? From their friends at school? Now that is scary.

It is not enough for me to just tell them what to expect. If I show them what it looks like to have a male who is seeking God treat them appropriately, they will know what is true and pure from what is false and manipulative. They need to see the difference between transactional affection and love. They need to hear from me that they are wonderfully and beautifully made. They need to know from me that they are prized and invaluable and need to be cherished. Dating in today's culture is so much more confusing and dangerous than it has ever been, and it is my responsibility to give my daughters an example of how an authentic man must treat them.

We have a nation full of young girls and women who are getting abused, mistreated, and taken advantage of, who have grown up in homes where their fathers have left their mothers or are cheating on them and everyone is shrugging their shoulders as to how we got here. I made the mistake of divorce earlier in my life, and I have the opportunity to improve, but I cannot do that on my own. I need God, a power greater than myself, to restore and reconcile all that I have broken.

Keeping them locked up, sheltered, and isolated protects them for a period; but they will all be adults on their own at some point. I have eighteen short years to lead and guide them on how to live a life that is fully satisfying and abundant.

> **Teenagers who are doing well are not doing well because they have the right set of rules around them. Teenagers who are doing well are doing well because God has a hold of their hearts. (Paul David Tripp)**

Similarly, my son needs to see me serving his mother and staying committed to her. If laundry needs to be folded or dishes need to be done, he needs to see me joyfully partaking in the house chores. This is not a favor to my wife. It is merely what needs to be done for our family. Rather than going out with the boys every weekend, he must see me continuing to swoon his mother and my wife and take her out on dates. The only way he will know how to be a godly husband is by observing it in my actions.

Our children will follow our example, not our advice.

My father's idol was education for me to be "successful" in life. Most of our interaction was about instruction. Another idol I see that parents have for their children to be "successful" is athletics. The amount of time spent in an activity is directly proportional to the value placed on it by parents. There is nothing wrong with teaching our children about things that are important to us. However, the purpose of the time spent in that endeavor must be to further cultivate the relationship with the child and not with the parent's desired end goal for the child. If the parent's ultimate goal in that activity for the child is worldly success, the child will believe life is all about performance, appearance, and control. From my personal experience and that I have observed with many others, this mindset leads to destruction.

The problem is that most men are not satisfied with "just being a father." We chase our careers, money, women, power, prestige, hobbies, and just about anything else other than being a father. We spend our time and energy on all these other pursuits that just do not matter in this world or the next. They are fleeting, pitiful attempts to fill the God-sized hole in our hearts and inevitably end in dissatisfaction and destruction.

There is nothing wrong with desiring to be great and successful in our careers, but we cannot do this to the exclusion of our wives and children. God wants us to be successful and do amazing impactful things in the world. In honoring God and serving our wives and children well while diligently working on our careers, God will take us higher than we ourselves thought possible. I have seen this transpire in my own life.

Working for fathers is almost always necessary to provide for the family. When I am driving home, I must shift my mindset. My day is not over. The most important part of the day is about to begin. I am about to return to the people who are most valuable in my life, and it is incumbent on me to be loving, patient, kind, compassionate, and caring. This is not easy. After working a long day in surgery or seeing patients in clinic, I must rely on God's strength and the Holy Spirit to work through me. On my own power, I will seek my own selfish desire of rest or entertainment and neglect my duties as a father. I am not perfect at this. No one is. But as I draw closer to the one true God, I progress each day.

In *The Knowledge of the Holy*, A. W. Tozer states, "What comes into our minds when we think about God is the most important thing about us." C. S. Lewis contended that statement in *The Weight of Glory* by responding, "By God Himself, it is not! How God thinks of us is not only more important, but infinitely more important. Indeed, how we think of Him is of no importance except in so far as it is related to how He thinks of us."

In reading those two statements, I believe ultimately, they are stating the same thing. For me, these can be combined into one sentence that combines both concepts. This is possibly the most critical point in this whole book:

What we BELIEVE when we think about God is the most important thing about us.

This drives any and all behavior in a person's life. It is not just what "comes into our minds," but it is what we truly BELIEVE about God and how God thinks of us that forms the basis of all thought and decision-making for an individual. Thus, what C. S. Lewis says is incorporated. What God thinks about us is infinitely important. However, a person's deepest inner conscience and heart must believe with full faith the true nature of God in order for it to have an impact on their actions.

This forms a person's belief system of who he/she is and what he/she is worth. It drives every single action of a human being. For me, my life was all about performance, appearance, and control, to please a God that I did not even believe in yet was still there spiritually in my heart. When my appearance to the world did not match what I knew to be true about myself, I did not feel loved by God and then drank to excess in an attempt to erase that feeling until it got to the point where I could not drink enough to do that.

You seek to imitate the kind of God you believe in. (Gregory Boyle, *Tattoos on the Heart*)

I have often heard people say, "My dad was an alcoholic, and he beat us all the time. I swore that I would NEVER be that way to my kids. And I turned out to be EXACTLY like him." "The apple does not fall far from the tree." "He was cut of the same cloth." "He is his father's child." "Like father, like son." Clichés carry on through time because they are true.

Consciously or unconsciously, we seek to imitate the kind of God we believe in. That concept of God begins and is implanted in our childhood, and the majority of that belief about God stems from the actions of our earthly father toward us. I am not minimizing the role of mothers in raising children. Mothers are critically important, and in fact, many children would be completely abandoned if it were not for the love and care of their mothers. The world would have been destroyed a long time ago if it were not for mothers. However, for whatever reason that cannot be understood, a child's concept of God is formed from the observation of the actions of his/her father.

That is why it is so critically important to learn about parenting from God Himself. There have been many books written on parenting over time, and I cannot say that society is any better off. The most important book about being a father was written almost two thousand years ago. It has not changed. I implore all of you who are fathers to seek God with all you heart and mind to become the father God created you to be. The impact will be felt not only in your home, but throughout the world for eternity.

32

SEEKING

When studying the Bible, it is very helpful to me not only to read and understand what is written, but also to realize and identify what is not written. The words in the Bible are breathed from God, are very specific, and need to be read and understood fully in order for them to have their full effect on my being and spirit. Studying those words and inserting things that are not specifically said or implied, which demonstrates what is not meant, aids me greatly in fully comprehending what God is actually saying in many specific verses.

One of my favorite verses in the Bible is Hebrews 11:6. It is a clear, concise promise that effectively communicates what I need to do in order to fully experience the immense reward God has for me in my earthly life.

> And without faith it is impossible to please him, for whoever would draw near to God must believe that he exists and that he rewards those who seek him. (Hebrews 11:6 ESV)

The first part of this verse instructs me that in order for me to draw near to God, I must have faith. Faith in that He is who He says He is. That information is found in the Bible. To have faith in God as He says He is, I must read, listen, absorb, study, and discuss this material with other people to embed it into my brain. The Bible is the book of truth. Therefore, the more truth I can impart into my thinking, the better my faith will be and enable me to draw near to God.

The second part of this verse is the promise that I have seen and experienced and drives my actions. It states, "He rewards those who SEEK him."

It does not say, "He rewards those who follow His rules."

It does not say, "He rewards those who understand Him."

It does not say, "He rewards those who repent of their sins."

It does not say, "He rewards those who exhibit good behavior."

It does not say, "He rewards those who wear crosses or shirts that say, 'Jesus.'"

It specifically says, "He rewards those who SEEK Him."

That is the key. Seeking God. Attempting to find God. God is already there, omnipresent, patiently waiting for us to come to Him. God does not go out to find us. It is our responsibility to go find Him.

A lot of Christians get tied up in the law, the same way the Pharisees did back in Jesus's day. They think that it is about behavior, following the rules, having intellectual knowledge of God's Word and memorizing it, or even merely stating that they believe in God. God rewards none of those things. All God merely wishes for is for us to seek Him, and therein His reward lies.

This is echoed in the Big Book (4th ed.) in the chapter "How It Works." It states on page 60

A. That we were alcoholic and could not manage our own lives,

B. That probably no human power could have relieved our alcoholism, and

C. That God could and would if He were sought.

The solution to the disease of alcoholism is found in God IF HE WERE SOUGHT. That is all that is required. It is just that simple. The question then becomes, how do we seek God?

The suggestions of AA clearly delineate how that is done. By getting a sponsor and calling them every day, we connect with another human being created in the image of God who has already demonstrated that they are seeking God by staying sober for at least one year. The sponsor's sobriety is the evidence that God is relieving that person's alcoholism and therefore proves the third point above, that God could and would if He were sought. This also generates faith in the sponsee because of what they have seen in their sponsor's life. It is the physical evidence of God's infinite power.

Going to meetings is another strong suggestion from AA. By going to meetings, we are continuing to seek God. The discussions at AA meetings are centered around the solution to the disease of alcoholism. The focal point of that solution is God/higher power. A power greater than ourselves. Many people call that many different things: universe, being, higher power, etc.; but whatever it is called, it is something human beings cannot fully grasp or understand, and therefore, ultimately it is God.

A person does not have to accept the word "God" to seek God. If they are seeking a "power greater than ourselves," they can call it whatever they want. God knows where that person's heart lies in seeking Him in that moment. The name that they place on their "higher power" is just semantics and representative of that person's point in their journey and has no reflection on God himself.

I believe that the Big Book is divinely inspired in the same manner as the Bible and that it is God breathed. Working steps and reading the Big Book is another suggestion from AA and represents another method for seeking God. Reading, studying, and discussing books like the Big Book and the Bible are vitally important. It is searching for the truth. It is no coincidence that the Bible is translated into more languages and is the most popular book in the world to this day.

The Big Book is phenomenal because it meets alcoholics where they are. That is exactly what Jesus has done with each and every follower—meet them where they are in their journey. Most alcoholics in active disease are not ready nor willing to talk about Jesus. A lot of people in the Bible were not ready nor willing to accept Jesus when they encountered him either. It is necessary to enter a person's life and journey from that person's experience, rather than trying to impose on them strict spiritual doctrine of where we think they need to be. All are welcome at the cross.

Some sponsors tell their sponsees to come up with their own concept of God/higher power. It does not matter what it is. The only requirement is to believe in something, ANYTHING, that has a power greater than themselves. There is no pressure to accept Jesus right there on the spot. They start with their own concept of God and then start the process of seeking.

That concept of God changes and evolves with them in their recovery. If they thoroughly give themselves to the AA program, that concept grows into "God as we understand Him." Notice the word "we" in steps 3 and 11. If the AA program is working for someone and they are staying sober, it is no longer a singular personal God to that person. It is "God as WE understand Him." Although the process started with that individual's specific concept of his/her own God, it evolves into who God really is, as long as that person continues seeking.

Our role as Christians is to assist others in whatever way we possibly can to seek God. It does not matter where a person starts from. I want to encourage them to seek God in truth in whatever way possible, where they are at in order to obtain their reward from God, as I have. I believe anyone who seeks God earnestly and with their full heart and mind will eventually find Jesus as well. He is the truth, the life, and the way. No one comes to God except through Jesus (John 14:6). However, most people do not take the time nor energy nor work to wholeheartedly seek God and, therefore, never find their true reward in their earthly life.

In the book *Seeking Allah, Finding Jesus*, Nabeel Qureshi supports my belief. He grew up Muslim, a devout student of Islam. His whole family was heavily involved in Islam. His journey intersected that of a Christian named David, and they became great friends. They truly loved each other. David demonstrated his love for Nabeel; he did not just verbalize it. They would have discussions about God and Jesus, and Nabeel continually sought the one true God. Persistently. Fervently. Without ceasing. After an amazing journey, Nabeel accepted and surrendered to the truth of Jesus Christ and became a devout Christian. If a person seeks God long and hard enough, the truth of who Jesus is and what He did will eventually be revealed.

It is written in the Prophets, "And they will
all be taught by God." Everyone who has heard
and learned from the father comes to me. (John
6:45 ESV) (Jesus speaking)

Seeking God today is easier than at any point in history. As
Christians, we do not have to define "seeking God" as reading the
Bible or going to church. I read my Bible, but that is only a compo-
nent of how I seek Him. There is an app called RightNow Media that
has Christian book studies I can listen to. I listen to the Bible, sermons, and Christian audiobooks while driving in my car. Inundating
my mind with the truth is how it gets renewed. For those who cannot read, the Bible can be heard from any device. The children's
song "Hear, know, do! Do what the Bible says!" effectively sums up
how abundant life can be had. The world floods our eyes, ears, and
minds with false promises. The more truth I can impart to my brain
and then heart, the more I know the one true God and Jesus Christ
whom He sent.

What is the "reward"? It is not financial or material. It is not
power. It is not fame. It is not security. It is not safety. The "reward"
may ultimately generate benefits in these other areas, but it is not the
ultimate "reward" referred to in Hebrews 11:6. To me, the reward is
best described in Philippians 4:7: "the peace of God, which surpasses
all understanding, will guard your hearts and your minds in Christ
Jesus."

It is not something that I can describe. The closest singular
word I would use for this feeling is serenity—the state of being calm,
peaceful, and untroubled. It "surpasses all understanding." By definition, I cannot fully understand it nor convey it in an appropriate
manner to do it justice. However, I will make an attempt here. I
would describe it as the ultimate contentment of life, fullness of joy,
feeling completely secure and safe, and freedom from judgment or
condemnation in all situations and circumstances in my life. It is the
best feeling I have ever had, better than any drug has ever given me,
and it does not dissipate. No matter what is happening around me,
if I get cancer or one of my children goes astray, the "peace of God"

consumes me; and I can feel all those things listed above. Jesus never promised me a problem-free life. In fact, Jesus said, "I have told you these things, so that in me you may have peace. In this world, you will have trouble. But take heart! I have overcome the world" (John 16:33 NIV). Notice Jesus says "in me you may have peace." In Jesus is the only way peace is found.

The intimate relationship with God through Jesus that I have now is the reward. If all I have in this world is that relationship, my heart, mind, and soul can be at peace. This relationship is the result of my journey to Christ through AA. It began in earnest when I envisioned my life with nothing of this world and only God by my side. Praying and meditating on this during that time led me to the knowledge that God was all I needed. From there, through the program of AA, my relationship with God through Jesus blossomed, continues to do so, and will continue throughout my earthly life.

As I am a human being, this "peace of God" can be shaken at times; but as I return to seeking God through Jesus, it returns in full force, which spurns me to want to seek God more. To know Him is to want to know Him more is indeed true for me. I still have an addict personality, and I want to feel good all the time. Now I know where I can find it.

John Piper has said his dad was the happiest person he had ever known. John Piper also said he knew that his dad was a devout follower of Jesus Christ. He knew those two things were connected.

He is most glorified when we are most satisfied in Him. (John Piper)

He calls this concept Christian hedonism. I would describe myself as a hedonist. I sought pleasure in everything the world promised would give me pleasure. Solomon had the same experience. In the Bible, he said that he denied himself no earthly pleasure. He and I came to the same conclusion. All of that is meaningless without God. Surrendering to God through Jesus and being close to Him is the ultimate pleasure. Nothing comes close nor lasts as this does.

I was repulsed by religion and Christianity most of my life. The message I heard was that being a Christian prevents a person from doing the things in life that bring the most happiness. I also heard that unless I accepted Jesus, I was a bad person and I was going to hell. I felt judgment, and not love, from most Christians that I encountered. Most Christians that I knew lived a life of drudgery, obligated to go to church, and resentfully refrained from things like drinking alcohol and sex.

What I know to be true today is that this is NOT the message of Christianity at all. Unfortunately, the Christians I encountered most of my life called on the name of Jesus but did not fully surrender to him. When I say surrender, I mean surrender every single part of their lives to him. Not just the parts they think they need help with. Jesus spoke of these people in Matthew 7:21 (ESV): "Not everyone who says to me, 'Lord, Lord,' will enter the kingdom of heaven, but the one who does the will of my Father who is in heaven."

Speaking the name of Jesus, but not doing the will of God, leaves many Christians stuck in this purgatory of human existence. It is a life of obligation, and not service out of joy and gratitude. It is a burden. Without seeking God daily through Jesus Christ, His son, and merely saying that one is a Christian is a miserable experience. Many Christians are just suffering through this life, blaming hardships on the fact that we live in a fallen world. They are not realizing that heaven is in the here and now today, but that only comes through seeking God through Jesus and DOING His will for us. It is not about missing hell and catching heaven someday. It is now.

> We are sure God wants us to be happy, joyous, and free. We cannot subscribe to the belief that this life is a vale of tears, though it was just that for many of us. But it is clear that we made our own misery. God didn't do it. Avoid then, the deliberate manufacture of misery, but if trouble comes, cheerfully capitalize it as an opportunity to demonstrate His omnipotence. (*Alcoholics Anonymous*, 4th ed., 133)

AW Tozer puts it this way in *The Knowledge of the Holy*: "By His nature He is inclined to bestow blessedness and He takes holy pleasure in the happiness of His people."

Heaven is not defined by gold-paved streets, angels playing harps, and light and airy music. The definition of heaven is knowing the one true God and Jesus Christ whom He sent (John 17:3). Conversely, the definition of hell is being separated from this. The painful truth is that we are born separated from God. When I lived my life not surrendered to God through Jesus, I employed many medicators (praise of people, image, fame, money, power, alcohol, drugs) to continue to live in the delusion that I was happy and free. Hell was the mental anguish, inner spiritual turmoil, and lack of peace I experienced living separated from God. Alcohol was the final medicator that brought me to the end of my selfishness and self-centeredness and guided me to the realization that life on this earth is not about me. It is about God. When finally surrendered to that fact and committed to seek Him and follow Jesus, I could enter the kingdom of heaven while living on earth.

That is why the day of salvation is today. The situation is urgent. My heart grieves those who do not have a relationship with God because hell is today. I cannot convince anyone of this fact. Only God can reveal that to a person, as He revealed it to me. My responsibility is to share with them the good news of the gospel, that salvation and peace is found through Jesus to be reconciled to God and assist them in their journey however I can.

> **There are only two kinds of people in the end: those who say to God, "Thy will be done," and those to whom God says, in the end, "Thy will be done." All that are in Hell, choose it. Without that self-choice there could be no Hell. No soul that seriously and constantly desires joy will ever miss it. Those who seek find. Those who knock it is opened. (C. S. Lewis, *The Great Divorce*)**

I pray that I have conveyed to you the abundant life that can be had TODAY through Jesus Christ. I pray that you will experience the most amazing life that is available to you on this earth. It may not be exactly the life that you have envisioned for yourself. It will be far better and more satisfying than whatever you have ever dreamed! You cannot see, hear, or imagine the happiness, joy, and freedom that come from a relationship with God through Jesus. I pray that you realize that this journey takes work, but the suffering is miniscule in comparison to the rewards that God has for you. I pray all of these things in the mighty and powerful name of Jesus. Amen.

APPENDIX

TREATISE ON ALCOHOLICS ANONYMOUS

Alcoholism and drug addiction are chronic, progressive medical illnesses that require compliance with daily treatment. AA is the progressive solution to the progressive disease of alcoholism and addiction.

The original twelve-step program described in the first 164 pages of the book *Alcoholics Anonymous* (a.k.a. the Big Book) is the most effective treatment for the disease of alcoholism and addiction. In a Cochrane Systematic Review published on March 11, 2020, Alcoholics Anonymous (AA) and Twelve-Step Facilitation (TSF) produced higher rates of continuous abstinence than the other established treatments investigated. It was also found that AA/TSF interventions have the potential to significantly reduce healthcare costs related to alcoholism and addiction.

Alcoholics Anonymous is the most effective treatment for drug addiction as well. A recent study in 2014 supports this fact. Two hundred seventy-nine patients were studied over a one-year period. One group was identified as alcohol being their primary substance of abuse. The other group included patients that had a drug (opiates, stimulants, marijuana) as their primary substance of abuse. They found that the abstinence rate was the same at three, six, nine, and twelve months posttreatment between alcoholics and the primary drug group. In the primary drug group, AA meeting atten-dance comprised 80 percent of their total twelve-step meetings. The authors state, "Findings suggest, that contrary to expectation, young adults [average age was approximately twenty years old] who identify cannabis, opiates or stimulants as their preferred substance may, in general, do as well in AA as NA (Narcotics Anonymous). This has significance in many communities where NA meetings may be less available or unavailable." There are three times as many AA meetings (60,000) across the United States than NA meetings (20,000).

Most states have physician health programs, such as the one I am affiliated with and described, that monitor and advocate for phy-sicians in recovery from alcoholism, substance use disorders, or other mental health issues. These programs require physicians to record and report AA or other twelve-step fellowship meeting attendance, usually ninety meetings in ninety days initially, then at least three per week thereafter for five years. Some of these programs have an astounding 90 percent drug and alcohol abstinence rate at five years, verified by random drug/alcohol testing. This provides strong evi-dence that AA and twelve-step recovery, particularly this treatment protocol, is the most effective treatment for alcoholism and addiction.

Some people may state that it is the random drug testing and possible loss of career that enables this high success rate. Any alcoholic or drug addict will tell you that random drug/alcohol testing and/ or threat of catastrophic consequences is not enough to persistently keep us sober. Josh Hamilton was a former crack addict and Major League baseball player, five time All-Star and American League MVP in 2010. In his book, *Beyond Belief*, he talks about when he was deep in his addiction, he would be smoking crack on the way to the drug test, fully knowing it would be positive, which means he would be suspended or expelled, yet not being able to abstain. If a person is truly an alcoholic/addict, random drug testing and/or risk of massive consequences will not prevent that person from drinking or using. The astronomical success rates of these physician health programs lie in the monitored compliance to treatment (AA or twelve-step recovery).

Relating this to cancer, another terminal disease, if I were to benefit from a specific treatment and survive because of it, it would be incumbent on me to publish my findings. It would be selfish, callous, and irresponsible of me to keep that treatment a secret for any reason. Just because I had been the recipient of that treatment should not preclude me from discussing it.

If the most effective treatment for this cancer was established and known, supported by scientific evidence, available in every city in the United States and throughout the world at NO COST, would it not be my responsibility as a physician to educate the public, medical community, and other physicians about this treatment?

I cannot be silent any longer.

My intent is that by admission of my disease of alcoholism and participation in AA, my prayer is to inspire others to follow the AA way of life and fulfill their dreams. Without talking about this experience, I would be leaving out the most integral part of the struggle and the blueprint for the solution. I have found not only sobriety, but also greater levels of joy, happiness, and satisfaction in becoming not only a physician as I was destined to be, but also an alcoholic who can relate to and help others overcome alcoholism and addiction.

In the chapter "The Doctor's Opinion" in the Big Book, Dr. Silkworth who specialized in treating thousands of alcoholics observed that even the most hopeless alcoholics could recover if they could obtain an essential psychic change brought about with the aid of a "higher power." The most efficient, effective process to that end is Alcoholics Anonymous.

The treatment for alcoholism and drug addiction is not medication. It is not therapy. It is not counseling.

It is Alcoholics Anonymous.

From the studies cited above, this is not merely my opinion. This is evidence-based medicine.

Most of my friends who are physicians do not know about AA's effectiveness until I share my story and how it worked in my life. They see addicts and alcoholics every day and prescribe naltrexone, Suboxone, Vivitrol, counseling, therapy, rehab, etc. All of that might add to the solution, but it is not THE solution.

Part of the impetus for me to write this book was the fact that I was certain I was an alcoholic for two years prior to rehab. I was surrendered to the reality of my disease but had no awareness or knowledge of the most effective treatment. Being a physician, I would think that I would be well versed on the most effective treatments for most diseases, but I did not for alcoholism and addiction. Had I known this earlier, I may not have needed rehab and just went to Alcoholics Anonymous on my own and started this journey (and saved a lot of money and pain).

Treatment centers are a costly, minimally effective treatment for alcoholism and addiction. I benefited greatly from my ninety days of rehab. However, the long-term effectiveness of my treatment plan is the continuation of my twelve-step program daily for the rest of my earthly life.

The financial burden of the opioid crisis is astronomical. We have free treatment available in almost every city throughout the United States with AA meetings and other twelve-step fellowships. There are no costs or dues for these programs. If there is any hope for slowing or eliminating the opioid crisis, it lies in Alcoholics Anonymous and programs that use the original twelve steps. There is not enough money to send everyone to treatment, especially when the solution already exists at no cost and is readily available for those who are willing.

As helping another alcoholic or addict is integral to keeping an alcoholic sober, it is our service work. We work for free. It does not take an MD, PhD, or any other advanced degree to help another alcoholic or addict stay sober. Almost everything I have learned about treating addiction and alcoholism, I did not learn in medical school. It takes experience, strength, and hope from living the program to transmit it to another individual. The paradoxical truth we find is that in helping another alcoholic or addict, the sponsor's sobriety is strengthened as well, if not more so.

> Practical experience shows that nothing
> will so much insure immunity from drinking as
> intensive work with other alcoholics. It works

when other activities fail. (*Alcoholics Anonymous*, 4th ed., 89)

No one knows what tomorrow holds, and I cannot state with 100 percent certainty that I will not relapse. If a person with cancer refuses chemo and radiation and subsequently dies, no rational person would state that it was the chemo and radiation that did not work. It is this way with alcoholism and addiction as well. If a person relapses, it is due to lack of compliance with treatment, not due to a failure of the treatment itself.

I can state with absolute certainty is that if I do relapse, it is NOT a failure of AA. It will be a result of me not "thoroughly" following the path, essentially being noncompliant in the treatment of my disease. In "How It Works," the first sentence states,

Rarely have we seen a person fail who has thoroughly followed our path. (*Alcoholics Anonymous*, 4th ed., 58)

There is one key word in that sentence: THOROUGHLY. Following the AA way of life consists of following many suggestions, the most important of these being

1. getting a sponsor and talking to him/her on an almost daily basis,
2. having a time for prayer/meditation throughout one's day,
3. attending twelve-step meetings regularly,
4. working the twelve steps all the way through, then continuing steps as directed by one's sponsor, and
5. helping others overcome their alcoholism or addictions.

This is by no means an extensive list of the actions that are required for success in the program, but these constitute the basics of "working the program." There is no cure.

It works if you work it.

Twelve-step programs require work. It is not easy, but it is a simple program of action, clearly delineated in the first 164 pages of the book *Alcoholics Anonymous*. Talking about it, thinking about it, reading about it will not keep an alcoholic sober. It is only by "working" the program that one can expect to be sober and lead a life that is happy, joyous, and free. This "work" becomes joy as one matures in the program. The actions above are no longer chores I must do. They become activities that I want to do, where joy is found.

Although this book goes into detail the why and how AA worked in my journey, one does not need to understand why or how it works. It starts with consistently going to meetings. Then, it is a matter of following the suggestions, fully and thoroughly, that results in a person's sobriety from mind- and mood-altering substances. Freedom from alcoholism and substance addiction will occur if the person merely follows through on the action steps suggested. Keep. Coming. Back.

Just do it. (Nike)

I know many, many people who started attending AA meetings with no intention of ever getting sober. They did it just to appease their family, or they were court-ordered to go to meetings. And yet many of them became sober and continue the AA way of life because their lives have improved so dramatically. Therefore, the motivation does not even matter many times. As long as a person continues to attend AA meetings, transformation happens, often without conscious awareness of it happening.

Miraculous turns of fate can happen to those who persist in showing up. (Elizabeth Gilbert)

If I do garner any kind of attention from this book, I want the reader to know that whatever glory might be attributed to me needs to be redirected to God. Although my life is the vehicle for this story, this book is not about me. The real subject of this book is the powerful hand of God, full of grace, mercy, and love. It is a story of how a person can submit to Him and fully enjoy the life that He has laid out for that individual. It is the story of a man brought from spiritual death to life. A miracle no less amazing than empowering a paralyzed man to walk.

The third tradition states, "The only requirement for membership is a desire to stop drinking." One does not even have to claim to be an alcoholic or addict to attend twelve-step meetings. I once heard a person in a meeting say, "I am not certain I am an alcoholic. All I know is that when I stop drinking, my life gets better, and when I start drinking again, my life gets worse." This begs the question, why would that person ever start drinking again? I am certain that any person who has a desire to stop drinking or doing drugs will obtain a better life if they follow the AA way of life, alcoholic or not.

To benefit from AA, one does not need to be a Christian, have any specific religious beliefs, or believe in anything at all. All one must have is a desire to stop drinking, doing drugs, or any other damaging behavior. AA will enable a person to stay sober if they work the program thoroughly. As the program is continued, a person's concept of "higher power" develops and enlarges, but there is no mandate to call it anything specific.

I pray that this book provides much-needed education about Alcoholics Anonymous. Because of my degree and position as a physician, not by any virtue innate to me, people look to me for information when it comes to medical diseases. I want to remove the preconceived notions the public has with AA. I had learned throughout my education that alcoholism is a disease that does not discriminate based on education, social status, race, gender, culture, or ethnicity. It is an equal-opportunity disease. However, I did not realize this was reality until I walked into my first AA meeting where other physicians were present. It removed any shame and guilt I had about having the disease of alcoholism.

I pray that others who read my story knowing that I am a physician will realize that as well. Alcoholics and addicts are your physicians, your police officers, your firefighters, your stay-at-home moms, your children's teachers and coaches, your pastors, your service workers, your neighbors, and your friends. We are all around you. There is no shame in being an alcoholic or addict, just like there is no shame in being a diabetic. Not only am I not ashamed of my alcoholism, I view it as the greatest blessing in my life because it opened me up to a whole new life that I had never dreamed of. I do not regret my past. It is my greatest asset in God's hands for me to help others.

PEOPLE ARE DYING. Today, it is estimated that one person dies an alcohol-related death every six minutes in the United States. Additionally, the opioid epidemic is taking hundreds of thousands of lives. One person in the United States dies of an overdose every seven and a half minutes. As devastating as that is, that does not count the cost, damage, and destruction of alcoholism and addiction in people's lives today.

I think that we are doing narcotic or other substance or behavior addicts a disservice by not introducing them to Alcoholics Anonymous. A good friend of mine went to treatment for crack addiction before he finally got clean. He has now developed an amazing program that led him to recovery and freedom that has helped many people, and I commend him for that. He told me the reason he developed his own program was he could not figure out why he did not get what everyone else was getting in treatment to become clean and sober. One day, I was quoting him some statements from the Big Book that are particularly impactful to me. After I did that, he said, "You know, I never really got into the Big Book."

I thought, *WHAT!* He went to treatment TEN times before he got clean and sober. It is my opinion that treatment did not work because no one ever handed him the book *Alcoholics Anonymous* and told him to read the first 164 pages because his drug of choice was crack, and not alcohol. Anyone who has studied alcoholism and addiction can tell you that the root of the disease is not the substance. The root is a spiritual malady. And that spiritual malady has been overcome by hundreds of millions of people over the past eighty years by thoroughly following the AA program.

We must be tolerant of those coming into the rooms of Alcoholics Anonymous who suffer from addictions to other substances. After all, the Big Book tells us that "love and tolerance of others is our code."

HUMAN LIVES are at stake. Xanax, Ativan, and other benzodiazepines are nothing but alcohol in pill form. The chemical effect to the body is the same. Opioids similarly produce a feeling of euphoria and numb feelings in a similar manner to alcohol. Therefore, it stands to reason that the principles that have helped alcoholics get sober for decades can work especially powerfully in opioid and other substance addictions.

From attending other twelve-step recovery groups for different substances and behaviors, it is true that the personality types who gravitate to different substances and behaviors are different. A sex addict cannot go into an AA meeting and start talking about the experiences that lead him there and experience true fellowship with others suffering from the same problem. Therefore, it is important to find the twelve-step fellowship for which a person has a specific addiction to experience community and understanding and share their experience, strength, and hope with one another.

But the basis of all the programs can be found in the first 164 pages of the book *Alcoholics Anonymous*. I feel it is ABSOLUTELY NECESSARY that ANYONE suffering from any addiction read and talk about those pages with another person.

My purpose is to be of maximum service to God and the people about me. I want this book to help as many people as it possibly can, those suffering from alcoholism and addiction, as well as those who do not. The truth is that everyone is addicted to something, so I believe that this book can help anyone.

Anyone who has been working a twelve-step program knows that we have found sobriety, but also a whole lot more.

A new life has been given us or, if you prefer,
"a design for living" that really works. (*Alcoholics
Anonymous*, 4th ed., 28)

This has been the most tremendous gift that I have ever received. I desire everyone to be happy, joyous, and free. That is why I feel it is important to educate people about Alcoholics Anonymous.

Just about everyone has a family member who has been affected by the disease of alcoholism and/or addiction. Instead of viewing that person as a loser who has no willpower or self-control, I pray this book changes the way that others relate to those with alcoholism and/or addiction. I pray that the reader will now view that person as a sick person, who has the potential to become the magnificent person God designed them to be. I pray that the reader will be able to employ what is revealed and learned from this book to obtain the abundant life that is promised to him/her. The life that has been uniquely, divinely designed and destined for that person by none other than almighty God.

ABOUT THE AUTHOR

J uris S. was born and raised in Chicago, Illinois, and its suburbs. He is a grateful follower of Jesus Christ who is also a recovering alcoholic/addict, retired professional competitive eater, former model, and ordained deacon. His heart's desire is to share the truth in love to help others discover abundant, extravagant life. He is a board-certified orthopedic spine surgeon. He lives a life beyond what he had ever seen, heard, or imagined with his wife and four children in middle Tennessee.

CPSIA information can be obtained
at www.ICGtesting.com
Printed in the USA
LVHW040739180621
690564LV00001B/36